THE POLITICAL ECONOMY OF EXPERTISE

THE POLITICAL ECONOMY OF
EXPERTISE

~

Information and Efficiency in American National Politics

KEVIN M. ESTERLING

THE UNIVERSITY OF MICHIGAN PRESS
ANN ARBOR

Copyright © by the University of Michigan 2004
All rights reserved
Published in the United States of America by
The University of Michigan Press
Manufactured in the United States of America
⊗ Printed on acid-free paper

2007   2006   2005   2004   4   3   2   1

A CIP catalog record for this book is available from the British Library.

Library of Congress Cataloging-in-Publication Data

Esterling, Kevin M.
The political economy of expertise : information and efficiency in
American national politics / Kevin M. Esterling.
p.   cm.
Includes bibliographical references and index.
ISBN 0-472-11398-4 (cloth : alk. paper) —
ISBN 0-472-03064-7 (paper : alk. paper)
1. Pressure groups—United States.   2. Policy sciences.   I. Title.

JK1118.E79   2004
322.4'3'0973—dc22   2004008127

To my parents and stepparents

Contents

Preface

WILLIAM REILLY [EPA Administrator]: I think, sir, we are undertaking something very ambitious and very innovative, and very novel here in many respects, and we don't want to screw it up. I think we want to do it right.
JOHN DINGELL [D-MI]: Right. I don't want you to screw it up.

—Hearings on the Emissions Trading Program, 1989

This is a book about the influence of policy ideas and public-interested expertise in U.S. lobbying politics. As such, this book is one attempt to address a major limitation in our understanding of contemporary politics: to date, political science has failed to articulate a coherent and compelling explanation of how and why democratic politics uses policy research and expertise as a way to produce public-interested legislation. Long ago, legal economist Richard Posner wrote,

> A serious problem with any version of the public interest theory is that the theory contains no linkage or mechanism by which a perception of the public interest is translated into legislative action. In the theory of markets, it is explained how the efforts of individuals to promote their self-interest through transacting bring about an efficient allocation of resources. There is no comparable articulation of how a public perception as to what legislative policies or arrangements would maximize public welfare is translated into legislative action. (1974, 340)

My intent for this book is to develop, in the words of Posner, just such a "precise and hard-edged theory" (1974, 343) of how public-interest legislation develops and to demonstrate that such an explanation is consistent with a wide range of observed practices of and outcomes from lobbying politics and the legislative process.

Specifically, I argue that under certain conditions, organized interest groups pressure Congress to use academic policy research and analysis to design public policies. Furthermore, interest groups tend to pressure Congress to enact those expert-informed policies that have a good chance of working well in practice and not to enact those policies that risk failure or entail too much uncertainty. The effect of these lobbying efforts is to further the public's larger interests by advancing policies that are effective, efficient, and well informed, but the public interest is largely a by-product of the process; interest groups organize this pressure for their own, private, or self-interested reasons.

This argument, while optimistic in tone, is not merely a set of aspirations for how interest groups ought to behave or what sorts of policies Congress ought to enact. Instead, in the pages to follow, I construct my argument in the "positive" tradition, where the conclusions follow from an underlying assumption that all political actors are pursuing their private self-interests. This is of course not to assert that legislators and lobbyists are motivated only by self-interest. Indeed, many of the prominent participants in U.S. legislative politics have substantive, professional, and intellectual interests in advancing good public policies. To the extent that this is true, I am glad to concede that my account understates the role of ideas in contemporary politics.

But it is interesting, possibly surprising, and even encouraging that one can focus on what are traditionally viewed as some of the most parochial organizations in the U.S. political system, especially interest groups and congressional committees, and can assume that these organizations are selfishly motivated, and yet the aggregate effect of their work still can be informative debates and enlightened legislation.

In this effort, I am able to articulate one possible mechanism—by no means the only conceivable mechanism—by which "a perception of the public interest is translated into legislative action," as Posner requires. Given the conclusions of my argument, which are largely optimistic, this book stands as a counterargument to many of the more familiar positive theories of regulation and public policy, such as the neoliberal Chicago school of economic regulation and political science's rational choice blame-shifting and distributive theories of congressional behavior. These existing positive theories of legislation forcefully argue that the self-interested efforts of interest groups and members of Congress lead to inefficient policies that are contrary to the larger public interest. In these positive theories of politics, democracy is incompatible with efficiency, and legislators have no use for research-based expertise that serves larger public interests.

One may well question why political science needs yet another take on the nature of the U.S. legislative process. Indeed, these existing positive theories of politics are well reasoned and internally coherent; they state predictions that are consistent with a large range of legislative behavior; they are widely cited and, I believe, compatible with the skeptical and often cynical views of democratic government that, for better and for worse, are deeply embedded in our culture. All the while, Congress often fails to comply with the prevailing theoretical expectations of the standard literature on positive political economy. Congress from time to time develops major legislation that is thoughtful, well informed, efficient, and in the public interest. And because these existing positive theories can explain only democratic failure and inefficiency, they are largely unhelpful in developing explanations for why Congress sometimes chooses to use expertise on behalf of the public interest and why sometimes it does not. Explaining the variation in important political phenomena is—or at least should be—at the heart of any social science enterprise.

To distinguish my argument from these more familiar theories, I reexamine a variety of embedded and often implicit assumptions in these established positive theories of politics regarding such concepts as democratic representation, citizen knowledge, and interest group preferences and motivations. I focus on the variable effects of research-based information, debate, and cognitive framing on complex problem solving in the democratic system. As a consequence, I identify the conditions where my argument applies and where it does not. More importantly, within this framework, I explain the success and failure of public-interested expert ideas in politics, which is a very important component of the success and failure of contemporary democracy itself.

This book is a product of the dissertation research I undertook as a graduate student at the University of Chicago. To outsiders, the concepts that appear in these pages may appear to be something of a social science grab bag. But this is a reflection of my training, as the University of Chicago embodies and institutionalizes interdisciplinary research in its best sense. For their help, patience, knowledge, and advice, I thank my dissertation committee members, Mark Hansen, John Padgett, and Cass Sunstein. I also thank those who commented on all or parts of earlier drafts: Scott Ainsworth, Frank Baumgartner, Chris Bonastia, Jay Hamilton, Marie Hojnacki, Bryan Jones, Howard Margolis, and Laura Stoker; my graduate school friends and current colleagues for many conversations that have produced much of what I know about political science and the political economy of expertise: Michele Berger, Rob Boatright, Tom Burke, Carol Caronna, Dan Carpenter, Nancy Crowe, Brian Finch, Ted Gayer, Zoli Hajnal, Michael Heaney, Yoi Herrera, Karen Hoffman, Ann Keller, Andy Kydd, David Lazer, Taeku Lee, Beth Leech, Doug Miller, Mike Neblo, David Peritz, Dean Spiliotes, Albert Yoon, and Kuba Zielinski; participants in the American Politics Workshop and in the Organizations and State Building Workshop at the University of Chicago for helping me develop my research; David Shaffer, a statistics student of mine at Dartmouth College, for very helpful research assistance; and my early influences who introduced me to the study of political philosophy and political science at my undergraduate institution, the University of Virginia: Michael Brint, Charles Jones, William Lee Miller, and Tim O'Rourke.

I am very grateful for generous financial support from several sources: a two-year postdoctoral fellowship from the Robert Wood Johnson Scholars in Health Policy Research program, a predoctoral fellowship from the Mellon Foundation, and a Hazen White postdoctoral fellowship in health policy at the Taubman Center at Brown University. I thank Jim Reische, Sarah Mann, Kevin Rennells, and Jeremy Shine at the University of Michigan Press for helping bring this book to fruition. Finally, I thank my family for their love and support: my talented and beautiful wife, Emily Garabedian; the late Clytie and Frankie Esterling; and my parents and stepparents, to whom this book is dedicated.

Finally, much of this book refers to "socially efficient" policies and in particular "market oriented" policies. If the reader has little or no familiarity with this research-based form of public policy intervention, I recommend reading chapter 5 first.

Abbreviations

The following list identifies the groups testifying in the areas of acid rain, school choice, and HMOs.

Acid Rain

AEP	American Electric Power
AES	A. E. Staley Manufacturing
AGA/INGAA	American Gas Association/Interstate Natural Gas Association of America
APPA	American Public Power Association
CFA	Consumer Federation of America
EEI	Edision Electric Institute
ELCON	Electricity Consumers Resource Council
NARUC	National Association of Regulatory Utility Commissioners
NCA	National Coal Association
NCAC	National Clean Air Coalition
NIEP	National Independent Energy Producers
NRDC	Natural Resources Defense Council
NRECA	National Rural Electric Cooperative Association
OOCC	Office of Ohio Consumers' Counsel
PSCI/ICARE	Public Service Commission of Indiana
PUCT	Public Utility Commission of Texas
UMW	United Mine Workers
VEPCO	Virginia Power/Dominion Resources
WFA	Western Fuels Association

WPPI   Wisconsin Public Power Incorporated

School Choice

AFT   American Federation of Teachers
CCSSP   Council of Chief State School Officers
LDF   Legal Defense Fund of the National Association for
                 the Advancement of Colored People
NAB   National Alliance of Business
NSBA   National School Boards Association
PTA   National Parent-Teacher Association
USCC   U.S. Catholic Conference

HMOs

AFL-CIO   American Federation of Labor and Congress of
                 Industrial Organizations
AMA   American Medical Association
ANA   American Nurses' Association
GHAA   Group Health Association of America
HIP   Health Improvement Plan of Greater New York

1

Democracy in an Age of Information
and Analysis

One of the core ends of democratic government is to enact public policies that address "structural" and "incentive" problems in the economy and in society. We often expect the government to lead efforts to clean up the environment, increase access to health care, improve the quality of education, and so on. Many of these structural problems can be described as "market failures," where individuals' and business firms' day-to-day choices lead to aggregate outcomes that as a society we wish to avoid (see Bator 1958; Mueller 1989, 11; Olson 1965). Since these private agents, acting on their own, cannot or will not meet society's aspirations, we often look to the government for constructive interventions.

Ideally, a well-designed democratic constitution should create incentives for the government to use the best available knowledge, research, and analysis to address public problems. All other things being equal, society should prefer to be governed by expert-informed rather than ill-informed policies because the former are often more effective and efficient in reaching social goals. To this end, academic researchers and professional analysts endeavor to apply the current state of research-based knowledge to solve the vast array of public problems, developing expertise-informed proposals with the intent of advancing the public interest. These policy proposals are often complex and technical and may include such methods as incentives regulation, economic deregulation, optimal risk regulation, and public goods and information production (see Stokey and Zeckhauser 1978). These interventions may seek to promote economic and social efficiency, to reduce externalities, and to produce public goods. In addition, many of these experts undertake empirical research into the quality of these policy ideas and their consistency with some vision of the public interest.

The recent rise of academic policy research and analysis indeed creates enormous opportunities for the state to intervene in ways that meet society's highest aspirations. At the same time, capitalizing on this expertise can present fundamental legitimacy problems for the democratic state (Heclo 1978). The complexity of many policy proposals and of debate before the government makes the policy process itself fundamentally inaccessible to ordinary citizens. Policy experts speak in terms of causal relationships between government action and real-world outcomes. Experts construct arguments that "tend to be long and complex, and focus primarily on the antecedents of a proposal. Because X and Y conditions exist, Z will occur" (Cobb and Kuklinski 1997, 93). Unlike policy experts, ordinary citizens often have at best a rudimentary or incomplete understanding of the empirical facts, basic assumptions, or causal logic underlying an expert policy idea or proposal. Few citizens expend the mental energy required to grasp the implications of complex policy when voting or otherwise evaluating the actions of government. And clearly, any theory of democracy would require accountability to ordinary citizens as a basic premise.

Many of the current theories of U.S. legislative politics are quite pessimistic about the capacity and willingness of Congress to use expertise in crafting legislation, given this accountability problem.[1] Much of this literature is informed by positive theories of political economy, such as the prevailing rational-choice theories of reelection-seeking legislators and the neoliberal theory of economic regulation. In these well-known theories of politics, constituents are said

---

1. There is a relatively new literature on the strategic transmission of information (notably Ainsworth 1993; Kollman 1998; Krehbiel 1992) that shares many similarities with yet has some differences from my argument. The similarities are obvious: in essence, this literature focuses on the communication of expert-based, empirical information in the political process, and the mechanics of my model in chapter 4 rely heavily on the signaling models found in this literature. The differences are more subtle: the models in this literature are based in the spatial framework, and for reasons I describe later, this literature ultimately can address questions only of distribution rather than of policy innovation and the construction of meaning in politics. (See Johnson 1991 for a fuller discussion of this distinction.)

to reward legislators only for delivering easy-to-observe benefits such as new spending programs or pork-barrel projects as well as overly simplistic regulatory policies that can be justified with superficial platitudes (Arnold 1990, 23; Mayhew 1974; Stigler 1975). Members of Congress are concerned first and foremost about reelection and so are only too happy to cater to citizens' apparent wishes and deliver these sorts of inefficient benefits and simplistic policies.

In this view, members of Congress will never use academic expertise to devise policies that are in the public's best interests. Instead, to the extent that public-interested expertise is cited in the policy process, it is used only instrumentally as a misleading symbolic gesture (Fiorina 1989; Mayhew 1974, 124–25) or as a rationalization or ruse to justify delivering inefficient subsidies to rent-seeking interest groups (Posner 1974; Stigler 1975).[2] And since members of Congress do not have incentives to promote the best interests of citizens and the nation, representatives will listen only to advocates who can construct politically appealing messages (C. O. Jones 1976). This in turn creates incentives for policy experts to abandon scientific norms as they participate in the policymaking process and to justify policies based on "sham science" and hack "advocacy analysis."

These widely cited positive theories of political economy present a rather bleak assessment of democracy that stands in stark contrast to the founding ideals of the U.S. constitutional republic: representatives advancing informed public policies. The standard view of Congress is of a legislature that systematically rejects the latest and best research and analysis on persistent social problems or of a body that uses research-based information only in a deeply cynical manner. And because public policies are uninformed, they are socially inefficient: citizens cannot have the information or expertise to know what is in their best interest, but they nevertheless reward only efforts to promote legislation that is within their immediate comprehension; Congress caters to citizens' opinions even when those opinions are ill informed and not in citizens' actual interests. In this view, the public-interest theory of legislation, which expects well-informed

---

2. For example, Stigler (1975, 115) writes, "The 'protection of the public' theory of regulation must say that the choice of import quotas is dictated by the concern of the federal government for an adequate domestic supply of petroleum in the event of a war—a remark calculated to elicit uproarious laughter at the Petroleum Club."

public policies, is naive and soft: given these assumed realities of democratic accountability, there is no mechanism or incentive to harness policy research and expertise for legislative policymaking, even though society becomes better off as its legislation and policy become more informed. Democracy simply parallels market failures with governmental failures.

This bleak view of democratic government contrasts with the intentions of the authors of the U.S. Constitution, such as James Madison, who believed that a well-designed government could channel the motives of government officials to act on behalf of national interests. Must legislated policy be inefficient and ill informed relative to the current state of policy knowledge in order to be politically acceptable or democratically legitimate? Is contemporary democracy indeed tied to forms of social regulation that deny the empirical complexity of social problems or that relegate all expert judgments to the publicly unobserved processes of administration?

∽

This book reconsiders this dilemma in the context of the politics of socially efficient policy, a type of expertise-informed policy where the aggregate benefits are expected to exceed the aggregate costs. One major form of socially efficient policy is known as market-oriented or incentives regulation, where the government seeks to remedy a market failure by creating incentives for private parties to make choices that are consistent with the public interest (Schultze 1977). Using incentives is often more efficient and effective in reaching social goals than "command-and-control" regulation, where the government attempts to compel private parties to conform to social goals in ways that are contrary to private interests.

In principle, these socially efficient policies should receive widespread endorsement in the majoritarian political process since, by definition, greater efficiency makes citizens and interest groups in the aggregate better off relative to the status quo. Congress could use this type of policy to reach desired social goals without increasing taxes or requiring new expenditures from businesses and other private entities. Socially efficient policies increase the pie instead of merely redistributing the available set of social resources. Such policies promise to do such things as clean the air at lower cost to industry, improve the quality of health care delivery at lower insurance rates, and improve grade school test scores without having to raise new taxes. Because they enhance welfare, socially efficient policies can appeal to a diverse set of interests, and policies that appeal to diverse interests are consistent with the type of common good that James Madison, in his republican theory of representation, envisioned that Congress would likely promote (1961, 325).

The established positive theories of political economy and congressional policymaking assert the strong claim, however, that Congress will never take this efficient-incentives form of regulation under serious consideration (e.g., Shepsle and Weingast 1984). The abstract policy expertise that informs these proposals is simply beyond the grasp of ordinary citizens and is difficult to communicate in the form of a sound bite. Political scientist Douglas Arnold, for example, claims that the incentives form of social regulation constitutes a "politically repellent" policy option for members of Congress (1990, 79–80). At about the time Arnold's widely read book was published, however, George H. W. Bush's administration had proposed to Congress a major incentives regulatory program of emissions trading as a way to address the acid rain problem, a highly salient issue throughout the 1980s (see chapter 6). And indeed, by 1990 a large majority of Congress had embraced this approach as the best solution to the seemingly intractable controversy (see R. E. Cohen 1992). Why would Congress choose a "politically repellant" policy to address a highly contentious and salient policy problem?

The standard theories of Congress cannot explain the legislative success of the 1990 acid rain emissions trading program. It could be argued that this program, as a single case, is only an empirical "error" for the established literature's otherwise systematic account of the government's failure to use expertise. The acid rain emissions trading program, however, is a prominent enough example of the use of the incentives form of regulation in legislation to merit examination. This program, based on the relatively arcane incentives regulatory logic derived from microeconomic price theory, was considered the principal reason for passage of the 1990 Clean Air Act Amendments, the most comprehensive regulatory act ever undertaken by the U.S. government. Finding a solution to the acid rain problem was the major reason Congress overcame ten years of otherwise fruitless debate over reauthorizing the act.

And the acid rain case is by no means singular. Prior research has documented the empirical importance of policy research and expertise for legislative politics, to varying degrees, in such diverse areas as transportation deregulation (Derthick and Quirk 1985), Superfund cleanup (J. T. Hamilton 1997), tobacco policy (Fritschler 1989), education reform (O'Day 1995), Medicare reform (D. G. Smith 1992), nutrition policy (Nestle 2002), and welfare reform (Baum 1991).[3]

The persistence that Congress shows in using expertise to advance the public interest, if only on occasion, suggests that the established theory and certainly its strong claims cannot stand as a complete explanatory theory. The standard positive account of legislative politics has had great predictive success, and its proponents have no trouble locating anecdotal empirical confirmation, since examples of ill-informed legislation abound. Indeed, it may be that democracy more often produces uninformed and inefficient outcomes than informed and efficient outcomes. But a good theory should not only predict typical or "modal" outcomes; a good theory should explain both success and failure or more generally explain the variance in the use of expertise in the legislative process irrespective of the number of observations that fall into the success and failure categories. Expertise in service of the public interest sometimes prevails in democratic politics, and so we must have some way to explain the occurrence of both democratic success and failure.

In this book, I develop one such explanation. I show that much of lobbying politics involves constructing what I call "causal frameworks" within which political actors can learn about their self-inter-

---

3. Other observable facts of the congressional policy process also are inconsistent with this standard view that scientific policy expertise is largely irrelevant to policy-making in Congress and in the larger political process. Most obvious are the recent developments of public policy as an academic enterprise and as an area of professional training (J. Goldstein 1993, 15; Skocpol 1987). In addition, research-based think tanks that do not have a political constituency are accorded particular influence and stature in policy decision making (Bimber 1996; Ricci 1993). Heclo and others have shown that contemporary "issue network" policy-making environments confer particular stature in the Washington lobbing community on groups with scientific policy knowledge and that recognized policy experts receive special access to Congress (Carpenter, Esterling, and Lazer 1998; Heclo 1978; Michaels 1992, 248).

ests in complex issues. Key to my argument is an assertion that many citizens, interest groups, and legislators have what are known as "extrinsic preferences" about public policies—they care about the effects of government interventions in an instrumental sense rather than the intrinsic moral, cultural, or symbolic qualities of the policies themselves. Outcomes are particularly important for interest groups: environmental groups want government actions to lead to cleaner air, trade associations want to raise the incomes of their member firms, and so on. If a group cares about the consequences of government interventions, then its preferences among available policies will depend critically on its beliefs regarding how government actions are causally connected to outcomes, or the means to the intended ends. That is, groups' preferences are intimately linked to a set of hypotheses regarding the expected consequences of government action.

I label this set of causal beliefs regarding the connections between a policy and its expected outcome the causal framework for the policy alternative. Every policy proposal, either explicitly or implicitly, contains a causal framework. In effect, a policy proposal is a set of hypotheses that if the government undertakes a set of actions (x), then a set of outcomes (y) are likely to occur. The hypotheses contained in the causal framework often are developed, researched, and best defined by policy experts in the research community. I assert that the politics of expert policy ideas—or of the political economy of expertise—depends on the informational properties of the available, expert-defined causal frameworks or, equivalently, the state of knowledge for the policy proposal. In essence, because political actors' preferences about policies depend on the hypothetical relationships between policies and outcomes, political actors also care about what is known about these hypotheses for each policy under consideration. This is to say that the prevailing causal beliefs regarding the expected impact of a policy will matter to political actors, but the extent to which these beliefs matter depends critically on the evidence indicating that the beliefs are plausible. If an analogy will help, the causal framework is like a road map, but drivers also want to know about the quality of the roads, traffic conditions, detours, relative safety, and possibly the scenery and attractions along the way. Drivers can select a route only imperfectly when relying only on a road map and do not want to arrive too late or harried, so they often will ask friends and colleagues about the details and aspects of alternative routes.

My explanation for how the state of knowledge—the informational properties of a causal framework—affects the behavior of political actors draws on concepts that will be familiar to anyone who has had an introductory statistics class (but should have intuitive plausibility for those who have not). In a causal epistemology, the state of knowledge has two major components. The first component is the degree of uncertainty in the causal framework, or experts' confidence in the hypotheses contained in the causal framework. All social processes have a random component, and so even if a policy is expected to make society better off, on implementation the intervention could make society worse off. Uncertainty is a function of the strength and quality of evidence regarding the program's effectiveness—conceptually, the size of the N in a statistical model.

The second component is the presence of conceptual or methodological ambiguity in the causal framework. Unlike uncertainty, ambiguity often cannot be resolved with additional empirical evidence. In the real world of social science, a given set of empirical results may be explained by different and even contradictory causal theories. In addition, different methods can confirm competing expectations even with the same data. In policy evaluation one expert may hold up a set of analyses and claim the results show that the policy will be a great success, while another expert may say that the results indicate that the policy will be a great disaster. Both uncertainty and ambiguity are variable and are subject to change over time as new research emerges. At any one time, however, these properties of the causal framework are exogenous to politics as the state of knowledge of the policy that has been socially constructed through peer review and other collegial processes in the policy research community.

It is often easy for Congress to learn about the hypothetical or expected outcomes of a policy alternative as embodied in its causal framework. These outcomes are often stated in the proposal itself: for example, if Congress were to adopt an emissions trading plan to control acid rain, firms could be expected to reduce sulfur dioxide emissions beyond the reductions achieved through command-and-control policies, and at lower cost. But Congress wants to know not just what the expected outcomes are from an intervention but also the likelihood that these outcomes will come about. Policies that entail too much uncertainty risk failure, and those that are ambiguous can result in unintended consequences such as increased divisiveness among groups or foreclosed opportunities to provide new benefits for groups and citizens. To complete the example, Congress will want to enact emissions trading for the acid rain problem if it is likely to work as promised but not if it is likely to go awry and create an environmental disaster at high cost to industry.

In general, it is difficult for Congress to know about the current, research-based state of knowledge for the full array of policies before it. In contrast, it is relatively easy for specialized interest groups to know about the state of knowledge for a policy, both because groups often have experts on staff that specialize in a narrow set of policies and because groups know very well how policies are likely to affect their special interests. The core question of the political economy of expertise is whether and under what conditions Congress can learn about the state of knowledge regarding the likely effectiveness of a policy from the assertions and arguments of interest groups.

Unfortunately, there is always the possibility that interest groups will attempt to exploit this dependence and try to convince members of Congress to enact a policy that is contrary to their constituents' interests but instead provides private benefits to the interest groups. I show that the research-based state of knowledge for a policy, which in the United States is exogenous to politics, sometimes gives an advantage to one side or the other in the structure and quality of competing lobbyists' arguments. In effect, the degree of uncertainty and ambiguity affects the groups' motivations for lobbying for or against a policy and for investing resources in a lobbying effort. Because groups' motivations to support or oppose a policy are correlated with the state of knowledge, Congress often can make inferences from debate among groups about the amount of uncertainty or ambiguity governing the policy. When this occurs, lobbyists' arguments in debates and in public hearings help Congress to make a correct decision and to avoid policies that risk failure or other unintended consequences upon implementation.

In effect, Congress and interest groups often find they have a mutual interest in solving complex policy problems by using the best research-based information and ideas available. And importantly, interest groups create this effective pressure out of self-interest: the theory behind the political economy of expertise does not rely on assumptions that interest groups act altruistically on society's behalf. If research gives an advantage to one side of a debate over the other among lobbyists, then, without anyone necessarily intending it, research has a positive impact on politics. This is often in the public interest: in many circumstances, interest groups pressure Congress to enact high-quality policies that are likely to work well in practice, and not to enact low-quality policies that risk failure or lead to further divisiveness among groups.

In part I of this book, I develop my argument about the political economy of expertise, or an explanation for the variance in the use and nonuse of public-interested policy expertise in the legislative process. I build the argument in three steps, considering in turn the interests of ordinary citizens, interest groups, and legislators in chapters 2–4. In part II, I set out a series of case studies to illustrate how the political economy of expertise works in practice under a variety of conditions. And I conclude by reconnecting the empirical results to larger discussions of expertise in democratic politics.

In chapter 2, I address the fundamental question of whether expert knowledge and ideas can ever be expected to influence legislative politics in a democracy. The tension between expertise and accountability in democracy is nothing new. Political philosophers have long noted that the manner in which citizens hold legislators accountable affects members' incentives to use knowledge and expertise in their work. I show that the theory of representation adopted will determine whether public-interested expert ideas can be expected to inform public debate among interest groups and legislation that emerges from democratic legislatures. Much of the established positive literature on Congress assumes (often implicitly) that representation in the U.S. Congress can best be described as a direct democracy. In a direct democracy, citizens require their representatives to enact policies that are immediately comprehensible. In this type of system, reelection-seeking legislators cynically cater to constituents' immediate demands for legislative benefits, even if these demands are based on ignorance, fear, or irrational biases and even if the policies that result run counter to citizens' present or long-term interests.

Political philosophers have long recognized these limitations of direct democracy as a form of governance. Indeed, the original authors of the U.S. Constitution explicitly designed the legislative branch to avoid the limitations of direct democracy and sought instead to institutionalize a republican form of constitutional democracy. In the republican mode of representation, legislators have incentives to exercise discretion and judgment and to construct well-informed solutions to complex and pressing national problems; citizens expect legislators to use expertise in their work. In this mode of representation, legislators who want to be reelected do not cynically cater to citizen ignorance but instead endeavor to develop reputations for quality, diligence, and trustworthiness among their constituents.

One limitation of republican democratic theory is that it does not supply a positive mechanism for why legislators use expertise to solve national problems. Republican theory states that citizens expect their representatives to use expertise as a part of their discretion, but citizens' relative ignorance prevents them from compelling legislators to use policy expertise on constituents' behalf. In chapter 3, I offer a positive theory for how the contemporary U.S. Congress, spurred on by a large number of interest groups, has incentives to use expertise to adopt expert-informed, socially efficient policies. Social efficiency is a causal framework for a policy alternative that, as an analytical matter, holds that the benefits from a government intervention should exceed the costs—the gainers should gain more than the losers should lose. My basic argument holds that socially efficient policies, because they enhance welfare, can attract support for an innovative regulatory program from a broad cross-section of interest groups. These policies are in the larger public interest because they create new opportunities to meet social aspirations and policy objectives (see Schultze 1977), but interest groups pressure Congress to develop these policies for self-interested reasons. And assuming that citizens exercise a republican form of accountability, Congress is free to experiment with socially efficient policies that make society better off to satisfy the demands of the largest number of interest groups.

Despite their theoretical appeal, these socially efficient policies sometimes fail to receive support even from interest groups that might benefit from the efficiency improvements (see Kelman 1981).

But on other occasions, interest groups strongly endorse these policies. In chapter 3, I show that the variable informational properties of the causal framework linking policies to outcomes can explain the variance in interest groups' support for socially efficient policies, which in turn helps to explain their overall place in legislative politics. The first property is the degree of uncertainty inherent in the causal framework. Assuming that interest groups are risk averse about prospective gains and risk acceptant about prospective losses (see Tversky and Kahneman 1981), the availability of empirical evidence in the form of policy evaluations strongly affects interest groups' motivation to lobby for and against efficient policies. The second property is the degree of conceptual or methodological ambiguity inherent in the framework.[4] Here, experts may propose competing or contradictory expectations. For example, a policy may be expected to perform well by one evaluation standard and poorly by another, or experts may use different methods to confirm competing expectations.

I show that, for better or worse, prospectively gaining groups need unambiguous and compelling evidence demonstrating the policy's likely effectiveness before they will mobilize their support, while prospectively harmed groups mobilize their opposition when less is known about the policy.[5] And assuming that Congress experiments with socially efficient policies as a way to satisfy interest group demands, one implication of this argument is that not only do interest groups pressure Congress to develop socially efficient policies that are well-informed by research and have a strong prospect of yielding the expected results, but they also pressure Congress not to develop "efficient" policies that look good on paper but are likely to fail in

---

4. Uncertainty and ambiguity are related in the sense that in some cases, more information and better analyses can resolve conceptual and methodological ambiguities. But uncertainty and ambiguity are analytically distinct because ambiguities often cannot be resolved with additional research-based information; in general, ambiguity can be resolved only through a consensus on theory and method in the expert research community.

5. It is relatively infrequent that a policy will be backed by clear and unambiguous scientific evidence; as a result, efficient policies often are unpopular in politics. Like the established theory, my theory predicts that efficient policies frequently will falter in the legislative process. Unlike the established theory, my theory can explain those cases when efficiency does prevail in the legislative process, like the emissions trading case I describe in chapter 6.

practice. In effect, interest groups pressure Congress to sponsor socially efficient policies that accord with the current research and state of knowledge, and interest groups do so for their own private reasons.

Chapter 4 considers how interest groups' motivations to support or oppose policies, as described in chapter 3, systematically translate into pressure on Congress to develop or not develop socially efficient legislation. Congress has strong incentives to experiment with analytical, socially efficient policies to benefit the largest number of interest groups and to advance citizens' interests in achieving pressing policy objectives, but these innovative policies may fail to deliver their expected benefits and may even make things worse relative to the original status quo policy.[6] Unfortunately, Congress lacks the analytical capacity as well as the private information that groups have on the effect of policies on their specific interests to know whether the policy is likely to succeed in practice. *

In chapter 4, I show that under some conditions, Congress can learn about the likelihood that a policy will yield its expected costs and benefits, or its relative chances of success in the real world, from debate among interest group lobbyists. The key to the argument is that, fortuitously, Congress's interests in enacting efficient policies are by and large compatible with those of many interest groups. If groups expect to benefit from the program, they also want Congress to enact policies that have a high chance of succeeding in practice and to avoid policies that have a high chance of failure. That is, interest groups' motivations for supporting or opposing a policy depend on the state of knowledge that governs the policy, such as the degree of uncertainty or ambiguity, and Congress often can make inferences about the state of knowledge from the arguments that interest groups make in debate. In signaling models, this is known as a separating equilibrium.

Unfortunately for Congress and for advocates of efficiency reform, these conditions for a separating equilibrium often do not exist. When there is ambiguity in the causal framework, interest groups can use the same empirical information and evaluation

---

6. An illustration of market regulation gone haywire is the current California power crisis; see, e.g., Charles Feldman, "The California Power Quagmire," http://www.cnn.com, January 4, 2001.

research results to make contradictory claims; thus, both sides pool on the same type of statement to Congress. In this case, the policy will appear too divisive, and members of Congress will not be favorable, all else being equal. In this way, I show the variable conditions for legislators' capacity and the propensity to use research and expertise. And, given the relative dearth of high-quality and compelling evaluation research relative to the quantity of theoretical policy research, my argument explains why the legislative process appears to be biased against expertise and innovative policies.

Chapter 5 introduces the case studies. In my argument, lobbying politics depends heavily on the expert-informed state of knowledge, such as uncertainty and ambiguity, conditions that vary across policies and over time. The case studies illustrate the politics surrounding three major congressional initiatives to enact socially efficient policies—in the areas of health, education, and the environment. Each case illustrates the pattern of debate in congressional committee hearings under a different condition set out in the theoretical chapters, which I label the certainty, uncertainty, and ambiguity conditions. This chapter gives some useful background information on the socially efficient, market-oriented policies that I explore in chapters 6–8 and provides the research design for the qualitative analysis of the case studies that follow.

The case study in chapter 6 examines the sulfur dioxide emissions trading program that Congress incorporated into the Clean Air Act and President George H. W. Bush signed into law in September 1990.[7] Congress embraced the emissions trading approach after years of struggling unsuccessfully to address the acid rain issue under command-and-control approaches: emissions trading "became the key ingredient in political trade-offs that eventually cemented an acid rain agreement" ("Clean Air Act" 1990, 230). In this case, a considerable amount of empirical evaluation research suggested that the emissions trading program would control the emissions that cause acid rain and would do so at low cost to industry. Environmental economists gathered this evidence from a decade of experimentation in the Environmental Protection Agency (EPA) with analogous emissions trading programs. The United Mine Workers (UMW) opposed

---

7. Clean Air Act §401(IV-A), 42 U.S.C.A. §7651.

the acid rain emissions trading program because, if the program worked as planned, it would remove a regulatory protection for high-sulfur coal. But the UMW was never observed to claim that the program would fail in a causal or empirical sense; instead, the UMW claimed that the program would work so well that an unacceptable number of high-sulfur coal miners would lose their jobs. In contrast, a wide array of organizations, including environmental groups, electric utilities, consumer groups, and state regulators, endorsed emissions trading as an empirically sound approach to acid rain control, and the program received widespread bipartisan congressional support. This case illustrates the politics of a research-based socially efficient policy under a relative degree of certainty in the causal framework.

The case study in chapter 7 examines a proposal that was considered despite a relative dearth of research-based empirical evidence: the 1991 Bush administration proposal to convert the Elementary and Secondary Education Act (ESEA) chapter 1 funding into an unrestricted school-choice voucher program. In the 1991 hearings, groups that opposed school choice—teachers' unions and school board representatives in particular—argued that a school-choice program would entail too many risks for the public education system since a true voucher program had never been tried. In response, the U.S. Catholic Conference (USCC), whose schools potentially stood to gain a tremendous windfall in new students from an unrestricted voucher program, was not observed to claim that school choice would likely reform public education or improve educational outcomes in the manner intended by the Bush administration. In this case, such a claim would have been untenable and unpersuasive because voucher programs were untested and very little research evidence existed to suggest that school choice improved educational outcomes. Instead, the USCC lobbyist focused her testimony on the normative importance of free choice in American society. And, perhaps for a variety of reasons, the Democrat-controlled committee decided to shelve the choice plan.

The 1990s subsequently saw a decade of experiments in voucher programs, most prominently in Milwaukee and Cleveland. The education policy community has deep conceptual disagreements, however, about the proper goals of education reform—principally,

whether programs should be evaluated at an individual level or systemwide. The second half of the case in chapter 7 examines the hearings on the George W. Bush administration's school-choice proposal
to illustrate the conditions where there is high-quality empirical evaluation information but considerable ambiguity in the research literature regarding the likely outcomes from such a policy. In this case,
groups on both sides of the debate used the available research to talk
past each other. This time, the Republican-controlled committee
shelved the voucher program. In terms of the overall argument,
chapter 7 illustrates two conditions: the first half shows debate under
uncertainty, and the second half shows debate under the ambiguity
that comes from experts' contradictory expectations.

Finally, the case in chapter 8 compares the testimony of an established professional group, the American Medical Association (AMA),
with other groups on the 1972 Nixon HMO proposal. In this case, the
policy research community was nearly unanimous in stating that
there was a considerable amount of empirical support behind the
HMO concept as a means of controlling rising health care costs. The
AMA lobbyists, however, invoked their professional authority to
assert that HMOs stood as an "untested experiment," taking a stand
contrary to the published evaluation literature. The AMA always
carefully invoked its professional authority when making claims contrary to the evaluation literature, trying to focus debate on the quality of care in HMOs, a dimension on which the group had a rhetorical
advantage. The lobbyists who supported the program— representing
group practitioners, nurses, labor unions, and insurance companies—lacked a similar rhetorical advantage; these lobbyists took
great care to support all of their claims with a literal reading of published evaluation data and results. The capacity of professional
groups to use their expertise to create methodological ambiguities in
the causal framework is seen in the contrast in the arguments of these
two sets of groups. The effect was that lobbyists on both sides of the
debate pooled on the same type of arguments both for and against
the policy. As in the 2001 school-choice case, the debate on HMOs
shed little light on the likely effectiveness of the policy, illustrating
how ambiguity in the form of competing expectations affects debate.

Chapter 9 discusses the cases and places the findings in the theoretical framework of chapters 3 and 4. The analyses of the testimony

show that the opposing groups were constrained from making research-based arguments in the 1989 acid rain hearings, which had unambiguous evaluations to show that the emissions trading program was likely to work well in practice, and that the supporting groups were constrained in the 1991 school-choice case, when there were no empirical evaluations to indicate its likely success or failure. In these two cases, supporting and opposing groups separated in the types of arguments they made in testimony. While hearings may more frequently resemble the "noisier" case studies like the 1972 HMO hearings and the 2001 school-choice hearings, I argue that the established literature is simply incorrect to assert that all hearing testimony is systematically unrelated to the evaluation research. The 1989 acid rain and 1991 school-choice cases show the conditions under which interest groups, acting out of self-interest, publicly pressure Congress in a manner consistent with the research-based state of knowledge.

I end by reconnecting the empirical discussion from the case studies to the broader context of constitutional democratic theory. While this book's specific research question is whether evaluation research systematically conditions lobbyists' arguments in testimony, this volume at root addresses the question of whether technical and analytical policy research has a place in the U.S. legislative process in both the empirical and the normative sense. Contrary to much of the established wisdom on Congress, I argue that contemporary republican democracy is considerably more resilient with respect to its ideals for enlightened representation than the established positive theories of congressional policy-making suggest. Innovative policies do not always and everywhere fail in legislative politics because of some fixed institutional flaws but because interest groups are often unwilling to endorse a policy when it is unclear if the policy will work in practice. Expert, socially efficient policy will sometimes prevail—a public-spirited policy outcome—even in the presence of many active private interest groups.

This optimistic view of democracy does not rest on naive assumptions about the human spirit or on some diffuse claims about the role of ideas in politics. Expert-informed, socially efficient policies in principle may succeed in U.S. politics even without assuming enlightened interest groups or a beneficent or omniscient legislature.

With sufficient information, interest groups may pressure Congress to enact research-based socially efficient policies for private reasons. Congress may look favorably on these expert-informed, socially efficient policies even when the legislature does not itself have the expertise to do comparative static analysis, hypothesis testing, or any of the traditional activities of policy experts in developing innovative policies. And most importantly, the system tends to weed out those proposals that may sound good on paper but are too risky to be tried.

There is no necessary contradiction between policy expertise and democratic accountability, either theoretically or empirically. The political system's apparent bias against expertise may arise simply from a lack of compelling policy ideas and solid research-based evaluation evidence in the academic study of public policies. The effect of uncertainty and ambiguity in the evaluation research is to create a bias in politics in favor of the regulatory status quo. If the cause of the frequent failure of expert-informed, socially efficient policy can be shown to be simply informational, then a political science perspective can encourage increased optimism among reform advocates as the scientific knowledge of policy effects accumulates.

PART I

~

THE POLITICS OF POLICY EXPERTISE

2

Policy Expertise and
Accountability to Citizens

In this age of information and analysis, public policy issues—as well as the accompanying policy alternatives, debate, and legislation—can be quite technical and complex. This complexity can make it difficult for citizens to understand policy issues and the implications of policy choices. Representatives have better access to policy analysis and information than do ordinary citizens just by virtue of holding office—through staffers, interest group communications, hearings, and Congress's other day-to-day activities. The information asymmetry between citizens and representatives makes it difficult for citizens to exercise democratic accountability. And as an empirical matter, the manner in which citizens hold their representatives accountable affects legislators' incentives to use policy expertise to advance the public interest (compare Fenno 1978 and Mayhew 1974).

Much of the prominent literature on Congress makes a strong claim that expertise is incompatible with democratic accountability. In particular, the literature on positive political economy argues that democratic politics is inherently biased in favor of ill-informed, inefficient public policies. This "democratic failure" is driven by the assumption, often implicitly evoked, that the U.S. legislative process can best be described as a direct democracy. In the several variants of the "hard-edged" or positive theories of legislative politics, reelection-seeking legislators invariably exploit citizen ignorance for personal gain. In one variant of the theory, legislators cynically mislead citizens by masking inefficient legislation with public-interested sounding platitudes. In another variant of the theory, members sincerely give constituents the inefficient legislation that they, through their ignorance, demand. Since electoral accountability is a stable feature of democracy, the leading theories predict that members of Congress should never use expertise in authoring legislation in a way that advances the public interest.

This established literature on positive political economy has had considerable predictive success. Congress indeed enacts unenlightened and inefficient legislation quite frequently, and it is relatively easy for researchers in this tradition to collect anecdotes and stylized facts to "confirm" that the theory is correct.[1] The problem with this established theory is that it is wholly incapable of explaining the instances when members of Congress do use public-interested expertise in developing legislation. In the next two chapters, I develop a model that can explain Congress's inclination and disinclination to use policy expertise under varying conditions—that is, I set out a causal mechanism that can explain both democratic success and failure.

In this chapter, I explore where the established literature has gone wrong. In many ways, accountability to citizens can lead members of Congress to seek expert advice and good information in developing legislation. In this republican mode of representation, representatives who use expertise can gain greater electoral security, can gain greater influence among their colleagues, and can better advance their careers in the legislature. Citizens can create incentives for members to sponsor informed legislation that is consistent with constituents' actual interests rather than their misinformed preferences.

The Tension between Expertise and Democracy

Modern democratic states intervene in the economy and in society in a wide variety of circumstances. Governments often take responsibility for providing public goods such as elementary education and national defense, for reducing pollution and other externalities, for

---

1. And thus commit the logical fallacy of affirming the consequent. It can never be said that a hypothesis is true because it agrees with the facts, but one can say that a hypothesis is false when the facts are inconsistent (see Blaug 1980, 15).

rate setting and promoting competition in incomplete markets such as in health care and public utilities, and by providing a social welfare safety net and otherwise preserving the social order (Katznelson 1996, 25). Each of these social and economic problems is caused by a limitation or failure in the market or in some social collective-action problem; in each case, the social structure leads to suboptimal conditions that cannot be overcome by individuals acting on their own (Arrow 1963; Bator 1958; Olson 1965; Stokey and Zeckhauser 1978, 298–308).[2] And according to the public-interest theory of legislation, democratic government will use its coercive power to advance citizens' aspirations for the kind of world they would like to live in, not the world that markets and individual choices happen to produce.

In the United States, the propensity of both state and federal governments to act on these complex policy problems has encouraged the development of policy science as an applied subdiscipline of academic social science (Bulmer 1987, 35; Skocpol 1987, 41). Policy science uses the systematic theory and empirical methods of economics, sociology, demographics, and political and other social sciences to illuminate the structural origins of complex social problems and to develop potential remedies (Sutton 1996, 203). The programs that experts develop often are based on abstract assumptions of complex social reality, and the proposed program designs state sophisticated hypothetical causal mechanisms relating the intervention into the economy or social order to possible outcomes (Wildavsky 1979, 126).

Like the other social sciences, policy science generally adheres to standards of scientific inquiry, and the accumulated knowledge on policy problems can be quite sophisticated, detailed, elaborate, and technical. Experts draw on this accumulated knowledge to propose policy solutions, which, because of peer review and other academic institutions, tend to be more effective and more socially efficient than the status quo policy, regulation, or program (Wildavsky 1979, 114).

---

2. A core tenet of neoclassical economics is that markets fail to perform efficiently in some circumstances. Market failure is the inability of private parties, acting rationally, to make simultaneous choices in Nash equilibrium that will make everyone better off (see generally Mueller 1989, 11). For example, high transaction costs and collective action problems create undesirable externalities (Bator 1958), information asymmetries allow for price and demand manipulation (Arrow 1963), and free riding inhibits the production of public goods (Olson 1965).

Nonexpert policies, in contrast, contain simple or direct regulatory methods that do not draw on the current state of knowledge and so tend to be inefficient because they misallocate resources and responsibilities, stifle innovation, and often are applied inconsistently (Lave 1981, 11).[3]

Policy science also shares with the other social sciences an empirical focus, so policy science practitioners view policy proposals as hypothetical solutions to social problems. Because social problems are complex in their origins, there is always uncertainty about whether the policy will have its intended effects. Perhaps the policy will work as described on paper, but there is always the possibility of failure, ineffectiveness, or disaster. Experts believe that they must understand the technical aspects of policies as an empirical matter if the policy can be expected to achieve its intended ends. Policy scientists try to learn the likely consequences of policies through systematic empirical research, evaluation studies, demonstration programs, and the like (Rose 1993; Wildavsky 1979, 35).

In contrast to experts, few citizens read policy journals or pore over mountains of technical analysis. And even if citizens were so inclined, they likely would find such analyses inaccessible. The theory and analysis that inform expert policy draw on specialized knowledge that is often communicated in the technical language of social science learned only through rigorous professional training. This training and background knowledge are necessary for understanding how each policy is likely to work in practice and which policy alternatives are desirable from anyone's perspective. Indeed, without the benefit of rigorous scientific training, citizens not only lack the capacity to comprehend analytical information but also tend to hold mistaken beliefs about public policy. Scientists and other well-informed policy

---

3. For example, the most efficient and least-cost allocation of pollution control responsibility is that allocation where the marginal cost of controlling emissions is equal across emission sources (Lave 1981, 15; Stokey and Zeckhauser 1978, 39). These marginal equalities cannot be achieved through direct government mandate. The government cannot make case-by-case standards because it does not know the marginal cost to firms to control emission sources, which is a function of plant characteristics and changing control technology. Experts commonly propose the solution of creating a market for emissions, which creates an incentive for each firm to achieve the least-cost control method and provides a mechanism for firms to control to the point where the marginal control cost is equal across emission sources (see, e.g., Tietenberg 1985).

experts often bemoan how citizens' beliefs tend to be inconsistent with scientific findings and expert opinion (Breyer 1993; I. Goldstein and Goldstein 2002; Margolis 1996).

Because of the background knowledge required, ordinary citizens have difficulty exercising their judgment on complex policy issues and possible alternatives on the government's agenda and particularly in identifying the most effective and efficient policy solutions. Public debate among citizens can never reach the level of expertise required for setting policy in complex social problems, in the sense of applying the current state of research-based knowledge as a means to reach society's highest aspirations. This is to say that citizens in contemporary democracy face a severe principal-agent problem, which Lupia and McCubbins (1998) label the "democratic dilemma." Legislators (the agents) and citizens (the principals) may or may not have similar preferences on policies, but legislators have information that the constituents lack about the quality of policies and which policy is in fact most in constituents' interest. Citizens clearly have trouble holding the government accountable for its actions when they cannot understand what government actions mean or how policies are likely to affect citizens' interests.

Accountability, however, is the hallmark of democracy. And since citizens' vote choices affect legislators' job security, members of Congress take their role as representatives very seriously (see Fenno 1978; Mayhew 1974). As I show next, the accountability mechanism that citizens employ can have powerful consequences for the government's ability to use policy expertise on behalf of the public interest.

The Established Literature: Government Failure to Parallel Market Failures

The prevailing positive theories of U.S. legislative politics forcefully state that democratic politics as practiced leads to inefficient and ill-informed legislation.[4] In each case, this result follows from an assumption, usually implicitly imposed, that U.S. legislative politics is best described as a direct democracy. In a direct democracy, legis-

---

4. For an overview of positive theories of legislatures and politics, see Ordeshook 1990; Shepsle and Weingast 1995.

lators respond to citizen ignorance simply by giving the people what they want. For example, Shepsle and Weingast (1984) argue that legislators' preferences are a direct function of (uninformed) district-level preferences. To these authors, democratic government is merely a means to translate district-level preferences into social choices. In these authors' words, "The geographical basis for representation determines, in a natural way, a political objective function for legislative agents. . . . Political institutions aggregate these preferences, usually through some voting rule or bureaucratic process, into political choices" (419).

While it is difficult for citizens to know what policies will make them best off, a kind of information that requires expertise to interpret and is extremely costly to gather, citizens gather information on legislator behavior very cheaply, since this kind of information is naturally produced in the course of an election campaign. Voters can use the information produced by challengers and communicated through the mass media to reward or punish incumbents for past votes and policy initiatives (Kingdon 1989, 60).[5] In this view, members of Congress deliver legislation that maximizes citizens' perceived benefits, even if citizens' perceptions of their wants and desires are misinformed or ill conceived (Arnold 1990, 47; McCubbins and Sullivan 1984).

In a direct democracy, representatives do not have incentives to use the current state of knowledge or the best thinking on policy problems to design policies and to draft legislation. To illustrate, consider the fate of a representative in a direct democracy who initiates complex or expert legislation and is called to task by a challenger during the next election campaign. The red-faced incumbent may try to argue that the expert policy in fact makes citizens and the nation better off than they would have been under simpler, inexpert policy alternatives. Typical voters can never know, however, if this claim is true or false because they cannot trace back the causal connections and empirical relationship between government action and real-world consequences (Arnold 1990). Even if voters could somehow master the causal argument, they could not compare the outcomes

---

5. What is important is the form of accountability that legislators believe citizens use when making voting choices. The discussion in this chapter takes on the incumbent's theory of voters.

from the expert policy to those that would have occurred, counter-factually, under the simpler alternatives.

In a direct democracy, legislators who promote complex expert policy that ordinary citizens cannot comprehend appear, at least on the surface, to want to limit or shirk accountability. Developing complex policies, where the programmatic means are not directly and obviously linked to stated policy ends, simply raises citizens' suspicions that their representatives are up to no good. By contrast, consider the fate of representatives who initiate simple or inexpert legislation. These incumbents will not be vulnerable to challengers' claims that the representatives should have sponsored some complex or expert policy, since voters with limited knowledge of policies cannot compare the outcomes of the simple policy to the expected effects of the expert policy. In addition, the simple policy allows for direct accountability.

When citizens exercise strict control over their representatives' behavior, as in a direct democracy, they create incentives for legislators to sponsor inexpert and uninformed policies, even though expert policies generally promise greater benefits and efficiency and more closely embody the current state of knowledge for policy problems. In this "delegate model" of representation, members comply with constituents' uninformed opinions even when those opinions run counter to citizens' actual interests. Under direct democracy, legislators maximize their chances of reelection by catering to citizens' ignorance, biases, and fears.

Recognizing this limitation, citizens in a direct democracy may instead simply give their representatives free rein to do whatever they like, but this also does not solve the democratic dilemma and in many ways makes things worse. In this "trustee model" of representation, legislators exploit citizens' ignorance. For example, the neoliberal Chicago school of regulation argues that in the absence of informed accountability, politicians give politically connected industries inefficient regulatory protection in exchange for campaign contributions or other forms of material support (Posner 1974; Stigler 1975). As another example, the rational-choice theory of "blame-shifting" legislators argues that legislators purposefully create inefficient regulatory programs so that the legislators may subsequently "help" citizens navigate all the bureaucratic red tape (Fiorina

1989). To get away with enacting this patently inefficient legislation that directly contradicts citizens' true interests, legislators simply manipulate constituents with facile platitudes and purely symbolic statements to the effect that Congress is pursuing the public interest when in fact it is not (Mayhew 1974, 132).

The trustee and delegate models of representation are two horns of a dilemma for direct democracies. In a direct democracy, what is important to the voter is clarity, that incumbents are taking strong stands on issues and taking direct action to address problems. But in the end, citizens are left holding the bag and have no means to encourage the government to advance social aspirations in any informed way.

Because the established positive theory of U.S. politics assumes that the legislative process is best described as a direct democracy, it paints a very pessimistic picture of Congress's capacity and willingness to consider, much less to legislate, enlightened policy. The result is the well-known "textbook" Congress that has no use for policy expertise.[6] Legislators sponsor mostly discrete, inefficient pork-barrel projects that are noncontroversial and are easy for citizens to observe and appreciate (Cain, Ferejohn, and Fiorina 1987, 213; Fiorina 1989, 46; Mayhew 1974, 127–28; McCubbins and Sullivan 1987, 306). Members assign their staff to constituency-service tasks rather than to gather research on the actual effects of policies (Mayhew 1974, 124–25). To the extent that members seek out research information, they do so to lend support for programs that they sponsor to satisfy district public opinion simply as post hoc legitimation (C. O. Jones 1976, 255; Schick 1976, 217–18; Weiss 1989, 411).

In this view, democratic representation leads to government failures that parallel rather than remedy existing market failures (Barke and Riker 1982, 102; Shepsle and Weingast 1984). There are several good reasons why citizens might choose to use direct accountability despite its limitations. One possibility is that citizens care foremost about the clear expression of social and moral values in politics— even more than about actual social welfare (see Aaron, Mann, and

---

6. In the textbook Congress, legislators' primary institutional concern is to find ways to impose the costs of inefficient legislation on each other's districts. Legislators use the committee system and jurisdictional rights to collectively impose inefficient distributions on each other (see Weingast and Marshall 1988).

Taylor 1994; Kelman 1981; Majone 1989, 142–43; McFarlane and Meier 2001). In this view, citizens see politics more as a forum for the expression of community values and ideological preferences than as a means to overcome market failure or to solve social problems (Dryzek 1994, 75). In this case, citizens prefer a simple policy that embodies a clear statement of social values to a complicated policy that promises more earthly rewards. In Weberian terms, this means that citizens favor the ethic of ultimate ends over the ethic of responsibility.

A second possibility is that citizens have a preference for inefficiency. It is not unreasonable for citizens to want some governmental largesse to flow to their district, particularly if the pork is flowing to other districts as well (McCubbins and Sullivan 1987). Because representatives are accountable to local districts, the flow of benefits is determined primarily by geographic pressures, and as a consequence, the size and distribution of pork-barrel projects do not meet the efficiency standards of a distribution that would have occurred in a competitive market (Weingast, Shepsle, and Johnson 1981).

At the same time, there are "bad" reasons for citizens to employ direct accountability in the sense that they are not behaving in a manner that is instrumentally rational for reaching their goals. In particular, given the low level of information that they possess on issues, citizens may mistakenly believe that the social world in reality is simplistic, easy to comprehend, and thus readily amenable to direct government intervention. Arnold, for example, asserts that "citizens conceive of the economic world as a less complicated place than economists do, and they are far more comfortable with single-stage policies that attack problems directly" (1990, 23). If citizens really do possess this bias for simplicity, they would mistakenly believe that expert, complex policies are neither necessary nor desirable. Their plain-folk intuitions about desired policies, at least in their minds, would suffice, and they would mistakenly believe that direct democracy is the best means to achieve social goals.

In *The Logic of Congressional Action*, Arnold argues that the emissions trading legislation I examine in chapter 6 is specifically the type of expert-informed, socially efficient policy that fits these conditions: citizens and legislators should hold a bias against emissions trading and in favor of easy-to-understand command-and-control environmental policies. First, Arnold argues that citizens have strong moral beliefs about the value of rigid and simple enforcement policies as a means to express society's right to a clean environment. Arnold states that with emissions trading, "Even if legislators suddenly became converts to the notion that effluent charges were superior to environmental regulations, they would still be reluctant to support such charges if they believed that future challengers might convince their constituents that they intended to sell 'licenses to pollute'" (1990, 24–25). Members of Congress are less vulnerable to attacks from challengers when they promote inefficient command-and-control regulation, since direct "prohibitions against emissions allow legislators to declare unequivocally that they are opposed to pollution" (80). Second, Arnold argues that citizens have an overly simplistic view of environmental problems: "Most people who are not economists prefer . . . interventions that attack the problems directly, contain either a single-stage or a very few stages, and are relatively easy to understand" (24). On both of these counts, the emissions trading program is a more "politically repellant option" for members of Congress than is the seemingly more direct policy logic of command-and-control regulation (79).

Shepsle and Weingast (1984) also evoke the assumptions of direct democracy to assert that Congress is unlikely to enact socially efficient policies. In their model, legislators' preferences for the size of a program and hence its relative efficiency are a function of district-level preferences. In the single-dimension case, under majority rule, the social choice for the program size will correspond to the preference of the median legislator's district. The size would be efficient only by the accident or coincidence that this particular district's preference corresponded to the efficient size. In Shepsle and Weingast's view, "This knife-edged condition is very stringent and unlikely to be observed in practice" (1984, 423). Congress therefore should rarely if ever have motivation to seriously consider a socially efficient emissions trading policy on its own merits (see also Fiorina 1982, 34–35; McCubbins and Schwartz 1987; McCubbins and Sullivan 1987, 309).

These expectations, however, were flatly contradicted in 1990 when Congress embraced the emissions trading program for acid rain control. This implies that the conditions that foster direct democracy assumed in the literature on positive political economy do not always hold true. Other forms of representation may govern the legislative process. The democratic process might be more enlightened than Arnold, Shepsle, Weingast, and the other prominent theorists of Congress envision.

Enlightened Democratic Representation

Years ago, Tip O'Neill stated that all politics is local. Many people interpret this phrase to mean that U.S. legislative politics can be reduced to questions of the distribution of local benefits, such as new dams, subsidized railway service, and extended hours at local post office branches. But what if, for example, a small community in upstate New York would like to reduce the concentration of sulfuric acid in its rain so that the residents can enjoy fishing in the local lakes and hiking in regional forests. While acid rain is very much of local interest, the problem is of national scope, involving sulfur dioxide emissions from factories and plants mostly in the Midwest. Reducing the concentration of sulfuric acid in the rain in upstate New York, it turns out, is a highly complex policy problem that no amount of localized pork-barrel benefits can remedy. The same is true if the community wants to improve educational practices in its school districts or to get high-quality health care at reasonable costs. There are times when representing local interests involves much more than simple questions of who gets what from politics.

On its face, it is a reasonable supposition that citizens desire to be governed by publicly interested legislation, even though they do not have the expertise to know how to construct such policies. It is likely that if asked directly, few citizens would say that they prefer policies that increase pollution at a greater cost to society or policies that increase overall health risks with no offsetting benefits. If citizens intend the public interest, then most citizens would probably be glad to hear that their representatives are using expert ideas to solve social problems.

Now recall the "good" and "bad" reasons why citizens might prefer a direct democracy where the government fails to promote policies that increase social welfare: citizens may foremost want a clear expression of values in legislation, may have a preference for inefficiency, or may mistakenly believe that the world is a simple place with few causal complexities. To say that citizens, under some circumstances, intend the public interest in increased social welfare is to say that these conditions for direct democracy do not always apply. Consider each of these conditions in turn.

First, it is by no means clear that citizens in today's society prefer policies that embody a clear expression of values to policies that promise to effectively attain social goals. Citizens do care about actual, real-world policy outcomes, such as clean air, educational attainment, access to health care, and so on. Since the Enlightenment and certainly in this day of information and analysis, most people believe in a rational, scientific view of markets, the social order, and the world generally, including the instrumental belief that society is susceptible to purposeful change and improvement (Polsby 1984, 159–60; Sutton 1996, 203). If anything, modernity places its naive optimism in favor of scientific, causal thinking (Galbraith 1967, 164). That is, citizens often expect politicians to follow the ethic of responsibility more than the ethic of ultimate ends. This is not to claim that citizens are merely pragmatic or to deny that citizens are ideological. But in today's society, ideology serves mostly as a heuristic for how parties and politicians propose to solve complicated policy problems rather than as an end in itself (Hinich and Munger 1996, 98).

Second, the preference for inefficiency sensibly can be related only to preferences regarding local-level projects and not to substantive regulatory programs intended to produce general benefits for the nation, such as improving public health or promoting environmental cleanup (Arnold 1981, 253). For substantive programs that produce general benefits, citizens should prefer efficiency to inefficiency, all else being equal, since an extra dollar unnecessarily spent on environmental cleanup cannot be spent on such things as programs that enhance health or improve education.

Finally, and most important, it is not clear that having little knowledge of policies causes citizens to believe that the world is a simple place or that social relations are easy to comprehend. The established positive literature on Congress simply does not consider the possibility that ordinary citizens may recognize their own ignorance (see Manin, Przeworski, and Stokes 1999, 13). In actuality, social problems nearly always have complex causes, and it is certainly conceivable that citizens recognize this complexity even if they cannot grasp it theoretically or analytically. Empirically, citizens hold multiple opinions on issues, generally recognize the complexity of issues, and can appreciate the merits of competing policy alternatives (Zaller 1992, 59). As people become more educated and sophisticated, they are less likely to believe that simplistic statements are good public policy and less likely to offer strong opinions on issues on which they are uninformed (Delli Carpini and Keeter 1996, 231). And citizens have experience to draw on: any optimism in the simplicity of social problems and their solution may have dissipated, for example, in the failure of the War on Poverty to rid society of poverty or in the repeated failure of states to meet clean air standards by specific dates set in the Clean Air Act.

Theories about politics are only as good as their assumptions. It is odd that the prevailing literature on positive political economy, otherwise steeped in rationality assumptions, would assume a form of irrationality on behalf of ordinary citizens. It is more compelling to develop theories of legislative politics that assume citizen instrumental rationality—all else being equal, citizens generally want Congress to enact the best possible legislation. As Alexander Hamilton wrote, "It is a just observation that the people commonly *intend* the PUBLIC GOOD. This often applies to their very errors. But their good sense would despise the adulator who should pretend that they always *reason right* about the *means* of promoting it" (1961, 432). Constituents may recognize that members of Congress are in a better position to gather information regarding alternatives and to know which is the best alternative for a given policy or regulatory problem. If citizens believe that social problems are complex, it is unlikely that they will believe that the optimal response will be in simple or one-stage policy designs. As Hamilton suggests, when citizens are instrumentally rational, they are more likely to be skeptical about simple policy proposals for seemingly intractable social problems.

When citizens are instrumentally rational and when they believe that their representatives are better informed than the general populace, as a general matter it is not in citizens' interest to bind representatives to the citizens' own expressed demands for specific policies since uninformed decisions can lead to unexpected disaster. Instrumentally rational citizens are likely to be happy to discover that their representatives have used expert approaches to solve difficult social and economic problems. Unfortunately, citizens cannot simply capitulate to representatives' judgment about the best policy, since legislators have their own goals, interests, and values; may experience organized pressure from interest groups; and can undertake actions that are difficult for citizens to observe. Citizens who are instrumentally rational have an interest in employing accountability in a way that encourages representatives to appropriately use expertise in their work.

As I have shown, many of the established positive theories of politics assume that citizens respond to this principal-agent problem by employing direct accountability. In practice, this implies that citizens use retrospective evaluations when deciding whether to vote for an incumbent. Under retrospective evaluations, citizens base their decisions on the perceived benefits of the incumbents' actions in their previous terms. Unfortunately, retrospective evaluations inherently limit incumbents' capacity to use expertise in their judgment and work. But citizens are not limited to retrospective evaluations to maintain accountability. Citizens instead may choose to use prospective evaluations of incumbents. With prospective evaluations, the incumbents' past actions in office serve only to signal the representatives' willingness and capacity to produce good public policies, as do other tangible and intangible indicators of the representatives' qualities, such as personality, demeanor, and background. If voters are instrumentally rational, then they will use prospective evaluations to choose the candidate most likely to enact well-informed policies after the election (Fearon 1999, 82–83).

Citizens can use accountability through prospective evaluations as a way to encourage representatives to use expertise in the public interest (Bianco 1994, 75). With this form of accountability, constituents do not need to understand the actual effects of incumbents' past actions to maintain accountability. Accountability through prospective evaluations requires citizens only to have the ability to select high-quality and highly productive representatives who also can be entrusted to work for citizens' best interests. And as I show next, when incumbents use expertise in their work, they improve their reputations for sponsoring high-quality legislation and for trustworthiness in exercising good judgment and consequently improve their chances for reelection (Bianco 1994; Fenno 1978).

Quality

Instrumentally rational voters by assumption want to select representatives who are well informed on issues, highly productive, and likely to promote economic and social well-being for the district and for the nation.[7] The use of policy expertise is correlated with or is an indicator of quality (Cobb and Kuklinski 1997), so when rational voters use prospective accountability, expertise enhances a representative's electoral security. This can be seen empirically. Members feel pressure to acquire information when developing legislation and making vote decisions (Ainsworth 1993; Krehbiel 1992), and the more salient and conflictual an issue, the more members feel pressure to search for information (Kingdon 1989, 231; Price 1978). Pushing for innovative legislation improves a member's chances of reelection (Hall 1996; Polsby 1984, 171) and discourages quality challengers from running (Fowler 1993, 180; Wawro 2000, 19).

Citizens should have little trouble determining whether candidates are well informed on important issues and whether incumbents have been productive while in office. Candidates' quality and productivity are relatively easy for citizens to observe. Information and elite judgments are readily available in campaigns and through the media (Alvarez 1998), through elite cuing (Lupia and McCubbins 1998, 206; Zaller 1992, 8–9), and through social networks, particularly acquaintances (Krassa 1990). Citizens have incentives to gather information about candidates, if not through a sense of civic duty or in the belief that their votes will affect election outcomes, then through interest in politics, for small talk, or for planning business investments (Wittman 1995, 10).

Perhaps as a consequence, the use of expertise increases members' influence among their colleagues, promotes members' advancement

---

7. While many models of Congress assume that voters only want to maximize district benefits, in fact most social and economic issues can be addressed only at the national level—district economies are linked, and social problems can move across district borders.

in the chamber and in the party, and enhances their enjoyment of the job. For example, a committee will have greater influence and increase its jurisdiction when it develops expertise on new issues (DeGregorio 1992, 981; Fenno 1966, 162; Kiewiet and McCubbins 1991, 5; Talbert, Jones, and Baumgartner 1995, 388). Having an expert understanding of issues improves members' influence in the chamber through cuing (Kingdon 1989, 84), improves members' standing in the party (Truman 1951, 333), and improves members' prospects of advancement to better committee assignment and leadership positions (Cox and McCubbins 1993, 126; Wawro 2000, 100).

Trustworthiness

Instrumentally rational citizens recognize that they do not always know the best policy and that their preconceptions may be wrong. Representatives do not necessarily violate citizens' trust by contradicting their opinions, predispositions, or direct preferences as long as citizens know that their beliefs and opinions may be poorly informed and legislators can show that they used wise judgment in their legislative activities. As Fenno and others have found, representatives feel they can contradict clear but misguided or misinformed district preferences if they have the trust of their constituents. To promote this trust, representatives need to offer constituents a coherent and compelling explanation of their actions to make the case that they used wise judgment given their better information (Bianco 1994, 53; Fenno 1978; Kingdon 1989, 49; R. A. Smith 1993, 185). Bianco (1994, 53) shows that explanations are not aimed at persuading citizens retrospectively that representatives' decisions were somehow superior to constituents' preferences, an effort that would only add a second layer to the principal-agent problem. Instead, articulating a coherent explanation and justification fosters the appearance of accessibility, credibility, and trustworthiness. Explanations are easier to construct and appear more credible if the policy is based on informed expert thinking about the underlying social problem (Cobb and Kuklinski 1997).

Empirically, citizens give representatives wide leeway to incorporate expertise into legislation. In general, constituents do not express preferences as strong as those of organized interest groups about the means chosen to implement policies. In pursuit of policy ends such as cleaner air, better access to health care, and so on, constituents impose only loose constraints on the policy means members choose to reach these ends (Kingdon 1989, 68). Members feel they have greater leeway to use their judgment when voting on technical amendments than on general legislation (J. T. Hamilton 1997, 746) and in allocating their legislative time and energy (Hall 1996, 58). Expertise plays a larger role in members' efforts to draft the technical substance of policy alternatives than when legislators are voting among alternatives (Whiteman 1985, 298).

～

The information asymmetry between representatives and citizens creates a rationale for citizens to defer to their representatives' judgment in the use of expertise to promote good public policies. Deference is instrumentally rational in the sense that allowing members to use their better information and judgment in their work does not always lead to the best possible outcome from government interventions, but refusing to trust representatives' independent judgment is even less likely to do so (Bianco 1994, 80). When citizens are instrumentally rational, legislators can be representative even when they contradict uninformed constituent demands to author innovative and informed policy solutions to pressing public problems (Manin, Przeworski, and Stokes 1999, 11).[8]

The assertion that citizens exercise rational deference to encourage the use of expertise in policy-making leads to a view of Congress that is organizationally very different from the "textbook" Congress portrayed in the established positive literature on the subject. This is the theme of an emerging positive literature that considers the role of information in legislative politics. Congress as an institution creates incentives for researching and drafting expert-informed policy. Con-

---

8. Interestingly, Jackson and King (1989, 1156) find that legislators are less constrained by constituency preferences as the constituency becomes better educated. This finding would be counterintuitive if citizens made use of retrospective evaluations in a direct democracy, since better-educated people would be better able to know when representatives deviated from constituents' more preferred policies. Citizens who are better educated are more likely to recognize the limits of their knowledge and thus more likely to exercise rational deference.

gress gives committees incentives to hold informative hearings (Dier-meier 1995, 347; Diermeier and Fedderson 2000, 53; Gilligan and Krehbiel 1987, 290; Krehbiel 1992, 85); it makes funds available for committee staff with expertise who take on responsibility for developing legislation (Price 1971, 319; Weiss 1989, 423–24); and it funds politically neutral research-support agencies such as the Congressional Research Service, (the former) Office of Technology Assessment, and the Government Accounting Office (Bimber 1996, 20). In addition, gaining expertise and authoring high-quality legislation helps members advance to better committee assignments (Wawro 2000) and gives members greater influence over colleagues (Kingdon 1989; Talbert, Jones, and Baumgartner 1995). As an empirical matter, the legislative process cannot be said to reject public-interested expertise through the logic of democratic accountability.

In other words, the role of the representative in U.S. politics is neither trustee nor delegate. Instead, I argue that representation in legislative politics often follows the republican principle, where legislators are expected to use better information and judgment to advance the public interest (J. Madison 1961; Pitkin 1967). Under the republican mode of representation, having an expert understanding of issues enhances members' electoral security. When legislators use information and expertise in their work, they improve their constituents' perception of their representatives' inherent quality as representatives and increase their capacity to construct coherent explanations of their actions in office. Citizens who trust their representatives will find it in their interest to encourage representatives to incorporate quality information and better judgment into legislation.

A Regression Study: Technical Expertise and Gaining Access

One way to gauge members' interest in policy research and expertise is to see whether they talk to experts as they develop legislation. Even though Congress has some organizational capacity to locate expert policy-relevant analysis on its own (through committee staff, support agencies, and so forth), members of Congress and their staff are generalists and are too short on time to do the research and analysis to discover firsthand the political meaning of available research (Bauer, de Sola Pool, and Dexter 1972, 412). If members of Congress are interested in learning technical information about policies, they and their staff will be willing to allocate some of their scarce time to talk to technical experts, and if they are not interested in technical information, they will ignore experts. As I discuss in the next chapter, and perhaps contrary to many people's impression of lobbyists, some lobbyists develop a genuine expertise, or a "technical knowledge," of policies. The question then is whether having a technical knowledge of policies gives lobbyists an advantage in gaining access to Congress, holding other relevant determinants of access constant.

To test this question, I reanalyze an existing survey of lobbyists (Heinz et al. 1995) that was conducted in the mid-1980s. Among its questions, the survey has a series of self-reports on the "importance" of access to Congress in the course of their work.[9] Two of these measures involve access through public hearings (the importance of preparing written testimony and the importance of giving oral testimony), and two measures involve access behind the scenes (the importance of supplying written documents and the importance of having informal discussions with official decision makers in their offices). To construct the dependent variable of legislative access, I use confirmatory factor analysis to construct a scale measure of overall access, which is the weighted sum of all four measures of access (the weights make use of the factor loadings that are estimated in the scale model). A lobbyist who scores high on this scale gains considerable access through any and all channels of access; a lobbyist who scores low gains little or no access. The question for analysis is whether lobbyists who have technical knowledge score higher on this overall measure of access, controlling for other relevant factors.

One possibility is that members of Congress are only giving access

---

9. One technical issue here is that these questions ask lobbyists the importance of access to "government officials"—members of Congress and their staffs as well as agency officials. In the statistical model, I examine the effect of expertise on gaining access among lobbyists who frequently lobby for changes in legislation and control for the effect of expertise on the access lobbyists may gain through the agency rule-making process. Because in these analyses I consider the effect of expertise only among those lobbyists who specialize in lobbying Congress, I simplify the discussion in the text to say that I am modeling lobbyist access to the legislative process.

to those lobbyists that use expertise in the service of a strongly held ideology, who only use research to support ideologically predetermined ends (C. O. Jones 1976). Given this concern, it is important to know whether ideologically driven experts gain access or whether all experts gain access including those who are ideologically neutral.

To evaluate the role of ideologically neutral and biased expertise for access, I construct two additional scales, one measuring lobbyists' degree of technical expertise and one measuring lobbyists' ideology. Lobbyists will score high on the technical expertise scale if their job leads them to have a technical knowledge of policies—that is, if their work involves frequent use of specialized and technical newsletters, professional and trade journals, and computerized databases. Lobbyists score high on the left-right ideology scale if they take the conservative position on a series of social and economic policy questions, low if they take the liberal position, and toward the center if she is centrist. I use these two scales first to construct a neutral expert score, on which centrist experts score high and ideologically biased experts and nonexperts score low. I also construct a biased expert score, on which ideologically biased experts (whether liberal or conservative) score high and centrist experts and nonexperts score low. I then regress the overall access scale on these two measures of expertise and a series of control variables to test the role of expertise for access.[10]

I find that technical expertise improves access to the legislative process for both ideologically neutral lobbyists and for ideologically biased lobbyists. In other words, expertise gives all lobbyists an advantage in gaining access over nonexperts, all else being equal. The first-difference standardized OLS effects are given in table 1. For comparison, I show the effect on access of lobbyists' political activity at the district level, which in this model is measured as the frequency of grassroots lobbying activity. The literature on access has established district political activism as substantively the largest determinant of access to Congress (see especially Hansen 1991). And indeed, the first-difference effect of district activism is the largest. Changing

---

10. The control variables are lobbyists' degree of political activity at the grassroots, a scale measure of their general or "nontechnical" knowledge of policies, ideology, amount of fund-raising, age, gender, income, education, party identification, and a series of measures of the characteristics of the organization that employs them and of the nature of the issues on which they work.

the district activism variable across its range increases access by a standard deviation: in terms of the scale of the task measures in the original survey, this is equivalent to increasing a lobbyists' access from "some" to "considerable." Holding all else constant, the degree of access that lobbyists gain from expertise are roughly comparable to the access gained from district activism. Technical expertise improves access for ideologically centrist lobbyists by 40 percent of the access gained from district political activism; expertise gains ideologically biased lobbyists (lobbyists with ideology scores three standard deviations away from the mean ideology score) 75 percent of the access gained from district activism.

In practice, both neutral expertise and biased expertise help lobbyists gain access to Congress, holding all else constant. That neutral expertise helps lobbyists gain access contradicts many of the stronger claims found in the established positive literature on Congress, which holds that members will not devote their scarce time to talking to technical experts who do not hold to a particular ideological agenda. In this view, using information provided by ideologically neutral experts will only complicate members' reelection efforts, since constituents will become suspicious of information that is not in the clear service of overtly political goals.

This analyses can rule out only the strongest claims of the established literature regarding the role of expertise in the legislative process. In particular, this analysis does not indicate whether the technical information that lobbyists provide is in any way accurate or credible. It does not explain the specific conditions under which expertise makes a lobbyist most effective in pressuring Congress for

TABLE 1. The Effects of Expertise on Access, Overall Access Scale

Theoretical Variable	Standardized Effect	Relative Effect (%)
Increasing Expertise		
Centrist Lobbyist	0.08^*	40
Strongly Ideologically Biased Lobbyist	0.16^*	75
District Level Political Activism	0.21^*	100
$N = 413$		
$R^2 = 0.32$		

Note: OLS estimates. Model also controls for lobbyist's general knowledge, ideology, fundraising activities, demographics, party identification, organization characteristics, issue characteristics, and participation in rule-making activities.
*Statistically significant at $p < 0.05$

or against specific policies or whether expertise as used in politics serves the larger public interest. These questions are the focus of the remainder of this book. These analyses do lend strong plausibility, however, to the claims of the emerging literature that shows that members of Congress are interested in learning expert information about policies.

Conclusion

In sum, members of Congress are less constrained by constituent demands in designing regulatory programs and policies than could be expected under direct democracy, as Arnold and other prominent theorists of Congress have assumed. Constituents do not strictly constrain members on the more technical questions of policy design, even on those topics where constituents have preferences about program outcomes, because constituents often will recognize that a correct policy regarding a socially complex problem will require expert thinking with which they are not familiar.

When representation is in the republican mode, citizens may intend to advance the public interest and expect representatives to use good judgment and act on the best available information. In this context, rational, utility-maximizing, reelection-seeking legislators do not necessarily cater to the public's ignorance, biases, or fears. Reelection-minded legislators instead use expertise to advance the public interest because doing so increases job security. Using policy expertise to author legislation enhances citizens' perceptions of representatives' quality and increases legislators' ability to explain their actions to constituents in a compelling way. Theoretically and empirically contrary to much of the positive literature on congressional policymaking, democratic accountability does not eliminate policy expertise from the legislative process.

This chapter claims only that citizens do not automatically reject expert approaches to public policy and that citizens are willing to grant their representatives leeway to incorporate better information and judgment into their work. Citizens do not have the anti-intellectual impulses ascribed to them by the established literature on positive political economy. For my purposes, I need to show only that the established literature simply has not settled the issue of Congress's use of policy expertise.

That citizens allow members to use expertise in their work does not explain why members do so, however. The republican theory of representation does not give a positive explanation for why members use expertise on behalf of the public interest. Given their low levels of information, ordinary citizens do not take to the streets demanding analytically optimal interventions. Perhaps explanations are easier to construct when based on expertise and the best thinking and research, but why do members enact policies that require explanation? The next two chapters show that interest group pressure and the need for collective action among interest groups is the mechanism for linking legislation with expertise in service of the public interest.

3

Policy Expertise and Interest Group Pressure

This chapter develops a "hard-edged" positive explanation that links legislative action with policy expertise—expertise that is intended to advance the public interest. I develop an explanation for why members of Congress sometimes use policy expertise in developing legislation yet sometimes do not. Policy research interests members of Congress because the theory that policy researchers develop often is the best thinking about how to solve persistent social and economic problems that concern a diverse set of well-informed interest groups. Assuming that citizens use a republican mode of representation (see chapter 2), then members of Congress are free to experiment with expert-informed socially efficient policies—public-interested policies where the aggregate benefits exceed the aggregate costs—to deliver benefits to the largest number of interest groups possible.

The core of the theory states that special interest groups, each acting in its own interest, in the aggregate prompt Congress to enact socially efficient legislation, but only when there is research-based empirical evidence to indicate that the policy is likely to succeed. When research clearly shows that the policy is likely to work as expected, to create new wealth and new opportunities to achieve social goals, groups that expect to benefit from the policy will pressure Congress to enact the legislation. When the research does not clearly show that the policy will work, groups opposed to the reform will gain the upper hand and pressure Congress not to enact the legislation. In effect, out of self-interest, interest groups pressure Congress to enact only those efficient policies that find unambiguous support in the policy research literature. Each interest group may be acting out of private or selfish interests, but in many circumstances, the aggregate effect of interest group pressure advances the larger public's interests.

Expertise and Collective Action in Issue Networks

At first glance, the assertion that organized interest groups pressure Congress to enact publicly interested policies may seem counterintuitive if not incredible. A common image of lobbying consists of interest groups pressuring committees for special interest favors at the expense of the common interests of society as a whole. For example, neoliberal economists assert that interest groups pressure the government for subsidies, usually in the form of regulatory protection for specific industries, and that the resulting transfer of income leads to deadweight losses in the economy (Posner 1974, 344; Stigler 1975). This image of interest representation as "subgovernments" operating contrary to public interests is well entrenched and is mostly reflexively assumed in the literature (e.g., Lohmann 1998; Mitchell and Munger 1991; Parker 1996). It would seem counterintuitive to claim that interest groups acting in their own self-interest pressure members of Congress to initiate expert, socially efficient legislation that furthers the public interest.

The image of a single group lobbying a single committee fails, however, to capture the aggregate effect of lobbying in the contemporary interest-representation system. Interest groups are often concerned with complex policy problems, and the aggregate effect of lobbying drives the system toward greater reliance on expert policy concepts and policy research. In contemporary lobbying, interest groups are deeply and profoundly influenced by expert policy concepts and ideas, not out of some philosophic love of knowledge but instead out of a desire to pursue their interests effectively on complex policy questions.

The Complexity of Interest Representation

As an empirical matter, interest representation among political organizations in Washington, D.C., is far more complex than standard lobbying models envision or assume. The number and diversity of interest groups has increased dramatically in recent decades (Gais, Peterson, and Walker 1984; Heclo 1978, 98; Walker 1983, 395).[1] In contemporary lobbying, organized groups represent the wide range of interests in the advanced capitalist economy and in a diverse society. Trade associations, firms, voluntary associations, professional associations, and unions represent nearly every conceivable interest in an organized, politically effective manner (Heclo 1978, 121; Salisbury 1984). Each group can have a radically different stake in any policy issue. Interest groups often compete with each other for members and for political support; thus, they often try to differentiate themselves strategically into narrow, specialized issue niches (Browne 1990, 477). Even within a niche, groups can express contradictory preferences (McFarland 1992, 59).

While each group is organized to represent effectively its particular interests, the aggregate effect of organized lobbying is to make it difficult for any group acting on its own to have any control over any significant issue or to capture the legislative process (Heinz et al. 1993, 381; Salisbury 1991, 378). Because so many competing groups exist, no one group can dominate the process through force or power. Each group is simply a node in a fluid, loosely structured issue network (Heclo 1978). Each group articulates a distinct interest, and as a result the system tends to deal with policy issues that are as complex and multidimensional as the fragmented interest-representation system itself. Issue networks have no dominant group to sort out or to integrate the diverse set of interests (Heinz et al. 1993, 22).

Social choice theory has long shown that when policy choices are complex and multidimensional, it is difficult for anyone to propose a policy that can enable a stable, long-lasting coalition for reform. In a multidimensional choice problem, under ordinary preference aggregation rules, each policy alternative potentially can be selected as the majority choice; individually rational decision makers may cycle

---

1. Hugh Heclo attributes the rise of issue network politics, or the general "politicization of organizational life," both to the emergence of new and complex social issues and to the federal government's tendency to rely on intermediary organizations—private and local governmental organizations—to deliver services as a way to avoid bureaucratic giantism (1978, 92). This has "pushed more and more policy concerns out of the federal government's own structure and into masses of intermediary, issue-conscious groups" (94).

among the choice alternatives in a manner that appears collectively irrational (Riker 1982, 19). Empirically, this is commonly recognized as the problem of gridlock among interest groups (Baumgartner 1989, 6; Heclo 1978, 105; Truman 1951, 366–67). Groups unsatisfied with a policy choice can always try to overturn legislation in courts, try to influence how regulatory agencies implement the policy, or simply start a new round of legislation (Loomis and Cigler 1986, 24; Lowi 1969, 26; Peterson 1990, 116; Walker 1991, 21; Weir, Orloff, and Skocpol 1988, 22).

This agenda cycling and gridlock create a collective-action problem among interest groups, since each group pursuing its own special interest cannot propose a policy that all groups can agree on. And, in the absence of government intervention to correct the underlying issue—whether market failure or some social structural problem— many groups become worse off.[2] Deadlock among groups forecloses opportunities for constructive government interventions in the economy or in society and thus closes off the possibility of legislation that may benefit the groups. When policies are unstable, the constituencies that groups represent cannot make long-term plans and cannot expect to capture any benefits from legislation and regulatory programs on a permanent basis. This collective-action problem among interest groups is not considered in the standard models that only envision a single group lobbying the legislature.

Framing Solutions to the Interest Group Collective-Action Problem

At the same time, the complex representation of interests, at least in principle, creates opportunities to resolve gridlock among interest groups. In a multidimensional problem, it is possible to convert a

---

2. Heclo (1978, 104) gives the example of the Carter energy plan to demonstrate the importance of containing issue network conflict for political actors: "Attempts to define the energy debate in terms of a classic confrontation between big oil companies and consumer interests were doomed. More and more policy watchers joined in the debate, bringing to it their own concerns and analyses: tax reformers, nuclear power specialists, civil rights groups interested in more jobs; the list soon grew beyond the wildest dreams of the original energy policy planners. The problem, it become clear, was that no one could quickly turn the many networks of knowledgeable people into a shared action coalition."

disjointed problem, or even a seemingly zero-sum problem, into a positive-sum problem through a creative solution that had not previously been envisioned (Rueschemeyer and Evans 1985, 48; Skocpol 1985, 15; R. A. Smith 1984; B. Stevens 1988, 144). Complexity allows for the possibility of mutual gains through improved efficiency or through solving interlocking problems simultaneously (Dryzek 1994, 75). New policy ideas can change a policy problem from one of redistributing existing resources to one of creating new wealth and new opportunities. But creative resolutions to complex problems are rarely obvious because people are "boundedly rational," and creative solutions to policy problems must be discovered (B. Jones 1994, 37). As I show next, democracy is a process that allows for and even encourages and fosters this creative discovery.

In a democracy, many if not most interest groups are organized to advance a private or "special" interest (Olson 1965). For complex policy problems, however, interest groups and politicians alike need to develop an understanding of the causal structure and mechanics of the underlying problem to effectively pursue their self-interests. Since people are limited in their cognitive capacities, they can, for the most part, attend only to some aspects of a complex, multidimensional problem and must ignore others to make the problem cognitively manageable (B. Jones 1999). In complex problems, people have to construct a simplification of the problem, or a causal framework that informs them of the relevant aspects of the choice problem. The causal framework tells lobbyists how they can hypothetically expect government actions to translate into real-world outcomes and consequently informs lobbyists whether their groups can expect gains or losses from a given proposal relative to the status quo (J. Goldstein 1993, 237; B. Jones 1994, 50; Legro 2000, 421; R. A. Smith 1984, 44; Stone 1989, 283).

A causal framework can be broken down into three analytical parts: the policy choice, the policy outcome, and the set of causal relationships that relate policy choices to outcomes. Some groups have intrinsic preferences regarding policies—that is, these groups prefer to have the government adopt policies for moral, cultural, symbolic, or ideological reasons, irrespective of the real world outcome the policies are likely to produce (see Aaron, Mann, and Taylor 1994). Most groups, however, care only about the actual outcomes of government interventions. Groups of this sort have extrinsic preferences regarding policies, or preferences about the consequences of government action rather than about policies. If a group has only extrinsic preferences about outcomes, the policy the group most prefers depends on its beliefs regarding the specific causal relationships that connect policies to expected outcomes. To say that interest groups care about outcomes is to say that interest groups care about causal theories, or the hypothetical relationships between government action and outcome. Since policy experts for the most part construct these causal theories, expert ideas and social science research matter and are central to lobbying politics. Or, if one prefers the old cliché, in contemporary politics, knowledge *is* power.

With regard to the case studies that follow, chapter 6 shows that in 1989 the United Mine Workers was neither for nor against regulating sulfur dioxide emissions as a means to control the acid rain problem; rather, the union favored a stringent command-and-control uniform emissions standard that protected the market for high-sulfur coal and opposed an equally stringent emissions trading program that made high-sulfur coal less marketable. Chapter 7 shows that in 1990, teachers' unions favored education reforms that reinforced bureaucratic control of schools and opposed reforms that weakened it. In both cases, these groups were neither for nor against an intervention in the environment and in education, respectively; instead, their support and opposition depended critically on the substantive causal framing of the policy.

The better lobbyists understand complex policy problems and how government actions are likely to translate into outcomes, the more effective lobbyists can be in achieving their groups' goals. By definition, expert-informed research provides the best and most accurate depiction of a policy problem given the current state of research-based knowledge. As a consequence, groups that self-interestedly pursue specific outcomes from government interventions seek out expert, research-based understandings of policies. This causes interest groups, as organizations, to develop technical and analytical capacities. Groups employ teams of technical experts and professional analysts to monitor and comprehend complex issues as they develop (Heclo 1978, 103; Salisbury 1991, 378; Wright 1996, 71). And perhaps more importantly, groups develop a network of contacts to discuss or debate policies with other groups that have similar interests (Carpenter, Esterling, and Lazer 1998; Heclo 1978, 117; Heinz et al. 1993, 411–12; Laumann and Knoke 1987, 251). In general, because of the complexities of policies, interest group politics is driven largely by policy ideas and expertise rather than by raw organizational or political power (Heclo 1978; Ricci 1993, 139–40).[3]

Groups that are effectively organized to pursue their interests have the capacity to find research-based solutions to complex problems, and this capacity offers a potential solution to the collective-action problem among interest groups. Expert policy framings can create positive-sum benefits for groups since a policy proposal that draws on policy expertise often happens to be a more optimal solution for a complex problem. Optimal policies can appeal to a wider cross-section of groups than nonexpert or suboptimal policies and thus can serve as the basis for a broad-based coalition among groups. It is much easier for a group to find support from other groups for policies that confer benefits broadly (Gambetta 1998, 23; Hojnacki 1997; Hula 1999). By sharing information and alternative perspectives, lobbyists can help each other improve the quality of the causal beliefs regarding a given alternative (Fearon 1998, 50; Manin 1987, 349; R. A. Smith 1984; Sunstein 1988, 1549). In the process, groups may discover new, innovative policies that reduce the number of dimensions on which participants disagree or that create positive-sum possibilities that had not previously been envisioned (Kingdon 1984; Knight and Johnson 1994, 282; Legro 2000, 421).

Rarely, if ever, are these creative or expert-based policies Pareto optimal, or desired by all groups. While many groups might expect to benefit from an expert-informed policy, some groups may be harmed or suffer some loss if the policy is implemented. Some groups may lose some regulatory protection or subsidy for their industry or other benefit derived from a suboptimal state of affairs. Other groups may oppose innovative, expert-informed policies for intrinsic or ideological reasons. These two sets of groups will organize an effort to oppose the policy in the political process. Those that may be harmed by a policy or that believe the policy is bad for soci-

---

3. Heclo (1978, 103) notes that "instead of power commensurate with responsibility, issue networks seek influence commensurate with their understanding of the various, complex social choices being made."

ety may try to reframe the debate by arguing that the goals the policy promises are not legitimate or not fair or equitable; manipulating the salience of choice and outcome dimensions to upset an equilibrium decision is an art known as heresthetics (B. Jones 1994; Riker 1986, 150–51).

These groups will often find it difficult, however, to defeat a policy backed by a broad-based coalition of well-informed interest groups in the majoritarian political process. In majoritarian politics, it is difficult to defeat a coalition that is broad based, so these heresthetic efforts do not necessarily hinder collective action or disrupt stable policy. Furthermore, opposition groups will have difficulty finding a new policy that would cause the coalition to become unstable through heresthetics, since this would require locating a new expert-based or creative idea to serve as the basis for a new coalition and such ideas are few and far between in practice.[4]

While expert ideas, as they are refined through discussion among interest groups, can lead to outcomes that groups collectively desire, perhaps just as often, efforts to reformulate policies through expert ideas do not lead to improved collective action among groups. When groups care about the outcomes of government interventions, their preferences about policies are defined by the hypothetical causal links between policies and outcomes. Consequently, interest group politics depends on the properties of the causal framework itself. As I show next, two informational properties can create barriers to collective action and the successful resolution of conflict through the use of expert ideas. The first barrier is uncertainty in the causal relationships linking policy to outcome, where a group will not agree to endorse an innovative policy because it fears that the policy will fail or not yield the expected benefits. The second barrier arises when there are conceptual and methodological ambiguities in the causal framework; such ambiguities can lead to disagreement regarding which policies lead to desirable outcomes.[5] The two barriers are very

---

4. Although I do not rule out this possibility, I consider the problem of competing frameworks later in this volume.
5. These two conditions match well with the discussion in Lave 1981. Regarding the availability of information and the extent of uncertainty, Lave says, "When dealing with uncertainty stemming from stochastic mechanisms or public attitudes, there is no substitute for careful, explicit modeling of the sources of variation in order to get estimates that will inform the decision makers" (31). Regarding fundamental dis-

different: uncertainty may be overcome with better and more complete information, but disagreement that is the result of ambiguity often cannot.

Uncertainty and Interest Group Mobilization

Expert policy proposals in theory can create positive-sum gains for many groups that have diverse interests. Unfortunately, whether a program will work as envisioned in the causal framework is unknown prior to enactment. Because of the complexity of most policy problems, there is always uncertainty about whether an innovative policy will produce its intended outcomes. Policies sometimes do not work as they seem to on paper but instead may succeed or fail as a result of systematic and random factors that cannot be known for sure prior to implementation. The proposition that a policy will achieve its stated goals is a hypothesis that may be true or false. The degree of uncertainty inherent in the causal links between policy and outcome depends on the state of knowledge found in the empirical evaluation literature for the policy topic. Information as evidence for the likely effectiveness of policies comes mostly from research-based evaluation studies of programs that are in some way analogous to the proposal under consideration (Kingdon 1989, 231; Rose 1993). These may be studies of small-scale demonstrations, agency experiments, analogous policies, private sector activity, applied policy research, and so on.

The availability of this empirical evidence and policy evaluation information regarding the likely outcomes of an intervention or, equivalently, the degree of uncertainty affects the aggregate support for and opposition to a policy among interest groups. Policies that have only weak evidence to show their effectiveness and that entail too much uncertainty tend to lack support in politics. According to Jack Walker, "Uncertainty and the fear of unanticipated consequences has always been a formidable barrier to reform" (1969, 890).

---

agreement on the interpretive framework, Lave writes, "The derivation of quantitative estimates for the effects of proposed policies is fraught with conceptual and practical difficulties. The level of theoretical knowledge, amount of past scientific work, and amount of agreement will determine the range of uncertainty surrounding each estimate" (45).

In contrast, policies with strong empirical support and demonstrated technical feasibility tend to prevail in the political process, all else being equal (Kingdon 1984, 139; Rose 1993). Thus, empirical evaluation information is an important explanatory variable in lobbying politics, since it systematically affects the overall degree of support for a policy among interest groups.

This aggregate effect of information on group behavior can best be explained using prospect theory, a well-developed theory for decision making under uncertainty. Prospect theory provides a link between evaluation research information and lobbying behavior. Groups that could expect to receive some gain or benefit from a policy once it is implemented are generally risk averse, meaning that they value a sure gain more than they value a lottery that has an identical expected payoff (Quattrone and Tversky 1988; Rabin 1998; Tversky and Kahneman 1981, 453). Consequently uncertainty reduces the support for a policy among groups that could expect to gain from the intervention. In contrast, groups that expect to suffer a loss or harm from the policy are loss averse and risk acceptant; losses are felt more strongly than gains in general, and losses loom even larger when the size of the loss is unknown in advance. As a result, uncertainty that arises from the absence of research-based information will tend to bolster the prospectively harmed groups' active opposition to the policy.

Prospect theory shows that uncertainty about a policy proposal differently affects the motivations of the prospectively gaining and prospectively harmed groups to invest resources in a lobbying effort. Prospective gainers need clear and positive evidence to show that the innovative policy is likely to succeed before they will mobilize their support, but prospectively harmed groups mobilize their opposition the less that is known about the policy. Because scientific evaluation information is often not definitive evidence either for or against a policy, this argument based on prospect theory gives an explanation for why opponents to a program are often observed to have an advantage in politics. But this advantage varies and is a function of the state of research-based empirical knowledge that varies across policy proposals and that can accumulate over time as research progresses. In general, high-quality research-based empirical evidence leads to collective action among groups that can expect to gain from the policy and tends to demobilize opponents to this collective effort. The implication is that research-based evaluation information is an important explanatory variable in lobbying politics.

Ambiguity

The discussion so far has suggested that many disagreements among lobbyists can be reconciled through more discussion, expert analysis, and better information, at least when the disagreements occur among groups that have extrinsic preferences or preferences about policy outcomes. Lobbyists are boundedly rational, and outcome-oriented groups may disagree with each other simply because they are misinformed or mistakenly have preferences for suboptimal policies. In this case, disagreement can be converted to agreement through a better conceptual framing and better empirical evidence on the efficacy of innovative policies.

This is not to say, however, that all disagreements can be resolved with better information, analysis, and open discussion. Expert analysis may produce several causal frameworks within which to understand a policy proposal, each of which may be equally well informed and compelling. Without a common causal framework, different experts can view information, arguments, or empirical results and come to radically different conclusions regarding the meaning and implications of these materials. Even if lobbyists were fully aware of the current state of knowledge for a policy proposal, they might have fundamental disagreements regarding social goals or the proper means to reach those goals and so may be unable to settle on a means for collective action. In this case, discussion and information can increase the salience of what is at stake and sharpen conflict between supporters and opponents (Sunstein 1988, 1555–56; Wildavsky 1979, 236). Discussion can expose new dimensions for disagreement, with the consequence that preferences remain intransitive and decisions unstable and subject to manipulation and gridlock (Fearon 1998, 57; Knight and Johnson 1994, 283–86).

One important source of ambiguity is when experts propose contradictory expectations for the relationships between policy choice and outcome. For many policy issues, the only relevant analytical question for outcome-oriented groups is whether the policy will work along a single dimension. For example, the environmental policy question in chapter 6, in simplified form, is whether an emissions trading program would reduce sulfur dioxide emissions at a reasonable cost. But on other issues, multiple causal frameworks may explain a given set of findings, and a policy may be expected to perform well by one dimension of evaluation and poorly by another (Wildavsky 1979, 131). To illustrate this conceptual ambiguity, chapter 7 describes a school-choice program where there were reasons to believe the program would benefit individual students who participate in the program but harm the school system as a whole.

Some groups may care only about one or the other outcome dimension, perhaps because of cultural or ideological intrinsic preferences that lead these groups to focus on one aspect of a problem to the exclusion of other aspects or because their private interests relate only to one dimension. In this case, information clarifying the outcomes along each outcome dimension can mobilize both sides of an issue, some believing that the intervention is likely to be a great success and some believing with equally good reason that the intervention is likely to be a failure. More important, groups interested in the full set of policy outcomes may be of two minds on whether to favor or oppose such a policy; this is because cognitively, it is difficult for people to trade off between separate outcome dimensions (B. Jones 1999). In this case, increasing information will paralyze the group, like a deer in the headlights, because it is facing both potential gains and losses. Chapter 7 illustrates this well with business groups that withheld support for the school voucher program, which they believed might increase aggregate test scores while potentially doing harm to the educational system as a whole.

A second major form of ambiguity arises from competing expectations among experts. These ambiguities primarily have methodological sources, where experts use the same data but different methods to confirm competing expectations for the consequences of a policy. The effect of this disagreement among experts as to the meaning of research results is to make it unclear which among multiple possible outcomes is likely to occur from a government intervention. As Lave (1981), Rose (1993), and others illustrate, policy experts may disagree about what quantities to place in the cost and benefit columns or even how to place costs and benefits on a similar scale. It may not be clear, for example, how to quantify the benefit from reduced particulate matter on the aesthetics of a state park or improvements to public health from cleaner air, but the monetary costs to industry are usually known precisely. Experts also can use different methods for estimating the likely effects of an intervention and can disagree over whether a given set of empirical findings was drawn from a similar population or set of circumstances. Either way, experts may dispute the likely impact of an intervention on methodological grounds. Groups often have the internal expertise and background knowledge and capacity to interpret statistical results and other research-based empirical evidence using competing methodological approaches. This methodological ambiguity can be seen in chapter 8, where a physician group reinterprets research findings using its professional authority to declare what empirical research findings do and do not demonstrate the appropriate practice of medicine.

In sum, ambiguity can have either conceptual or methodological sources. Either way, in the presence of ambiguity new information about how the policy is likely to work in practice simply leads to even greater disagreement and reduced collective action among interest groups (see Legro 2000, 426). In this case, having more and better evaluation information and evidence for program effectiveness can mobilize groups on both sides of the issue for different reasons. Groups that have extrinsic preferences and that care about the full set of outcome dimensions will become paralyzed as they gain more information. These forms of fundamental ambiguity often but not always exist, so like uncertainty, ambiguity in the causal framework is an important explanatory variable in lobbying politics.

Socially Efficient Policy as a Means to Resolve Gridlock among Groups

One important policy framing that potentially can resolve gridlock among a diverse set of interest groups is a type of regulation called socially efficient policy. A policy is socially efficient when the benefits from the policy are large enough that those who gain a benefit could compensate those who suffer some loss and still come out ahead, even if the compensation in practice is not carried out. Technically speaking, such a policy meets the wealth-maximization or Kaldor-Hicks criterion for efficiency (Stokey and Zeckhauser 1978, 137; Wittman 1995, 4–5). Efficiency is a research-based, analytical property of a policy: a policy is inefficient, for example, when its marginal benefits do not equal its marginal costs and gains may be realized in a more efficient program (Stokey and Zeckhauser 1978, 141). If a policy is socially efficient, the aggregate benefits flowing to groups are increased (the pie is expanded rather than sliced in a new way), even without increasing taxes or imposing new financial burdens.

A socially efficient reform makes the gainers gain more than the losers lose, so socially efficient policies—at least in principle—can attract the support of interest groups with otherwise radically diverse interests (Hahn and Hester 1989a, 143).[6] Because of their positive-sum properties, socially efficient policy proposals in theory can make even traditional interest group antagonists jointly better off than they currently are under an inefficient regulatory status quo (see, e.g., Mueller 1989, 9–10; Quirk 1989; VanDoren 1989). Socially efficient policy may promote agreements among a diverse set of organized groups because, by the assumption that the policy increases welfare, more of the segments of the economy and society can be made better off relative to the regulatory status quo (see Skocpol 1985, 15). However, an efficient policy can make a diverse set of groups better off but is neither necessary nor sufficient to do so. For example, a reform that benefits one group considerably and harms many groups slightly may be efficient by the wealth-maximization criterion. The socially efficient policies that attract the support of a larger number of groups will tend to be the ones that survive in majoritarian politics and in policy communities, however, and those that benefit few groups will not (Kingdon 1984).

Some groups may benefit from an inefficient regulatory status quo—perhaps one that artificially raises prices or creates barriers to entry into a market. Groups that receive a deadweight benefit or rents from an inefficient policy or from the unregulated status quo can be counted on to oppose efficiency improvements because such groups are not necessarily compensated for their losses. Political

---

6. One well-known example is airline deregulation, which benefited consumers, the business community, antiregulatory conservatives, free-marketers, and advocates of smaller government (Derthick and Quirk 1985, 47).

actors generally are loss averse, weighing expected losses more heav-ily than possible gains, and thus can be expected to particularly stren-uously oppose efficiency reform (Tversky and Kahneman 1981, 454). These groups may try to reframe the debate to focus on the fairness or equity of their prospective losses. Often but not always, however, the rents that efficient policies eliminate are viewed as illegitimate gains or are otherwise socially undesirable. While rent seekers' oppo-sition to efficiency reform is often vigorous, it is frequently difficult for them to argue persuasively that preserving the deadweight rent that they privately enjoy should trump the more general interest in realizing the social benefits of efficiency that many other groups could enjoy.

The opposition of rent seekers notwithstanding, socially efficient expert policy can facilitate agreements among diverse interest groups and so reduce intergroup conflict regarding the direction of public policy. Becker (1983) provides a general model that shows that groups favoring efficiency have an intrinsic advantage in pressuring for policy change over groups opposing the efficiency improvement. And as a result, groups supporting efficient reform should be more effective in pressuring Congress to enact and reauthorize efficient programs than groups attempting to prevent or overturn the efficient reforms.

The Becker Model: Efficiency and the Intrinsic Advantage

Becker's (1983) general model of interest group pressure shows that the relative effectiveness of a group in producing pressure, all else being equal,[7] is a function of the relative efficiency of the policy the group endorses (see figure 1). Becker's framework defines any policy by a set of functions: a cost function (C) describing the amount of harm inflicted on some groups, and a benefit function (B) describing the amount of benefit conferred on other groups. Together, these functions imply an aggregate redistribution of social, economic, or policy benefits from the harmed to the benefiting groups. In figure 1,

---

7. Becker (1983) shows that group effectiveness is a function of organizational fac-tors (e.g., ability to control free riders, number of members, the relative effectiveness of competing groups, and so on) as well as the nature of the policy at issue.

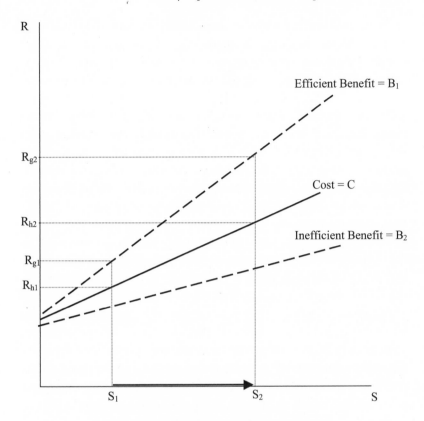

Fig. 1. Efficiency advantages the gaining group
(graph derived from Becker 1983)

for example, a policy S_1 redistributes by "taxing" a harmed group h the amount R_h and benefits a gaining group g the amount R_g. Given the cost and benefit functions, the redistribution may be efficient in the aggregate by a welfare-maximizing criterion, where the aggregate benefits exceed aggregate harms ($R_g > R_h$), as well as efficient at the margin, where the increase in benefits is greater than the increase in harms (the slopes $B' > C'$). These functions combine to provide the causal framework that links government actions to outcomes: the policy is positive-sum; groups know whether they should gain from or be harmed by the policy; and the gainers should gain more than the losers lose.

As Becker shows (see the appendix to this chapter), when the proposed policy is efficient at the margin ($B' > C'$ in figure 1) and there is full information, groups that would benefit from the efficiency improvements gain the most per unit of resource expended in a lobbying campaign (since $dR_g > dR_h$) and thus should have a greater willingness to invest scarce group resources in the lobbying effort than groups that will be harmed by the efficiency improvement. As a consequence of the difference in the marginal payoff to each side of the issue, by Becker's logic, the relative payoffs from the efficient policy motivate the groups that would benefit from the efficiency to support the proposal more than the relative payoffs motivate groups that would suffer a cost to oppose the proposal. This relative advantage is what Becker calls the "intrinsic advantage" for groups that stand to gain from efficiency. Gainers invest their scarce resources to lobby on the issue, while the harmed groups divert their resources to lobby more productively on other issues.[8]

Assuming Congress responds to the aggregate pressure from interest groups, according to the Becker model, lobbying politics should lead Congress to enact socially efficient policy. This theory of lobbying reconciles the government's role as a provider of public goods and facilitator of market efficiency with the reality of interest group pressure and is a positive theory for Congress's incentives to use public-interested policy expertise in the form of socially efficient legislation (Becker 1983, 384). And furthermore, once enacted, socially efficient policy should be relatively stable. As Wittman (1995, 117) explains, "By definition, the cost that a wealth-maximizing law imposes is less than the benefit it brings. Therefore, other things being equal, pressure for change is the least when laws are efficient." Lave (1981, 7) notes that opponents have fewer grounds for challenging an efficient policy in court and that courts give more deference to policies that have solid grounding in efficiency-based expertise. In other words, socially efficient policy can resolve gridlock and the collective-action problem among interest groups.

At first glance, efficient policies, which enhance welfare and can

---

8. Whether a group invests in the issue depends on the marginal benefit of the issue relative to that of other issues. The intrinsic advantage is a relative rather than absolute advantage.

appeal to a wide cross-section of interest groups, might be assumed always to prevail in majoritarian politics: in principle, a cross-section of groups that could expect to benefit from these policies should mobilize to support the innovative programs, and Congress (all else being equal) should favor them as a way of maximizing the benefits it can deliver to interest groups. While this intrinsic advantage for groups favoring efficiency is true as a deductive result, it raises the questions of why interest groups often do not support efficient policies in the political process (Kelman 1981; Robertson 1991, 65) and of why these policies often fail to gain support in Congress (Arnold 1990).[9]

As I show next, the nature and availability of research findings systematically affect interest groups' motivation to lobby for or against socially efficient policies and programs. Becker's model makes two key assumptions, and these assumptions do not always hold: that groups have no uncertainty about how an efficient policy will work in practice and that there is no ambiguity in the causal framework to interpret the implications of government action. I argue that these two conditions defining the state of knowledge for a policy affect interest group support for and opposition to a policy, which in turn affects Congress's interest in developing efficient policies as a means to benefit interest groups.

Becker Amendment 1: Uncertainty

Policies can go awry. After a policy that is intended to be socially efficient is implemented, the aggregate benefits indeed may exceed the aggregate costs, but it also is possible that the policy will fail and all groups may become worse off. The expected impact of a policy is only a hypothesis. Uncertainty plagues socially efficient policies in particular, since they tend to be theoretical, complicated, counterin-

---

9. One possibility is that policies that meet the welfare-maximizing criterion also are inefficient at the margin ($B' < C'$ in the appendix notation), and thus the intrinsic disadvantage to gaining groups can be derived from the Becker model itself. The goal in this chapter, however, is to amend the Becker model to take into account uncertainty and ambiguity.

tuitive, indirect, and roundabout (Arnold 1990, 24; Schultze 1977, 78). Uncertainty, therefore, should affect groups' relative support for a socially efficient policy.

The effect of uncertainty is easily demonstrated within the Becker model framework, and I offer the argument as an extension of the model. Assume that the causal framework is unambiguous, so the only relevant question is whether the policy is likely to work as planned. The benefit and cost functions in Becker's framework are defined by a set of parameters, and under limited information the point estimates for the parameters of each function have corresponding variances and covariances. The policies' parameters, that is, are states of the world that must be estimated. Without loss of generality, assume that there is uncertainty only regarding the marginal benefit of a policy; the marginal costs are fixed.[10] The state of knowledge about a policy is therefore a distribution over the range of possible marginal benefits that may be gained from the policy once it is implemented, with expected value equal to the true marginal benefit of the program and variance that is a function of the state of research-based empirical knowledge. In this case, the marginal benefits from the proposed efficient policy may be bigger, the same, or smaller than expected when the policy has been enacted. Or in terms of figure 1, it is not known whether the policy will turn out to have benefit function B_1, benefit function B_2, or anything in between.

In this case, the key variable for interest groups' motivation to invest resources to support an efficient policy is the relative availability and strength of research-based empirical evidence in the form of policy evaluation information, which affects the standard error of the marginal benefits or, equivalently, the amount of uncertainty surrounding the proposal. The outcome distribution regarding marginal benefits is a function of inherent stochastic processes and the state of scientific knowledge, so the function parameters vary across policies and over time. When the evidence clearly indicates that the efficient policy will work in practice, all parties to the decision can expect the marginal benefits to exceed the marginal costs, and everyone will recognize that the policy is likely to be socially efficient, as

---

10. This is consistent with many analysts' claims that benefits are more difficult to quantify than costs; see Lave 1981. In addition, allowing the marginal costs to vary has the same implications.

envisioned in the original Becker model. When little is known empirically about the policy, it is possible that on implementation the realized marginal benefit will not exceed the marginal cost, so the policy may not realize its efficiency promises in practice.

First, consider the effect of uncertainty for groups with extrinsic policy preferences, or those groups with preferences exclusively about policy outcomes. Given this uncertainty, within Becker's framework, investing resources to advocate or oppose an efficient program is a gamble for groups with extrinsic preferences, and this gamble affects these groups' decision making. According to prospect theory, both the expected value and the amount of uncertainty in the outcome distribution will affect outcome-oriented groups' perception of the benefits and costs of a policy and consequently their willingness to invest resources in a lobbying effort to support or oppose the proposal. Prospect theory demonstrates that risky gains appear to be even less valuable and risks of losses appear even more costly than risk-free gains and losses (Tversky and Kahneman 1981). Formally, this implies subtracting some portion of the variance of the outcome distribution from prospective gainers' expected benefits from the policy and adding the variance to the prospectively harmed groups' costs.

If Congress were to choose to enact the policy, one can think of the outcome as a draw from the policy's outcome distribution of relative benefits and costs. Assume that interest groups privately know the expected value and the variance of the outcome distribution (again, the standard error of the policy's marginal benefit B), so the likelihood that a policy may succeed or go awry (technically, the degree of confidence) is a known quantity for the group. If the policy is efficient, the marginal benefits for groups will exceed the marginal costs (that is, if the true benefit function turns out to be B_1). If the prospectively gaining group is not confident that the program will succeed as expected, it will become less likely to invest resources to advocate the policy alternative because the group is risk averse and uncertainty diminishes the value of the prospective benefit from the proposal. At the same time, uncertainty will tend to bolster the prospectively harmed group's active opposition, because this group is risk acceptant and uncertainty augments the apparent costs of the policy. Uncertainty or lack of information motivates the harmed groups more than the benefiting groups and, therefore, contrary to the original Becker result, tends to give the advantage to the prospectively harmed groups.[11]

Next, consider interest groups with intrinsic preferences regarding policies. Here, groups may have moral, ideological, symbolic, or private reasons to support or oppose the policy irrespective of how the policy is likely to work in practice. These groups are intrinsically motivated to support or oppose the policy, independent of the available evidence or the current state of knowledge about the effectiveness of the policy.

The full logic regarding the effect of evaluation information and uncertainty on interest group mobilization is summarized in table 2 and is stated more formally in the appendix to this chapter. As a general proposition, among groups that have extrinsic preferences about policy outcomes, uncertainty advantages the opponents and certainty advantages the supporters. In effect, improving the state of knowledge with more and better evaluation research lends an advantage to those groups that could expect a private benefit from the efficient policy; in turn, these groups will more effectively pressure Congress for the efficient reform. Because carefully researched evalu-

TABLE 2.   Information Affects Activity: Uncertainty

	Supporters	Opponents
Strong Evidence		
Extrinsic Preferences	Vigorous	Moderate
Intrinsic Preferences	Vigorous	Vigorous
Weak Evidence		
Extrinsic Preferences	Moderate	Vigorous
Intrinsic Preferences	Vigorous	Vigorous

11. It is of course possible for the research to show that the program is expected to be inefficient or that the marginal benefits are expected to be less than the marginal costs (that is, research shows the policy is likely to be B_2). In this case, no groups should support the policy. It is straightforward to show that groups opposed to the efficient policy will have the advantage when the research shows that the policy is likely to fail. Here, I assume that policies demonstrated to be inefficient are discarded in the political process, at least among groups with extrinsic preferences for efficiency. And even if the outcome were to approximate the status quo, no group should support the proposal because of an effect known as the status quo bias (see Quattrone and Tversky 1988, 724; Rabin 1998: 14; Ritov and Baron 1992).

ation information often does not exist for innovative policies, the groups that are likely to suffer a loss or economic harm from an efficient policy reform often are advantaged in politics. This may account for the apparent anomaly, for example, that industry groups have not given emissions trading proposals much support over the years despite the prospect that such plans will reduce emission-control costs or that national-level business associations have not strongly endorsed school choice. But information is a variable; because evaluation information sometimes is credible and convincing, the groups that could expect to benefit from the efficient policy will sometimes get the upper hand.

Becker Amendment 2: Ambiguity

Some forms of disagreement can be reduced or resolved with more information and discussion if the underlying source of the disagreement is a suboptimal causal framework within which lobbyists understand their preferences regarding policy alternatives or if the source of disagreement is simply a lack of information. But not all disagreement can be resolved through more information and discussion. There are times when the causal framework itself is fundamentally ambiguous and in this context additional information may not resolve disagreements. As I have shown, experts may propose contradictory theories or competing methods within which they interpret the results from previous evaluation studies. Like uncertainty, ambiguity affects groups' preferences about policies and their motivations for supporting or opposing them.

The Becker model is easily extended to accommodate causal ambiguity. Recall that in Becker's original model, there exists a single cost function and a single benefit function and that the comparison between costs and benefits is unambiguous (for example, as if all relevant policy outcomes such as taxes and subsidies were quantified by money). That is, to Becker, a policy can have either a benefit function like B_1 or B_2 but not both, and further, the magnitudes of the parameters describing the functions are known and unambiguous. Each of these assumptions is often violated in practical politics.

First, ambiguity may stem from having multiple dimensions by which to evaluate the outcomes of a policy, and a policy may be expected to have a high marginal benefit along one dimension and a low marginal benefit along another. To illustrate the effect of this conceptual ambiguity in the Becker framework, assume that the costs are well known but that a program has two different goals; furthermore, by one goal or benefit function, the marginal benefits exceed the marginal costs, and by the other goal they do not. In such a case, the benefits may be described both by B_1 and by B_2. Some groups will focus their attention on one or the other of these outcome dimensions for private or intrinsic reasons (see Baumgartner and Jones 1993). Here, supporters will use arguments that will call attention to the marginally high benefit function B_1, and opponents likewise will call attention to the marginally low benefit function B_2. In this case, information lending clarity to the likely outcomes will only worsen disagreements and fuel both sides' claims. In addition, groups that have extrinsic preferences and care about both outcome dimensions will tend to be of two minds, and information will tend to increase these outcome-oriented groups' ambivalence.

Second, in practice the expected size or magnitude of the costs and benefits is subject to interpretation, which can lead to competing expectations among experts regarding the likely outcomes of an efficient policy. As a matter of methodology, experts may disagree about the scale of the benefits and costs, what specific benefits and costs should be accounted for in evaluating programs, whether and how previous findings apply to the current policy issue, and so on. With this methodological ambiguity, the available analytical information and empirical evidence does not help to clarify the hypothetical links within the causal framework that connect government action to outcomes. In essence, ambiguity allows for competing beliefs about the effects of and desirability of a government intervention.

In either case (see table 3), when there is ambiguity in the conceptual framework, supplying better evidence will mobilize all groups—both supporters and opponents—that have private or intrinsic reasons to focus on one or the other outcome dimension. In the strong evidence case, evaluation information only worsens disagreements among these groups. For groups with extrinsic preferences desiring an overall improvement from the government intervention, high-quality evaluation information may simply increase ambivalence. In the weak evidence case, the same logic of the weak evidence case in table 2 applies. Those who can expect to benefit from the policy are risk averse and may not be certain that these benefits will be realized in practice. Meanwhile, those who expect some harm are loss averse and risk acceptant and so will be vigorous in their opposition. Among groups with extrinsic preferences, the potential gainers will withhold support, and those who may experience a harm will be active in their opposition. Overall, like uncertainty, ambiguity only increases the advantage opposition groups have in lobbying politics.

Conclusion

Expert policy ideas and research directly affect interest groups' motivations when lobbying Congress. Under favorable conditions, interest groups act out of self-interest to pressure Congress to enact socially efficient policy. When research-based information exists and unambiguously shows that the policy is likely to create efficiencies in practice, groups that could expect to gain from the program will pressure Congress to enact the policy. The absence of research-based information or the lack of a clear causal framework connecting government action to outcomes reduces the support for a policy among groups with extrinsic preferences for the benefits that they may derive from expert policy. While clear and unambiguous evidence in support of innovative policies often does not exist, the amended Becker model shows that inefficient policy is not a necessary result of democratic politics, and the legislative process sometimes can be expected to produce efficient public policy through interest group pressure.

TABLE 3. Information Affects Activity: Ambiguity

	Supporters	Opponents
Strong Evidence		
Extrinsic Preferences	Moderate	Vigorous
Intrinsic Preferences	Vigorous	Vigorous
Weak Evidence		
Extrinsic Preferences	None	Vigorous
Intrinsic Preferences	Vigorous	Vigorous

As a simplification, this chapter assumed Congress was an institutional black box and merely responded to the aggregate sum of interest group pressure. Assuming that Congress is a black box, the Becker model provides a positive theory that can link socially efficient policies to legislation. Overall, if society wants Congress to enact efficient policies that clearly will work and not to enact policies that will likely fail or are only ambiguously related to the public interest, interest groups often pressure Congress to act in a manner consistent with the public interest. The next chapter shows that Congress has its own incentives and capacity to develop socially efficient policies.

APPENDIX
The Intrinsic Advantage from Efficiency

An analysis of noncooperative competition among pressure groups can unify the view that governments correct market failures and what has seemed to be a contrary view that governments favor the politically powerful. (Becker 1983, 384)

Becker's logic for the relative advantage conferred by efficient policy is illustrated in figure 1, a graph derived from his more general model for competition among interest groups. The Becker article is difficult to decipher, and this chapter appendix gives a brief summary of his model and my extensions.

For simplicity, assume that there are two groups, {h, g}, organizationally equal in every respect, and that the policy proposal at issue is to impose some cost on one group (group h, the prospectively harmed group) to provide some benefit to the other group (group g, the prospectively gaining group). The vertical axis in figure 1, labeled R, represents the gains or losses for each group from the policy. R_h represents the cost of the proposed policy to group h, and R_g represents the benefit to group g.

In Becker's framework, every policy proposal implies a pair of functions: a benefit function for group g, called B(S), and a cost function for group h, called C(S). One can think of any policy as a proposal to redistribute social, policy, or economic resources from h to g, and this implies an accounting identity $S_h = S_g$, where S is the total amount redistributed. The policy proposal in figure 1, in effect, is to move the status quo from S_1 to S_2, say, using the policy $\{C, B_1\}$. Under an efficient policy, by definition, the benefits to group g must exceed the costs to group h, or $R_g > R_h$. Geometrically, any function B to the left of C meets the wealth-maximization definition of efficiency. So, for example, $\{C, B_1\}$ in figure 1 is efficient and $\{C, B_2\}$ is inefficient by the wealth-maximization criterion. Group g favors moves to the right on S, and group h opposes moves to the right.

The cost (C) and benefit (B) functions describe the absolute and marginal efficiency of the policy proposal and together provide a framework for analyzing the politics of efficiency policy. Under full information, when a policy is efficient at the margin—that is, when the marginal benefits are greater than the marginal cost (which requires $B' > C'$)—the group that will benefit from the policy has what Becker calls an "intrinsic advantage" in lobbying politics. Consider the efficient policy $\{C, B_1\}$ in figure 1 ($B_1' > C'$, $C'' = B_1'' = 0$). By increasing S from S_1 to S_2 under policy $\{C, B_1\}$, the marginal benefits to g are greater than the marginal costs to h since the vector $R_{g1}R_{g2}$ is longer than $R_{h1}R_{h2}$ (i.e., $dR_g > dR_h$), and so group g's efforts to increase its benefit have a higher marginal payoff than group h's efforts to prevent its cost increase.[12] As a consequence, group g should be more inclined to invest its scarce resources in supporting this policy than in other, less efficient uses of its resources. Group h is likely to divert its resources to lobbying for or against other policies where it will have a greater marginal impact. Thus, group g has a greater motivation to act on this policy than does group h.

AMENDMENT 1: Information

The parameters to functions B and C are states of the world, are uncertain, and so have sampling distributions. The effect of limited

---

12. Of course, this logic of the advantage conferred by efficiency is not limited to linear benefit and cost functions. A function that has a downward bend (concave, or $B'' < 0$) is marginally efficient up to the point where $B' = C'$ and then is marginally inefficient beyond that. (Policies of this type can be accommodated in the lobbying model that follows.) Policies where B is to the left of C and $B'' > 0$ are at all points wealth maximizing and at some points marginally efficient and thus behave similarly to policy $\{C, B_1\}$. In general, at any point S, decreasing the marginal efficiency of the cost function (raising C') improves the advantage for group h; increasing the marginal efficiency of the benefit function (raising B') improves the advantage for group g.

information is to subtract benefits from group g's utility (v_g) and to add costs to group h's utility (v_h):

$$dR_h(C) = v_h(E(C'), SE(C'))$$
$$dR_g(B_2) = v_g(E(B'), SE(B')) <? > dR_g(B_1)$$

where E(.) is the expected value, SE(.) is the standard error. According to prospect theory, $dv_h/dE(C') < 0$, $dv_h/dSE(C') < 0$, $dv_g/dE(B') > 0$, $dv_g/dSE(B') < 0$, and $|dv_h/dE(C')| > |dv_g/dE(B')|$.

For simplicity, assume that marginal costs are easy to quantify, but marginal benefits are difficult to quantify, so only B' is characterized by a sampling distribution. Assume $\{B_1', B_2'\}$ in figure 1 is the 95 percent confidence interval for B'. By the logic stated earlier, it is a relatively bad investment ex post for group g to invest resources to support policy B whenever B' < C', because in practice group g did not have an intrinsic advantage over group h. The probability of group h's intrinsic advantage is given by the probability area to the left of C', or $p(B' < C') = \alpha$; This area increases as less is known about the policy and decreases as more is known about a policy (i.e., $d\alpha/dSE(B') > 0$).

> *Proposition 1:* This amendment to the Becker model implies that increasing uncertainty for the policy (SE(B')) reduces the motivation for group g to support the policy relative to the motivation for group h to oppose the policy; adding information has the opposite effect.

Chebechev's inequality implies that this logic works for any sampling distribution for B'. In addition, a two-tailed outcome space (which may occur, for example, when B'' < 0 and C'' = 0; see n.14) yields the same logic but only gives a greater advantage for opponents since the effect of a two-tailed outcome space is to increase the size of α.

AMENDMENT 2: Ambiguity

The Becker model assumes that there is a single dimension to evaluate the benefits of a policy, but empirically this is often not true in practice. Assume there are two metrics by which one may assess the social efficiency of a policy, given by B_1 and B_2. Or equivalently, assume there are two studies that use different estimation methodologies, different samples, or whatever, where the estimated benefit in one study is B_1 and in the other is B_2.

> *Proposition 2:* When there is ambiguity about the efficiency of a program, groups on both sides are mobilized with evidence to support their conflicting claims; supplying more information will only heighten disagreement.

4

Policy Expertise and
Congressional Learning

Chapter 3 showed that under some circumstances, interest groups pressure Congress to enact expert-informed socially efficient policy. For simplicity, that discussion treated Congress as if it were a black box: under this assumption, socially efficient policy prevails as long as Congress responds to the collective pressure from self-interested organized groups. Legislation does not emerge spontaneously, however, and Congress has considerable autonomy and discretion in how it chooses to address problems on its agenda. As I show in this chapter, Congress can choose to develop expert-informed, socially efficient policies to resolve collective-action problems among interest groups. In addition, under the republican mode of representation set out in chapter 2, Congress has incentives to use expertise and judgment as a way to advance the national interest. That is, Congress can strategically use socially efficient policies to satisfy the interests of both organized groups and constituents simultaneously.

But despite this autonomy, Congress still depends fundamentally on interest groups. To achieve its goals, Congress needs to know that the policy will work after implementation, that it will not be a disaster, that it will improve social efficiency in a manner that will benefit interest groups and advance constituent interests. For example, Congress will not want to develop and enact a policy that creates an environmental disaster at high cost to industry. If Congress could both

see into the future and read interest groups' minds to see how policies are likely to work when implemented, then Congress indeed
could have complete autonomy. Congress would simply implement
policies that are socially efficient, and groups and society would reap
the benefits from newly gained efficiencies. Congress unfortunately
lacks these analytic capacities. Often, only specialized interest groups
have the capacity to say if a policy can be expected to be efficient,
based on their internal analytical capabilities and their private interests. And they can broadcast Congress's successes and failures to constituents.

The question for this chapter—indeed, the central question of this
book—is whether Congress can learn from public debate among
interest groups about the likely effectiveness of policies or whether
interest groups will only exploit their informational advantage to
confuse and mislead Congress. In effect, the question is whether the
pressure interest groups bring to bear on Congress out of self-interest is meaningful for Congress and can provide Congress with the
information it needs to govern effectively.

In this chapter I show that under a variety of conditions, debate
among interest groups can reveal whether a policy is likely to be
socially efficient and in the public interest. Even assuming that all
lobbyists intend to advance only their groups' private interests, the
aggregate effect of debate can be to expose falsehoods, biases, limitations, and blind spots in the arguments of competing groups. In
some circumstances, interest group debate is informative for Congress, and in such cases, groups pressure Congress to make decisions
that correspond with the current state of knowledge in a manner
consistent with the public interest. Unfortunately, the conditions
necessary for an informative debate do not always hold, and debate
does not always help Congress reach decisions. Debate sometimes
will reveal fundamental disagreements among groups or disagreements that cannot be reconciled by additional information, analysis,
or discussion. In general, Congress's ability to learn about the likely
effects of policies from debate among interest group lobbyists varies
across identifiable circumstances, such as uncertainty and ambiguity;
hence, its propensity to develop socially efficient policies varies
across these conditions as well.

Complexity and State Autonomy

The argument that interest group pressure leads to socially efficient policy outcomes, as set out in chapter 3, simply assumes that Congress is an institutional black box that responds to the demands of interest groups, a simplification that underlies most theories of pluralism (Latham 1952). Congress, of course, is much more than an institutional black box. Constitutional framer James Madison envisioned Congress as a creative force for solving national problems, a view articulated in his "extended sphere" concept of representation in the U.S. Congress (see also McConnell 1966, 114; Pitkin 1967, 218). This is the foundation of his theory of republican representation. Madison wrote,

> In the extended republic of the United States, and among the great variety of interests, parties, and sects which it embraces, a coalition of a majority of the whole society could seldom take place on any other principles than those of justice and the general good. (1961, 325)

In Madison's view, democratic government is much more than a set of institutions and procedures for aggregating individual or "factional" group preferences: by the design of the Constitution, members of Congress must search for policies that are broadly appealing and are based on diffuse or widely shared values.

Using the reasoning set out in chapter 3, Congress clearly can purposefully use expert, socially efficient policies to engineer agreement as a basis for collective action among groups.[1] When policy problems are complex, Congress can use its agenda-setting power to shape the political landscape as much as it responds to interest group pressures.

---

1. Empirically, Congress favors policies that have the backing of a broad and diverse coalition of interest groups (Loomis 1986, 260). But Congress often takes on an entrepreneurial role to reduce disagreement and solve collective-action problems among groups (B. Jones 1994, 23; Walker 1991). Congress may use its staff and capacities to craft alternative proposals (Wawro 2000) or may simply adopt policies crafted by interest group policy entrepreneurs (Loomis 1986, 270; Mintrom 1997), through debate processes (Habermas 1998), or by other public officials (Peterson 1990, 42).

Congress can simply change the content of policies on its agenda to induce a change in the degree of support or opposition to a policy (Baumgartner and Jones 1993; B. Jones 1994, 13; Salisbury 1991, 377; Wright 1996, 172–73). Congress as an autonomous institution has the capacity to propose solutions to complex social problems and thus to change divergent preferences to convergent preferences in lobbying politics.

Of course, not all issues are potentially positive-sum. The multidimensional complexity of some policy choices may be masked by an ideological simplification of the policy problem (Hinich and Munger 1996), or certain moral aspects of the policy choice may trump social welfare considerations (McFarlane and Meier 2001). But for many complex policy problems, it is possible for Congress to improve social efficiency by changing a policy from a suboptimal to an optimal policy framework. Congress can select a policy that converts intransitive to transitive collective preferences through better and more optimal policy framings (Knight and Johnson 1994, 282; Przeworski 1990, 23–24; Richards 2001, 262). Because expert-informed socially efficient policy can appeal to diverse groups, Congress may prefer to experiment with this style of reform than to continuously revisit the command-and-control regulatory status quo and engage in the cycling that occurs when interest groups cannot act collectively.[2] In this sense, policies that offer the prospects of positive-sum gains for groups—or socially efficient policies—are consistent with the sort of policy Madison expected Congress to embrace.

Of course, Congress is interested not just in satisfying group preferences but also in attending to the interests of the ordinary citizens to whom legislators are ultimately accountable. If at all possible, Congress would like to simultaneously satisfy the interests of both constituents and organized groups (see Denzau and Munger 1986). In the republican mode of representation, promoting expert-informed, socially efficient policies is consistent with members' elec-

---

2. Political leaders may attempt to reduce the level of intergroup conflict through other strategies as well. Baumgartner (1989, 128), for example, found that those currently in control of a social policy tend to define issues as technical rather than political in nature to prevent the expansion of conflict or to adopt programs to reduce the number of competing groups.

toral interests.[3] Because they enhance welfare, efficient policies promote national interests by creating new opportunities to meet society's aspirations for public policy (Sunstein 1988, 1554). All else being equal, the public prefers efficiency to inefficiency since every dollar spent on, say, environmental cleanup cannot be spent on education or health care. Of course, if greater efficiency harms a specific district interest, such as a local industry that wants to preserve a regulatory protection, the member for that district will oppose the efficiency reform. Absent these specific local pressures, members can advance the national interest and consequently improve their chances for reelection and the advancement of their careers when they develop policies that improve social efficiency.

Congress has an interest in socially efficient policies because, by coincidence, these policies benefit interest groups and at the same time are in the larger public interest. But this happy coincidence is often something of a house of cards. Congress wants to enact efficient policies that are likely to work as expected and does not want to enact efficient policies that are likely to fail in practice or pose the strong possibility of disaster. Congress will not be interested in enacting an innovative program that is likely to fail because the program will not deliver benefits to groups and because members would be vulnerable to interest groups' claims of sponsoring poor-quality legislation. Interest groups will punish Congress by broadcasting to constituents that Congress has enacted policies that are contrary to the national interest. In addition, all else being equal, Congress would like to avoid policies that engender divisiveness among groups. When a policy is too divisive, Congress cannot be sure that the policy will ultimately improve efficiency; the policy may be foreclosing rather than expanding opportunities to meet social goals.

Thus, Congress will favor policies that are expected to be both socially efficient and demonstrably effective, and Congress would like to avoid policies that have the prospects of unintended consequences such as failure or divisiveness. Writing legislation that has a

3. Chapter 2 shows that constituents often trust their members to use expertise to advance the national interests. Using public-interested expertise increases members' ability to construct explanations, and having appealing interpretations is consistent with their reelection incentives (R. A. Smith 1984, 49). In addition, authoring high-quality legislation helps representatives advance in their legislative careers (Wawro 2000).

realistic chance of enhancing efficiency and social welfare requires expertise. It is relatively easy for Congress to know the expected outcomes of an innovative policy proposal (i.e., the hypotheses implicit in the causal framework). The policy proposal itself often spells out these expectations: a school voucher program should create effective schools, emissions trading should clean the air at the least cost, and so on. But it is much more difficult for Congress to know the research-based state of knowledge that governs the expectations set out in the causal framework—in particular, whether the policy is likely to succeed and meet expectations or if it will have nasty unintended consequences, such as a dysfunctional school system or an environmental disaster. Unfortunately, Congress lacks the internal analytical capacity to make informed decisions on the full array of issues before it or to know enough about the state of research-based knowledge that is behind the proposal to avoid unintended consequences.

One possibility is that Congress could simply empanel academic experts to report the current state of research-based knowledge on each issue, perhaps conducting a seminar of sorts to learn about the causal framework and the corresponding informational properties for each policy proposal. This approach would fail to help Congress avoid unintended consequences, however. What matters to Congress is not an abstract academic understanding of the policy issue but instead how policies impact specific groups. In practice, interest groups are in the best position to say if a policy is likely or unlikely to enhance welfare in any effective manner. Because interest groups have specialized interests and because staff and extensive contact networks give interest groups a capacity to learn about the technical aspects of policies, interest groups generally are more knowledgeable about public policies than is Congress. Furthermore, groups know how alternative policies intersect with the groups' core interests and whether the groups specifically can expect to benefit from the innovative program. To make informed decisions, Congress must learn from interest groups about the likely impact of policies.

Interest groups and Congress are thus asymmetrically informed regarding the expert-informed state of knowledge. Groups are in a better position to know whether a policy is likely to work or to be efficient in practice and to resolve conflict among interest groups.

Given this information asymmetry, Congress needs to rely on interest groups for substantive advice in developing innovative legislation that has the prospect of enhancing efficiency (Schlozman and Tierney 1986, 97; Weiss 1989, 423–24). This is well illustrated in a quotation from Representative Edward Markey (D-MA) in the hearings on the emissions trading program described in chapter 6:

> I don't contend to be able to understand this whole concept of transferring of allowances and I'm going to have to be educated a little bit more on it—and the experts in the room could perhaps identify themselves, whoever totally understands how this whole transfer of allowances is going to work. . . . I would be interested in how the rules and regulations would be developed and what people's sense is of how the program would work, because I'm quite confident that there's a certain amount of ambiguity that is still inherent in the philosophical approach which we're hearing.[4]

Congress therefore is only a semiautonomous actor. Congress does not depend on any particular group, sector, or faction for political support but does depend on the system as a whole providing necessary information. Given this dependence, the question is whether and under what conditions Congress can exercise its capacity to solve collective-action problems among interest groups and advance the national interest through improved efficiency in public policy. More generally, can Congress govern in this era of increasing policy expertise and develop creative solutions to pressing social problems using information and advice provided by interest groups?

The Informative Nature of Public Debate

Socially efficient policies often engender much controversy. While efficiency in principle promises that the aggregate benefits from the policy will exceed the harms, this is of little solace for the specific groups and individuals who suffer the harms. In addition, like all innovative policies, efficient policies are only hypothetical solutions

---

4. U.S. House of Representatives, *HR 3030 Clean Air Act Reauthorization Hearings*, pts. 1–3, September–October 1989, p. 694.

to policy problems. Groups on both sides of the debate have incentives to persuade Congress that the policy is either desirable or undesirable, depending on their specific preferences, as a means to pressure Congress to enact or not enact the policy.

Lobbyists can pursue two different argumentative strategies or make two different types of arguments that potentially can matter for Congress (see table 4). On the one hand, lobbyists can make research-based instrumental arguments that seek to establish the causal relationships and the likely implications of government actions. Instrumental arguments address whether the policy is likely to yield its expected outcome and relate to the causal effectiveness of the policy based on the quality of the policy's internal design. Instrumental arguments focus on the program's internal logic using objective and scientific "information describing or explaining how the policy under consideration will operate" (Webber 1984, 112). These arguments are objective in the sense that they are falsifiable, research- or evidence-based causal claims: if government undertakes policy X, then outcome Y will or will not occur. For example, a lobbyist who favors the policy might argue that the socially efficient policy will be effective in an instrumental sense: it will enhance welfare, has a good-quality design, and is easy to implement. A lobbyist opposed to the policy might make instrumental arguments that it will fail miserably, has a flawed design, and is not an efficient means to reach the stated goals (Arnold 1990, 97; Robertson 1991, 57).

On the other hand, lobbyists can make normative arguments regarding the desirability of the policy (independent of the outcome) or of the outcomes (independent of the policy). In this sort of argu-

TABLE 4. Types of Arguments in Debate

Instrumental Arguments	Statements that focus on the quality of the causal logic behind the program or the structure and efficacy of the causal linkages between policies and outcomes
Normative Arguments	Statements that the program is desirable or undesirable for reasons external to the analytical program logic contained in the proposal, the desirability of the policy independent of the outcome, or the outcome independent of the policy

ment the outcome itself or the policy itself is deemed good or bad, legitimate or illegitimate, desirable or undesirable. Policy X is good or bad independent of outcome Y, or, assuming Y occurs, Y is deemed either good or bad (Bohman 1990, 95; Johnson 1991, 183). Normative arguments refer to the program's external effects or intrinsic desirability using an argument that "pertains to ideological, ethical, and political considerations important to selecting an alternative policy but not in understanding the mechanics of a policy" (Webber 1984, 112). In this definition, a normative argument or assertion of whether a policy is desirable is generally not falsifiable. For example, a lobbyist might argue that the distribution of the wealth that will result from improved efficiency is itself unfair. The lobbyist may concede that the program will yield its expected outcomes but then argue that the inequities in the final distribution trump society's gains from increased efficiency. Alternatively, a lobbyist could use free-market metaphors to argue that a socially efficient policy, such as one based on free choice and market incentives, is inherently desirable as something distinctly American, irrespective of the consequences of the policy.

As table 4 summarizes, each argument type focuses on a different aspect of the policy choice. Instrumental arguments focus on the quality of the internal logic or the policy design as a causal and empirical matter, while normative arguments focus on aspects of the policy choice that are external to the program's design—in particular, the intrinsic desirability of the policy or of the outcome. By this definition, normative arguments do not depend on or even speak to the causal framework and the current state of knowledge, so Congress cannot learn about the likely outcomes or the prospects of failure or unintended consequences from normative arguments. This simplification in the debate space helps to focus the discussion on the role of policy expertise in debate and relies on the familiar assertion that policy experts can use their tools to show the best means to given ends but cannot show which means or ends are intrinsically desirable.[5]

If Congress believes lobbyists' statements that the policy has a good-quality causal framework—that is, the policy will succeed in

---

5. To the extent that normative arguments are falsifiable, they simply will behave similar to instrumental arguments, as I describe subsequently.

practice and will create new gains from efficiency—Congress is likely to enact the policy unless the legislature is somehow overcome by the available normative arguments about the intrinsic desirability of the policy or of the outcomes. If Congress believes lobbyists who argue that the policy will fail to work in practice, and result in some form of disaster, then Congress will choose not to enact the policy. It is possible, however, that interest groups will try to exploit this dependency or strategically muddy the waters to confuse Congress and use inaccurate instrumental arguments to advance private interests. Interest groups might even use hack, nonscientific, or "advocacy" analysis to misrepresent the true state of research to Congress to gain any advantage in the process.

For example, assume the truth is that the policy under consideration, if it were implemented, would be efficient and effective in producing new wealth and new opportunities to meet social aspirations, such as improving the quality of health care while holding the line on insurance rates. If this policy were implemented, the benefits to some groups (business trade associations, consumer groups, health advocates) would exceed the harms imposed on others (professional physician groups). Those who expect to be harmed by the policy, along with groups that are intrinsically opposed to the policy, could try to convince Congress that the policy is undesirable. Normative arguments regarding the equity or fairness of the policy only go so far, however; these arguments may or may not resonate with Congress. But if the group could convince Congress that the policy will fail (contrary to the truth), then normative arguments are potentially useful but not necessary. If Congress believes the policy will not produce the expected benefits, Congress simply will shelve the policy and not consider it further. Now, assume the truth is that the policy will fail miserably if it were implemented—for example, it will worsen health care at higher cost. For similar reasons, groups that favor the policy for intrinsic reasons (but not extrinsic reasons) would like to mislead Congress into believing that policy will be a great success.

The central question, then, is why a group opposed to a policy would ever concede that the policy should work in practice. Alternatively, why would a group that favors a policy ever concede that the policy might fail to deliver on its promises? Why would a group ever limit its arsenal of arguments to nonfalsifiable normative arguments, which in practice have only limited effectiveness in persuading Congress? I show next that this sort of information that Congress needs to govern effectively and to develop innovative policies in the national interest often is revealed through the processes of public debate among lobbyists. In general, democracy requires political actors to persuade each other to support a position or to persuade members of Congress to write a policy in one way rather than another, since democracy does not offer legal or procedural means to compel others involved in majoritarian politics to do what one wants. Influence in a democracy therefore depends on the capacity to persuade, which creates incentives for lobbyists to make compelling, well-informed, and public-interested arguments.

The politics of public debate has received comparatively little attention in the empirical literature on American politics. One reason for this neglect is the dominance of the (full information) spatial framework for analyzing political institutions and decisions (e.g., Shepsle and Weingast 1984). In this framework, political actors have preferences over policies that are, by definition, self-evident. Rational debate is not necessary and is even a waste of time in this context because political actors already know their positions; persuasion simply cannot occur. Knowing the preferences of each legislator, the aggregation rule, and any institutional constraints enables the prediction of the outcome of the legislative process with certainty. To the extent that rationales are offered, they can be sensibly understood only as misleading rationalizations for positions that legislators and lobbyists take for political or private reasons (Posner 1974). In this view, democracy in practice is not the idealized Athenian version of government by discussion; instead, democracy is coextensive exclusively with the institutions and procedures used for aggregating individual preferences.[6]

It is true that debate is fruitless on some topics; for example, some issues will have an ideological or moral simplification that resists new information or arguments (Bohman 1990, 100; Knight and Johnson

---

6. For example, Ordeshook (1990, 20) states, "The central questions of politics, then, concern how political institutions (such as elections, representative assemblies, and committees) together with the procedural details of the institutions translate preferences . . . into a social decision."

1994, 286). For these sorts of issues, legislators and lobbyists know with certainty the position they want to take before listening to any debate, since all that matters to them is their opinion or political intuition. But many issues do not turn merely on opinion or intuition. Chapter 3 shows that for complex policies, because the consequences of government action are often hard to anticipate, political actors need to understand the likely consequences of a policy through a causal framework to pursue their interests effectively. A main purpose of debate is to offer compelling rationales by which to establish an understanding or a causal framework within which people can pursue their interests on issues that are new to them and beyond their immediate comprehension. On complex issues, persuasion is possible in this sense of mutually constructing concepts within which the consequences of policies may be understood and preferences defined, even when participants themselves self-interestedly seek objectives.[7]

Because Congress wants to avoid unintended consequences, such as a disastrous or unusually divisive policy, it wants to learn about the causal framework to illuminate the likely consequences of the intervention, given the current state of research-based knowledge. In this case, the instrumental arguments lobbyists make to Congress are not idle comments but instead can inform Congress about the objective properties of policies that Congress can use in its decision making— in particular, the causal relations linking government action to real-world outcomes. I show next that, at least in an idealized debate where groups know the outcomes of policies with certainty and the truth is demonstrable (as envisioned in the original Becker model), public debate constrains lobbyists' capacity to mislead Congress with demonstrably false information. At least in this simplified debate world, groups have a hard time exploiting their information asymmetry for three reasons.

First, because they have a self-interest in persuading others, especially legislators, lobbyists have incentives to use high-quality analy-

---

7. Rothenberg (1992, 226) illustrates this well in his study of Common Cause. He shows how Common Cause was effective in using technical policy analysis to persuade Congress on the issues surrounding the MX missile, a policy with which legislators have little firsthand experience, but was not effective in using analysis to persuade members on campaign finance reform, an issue with which they have considerable experience.

sis and information to construct instrumental arguments. The likely efficacy of policies is not merely a matter of opinion or normative beliefs but instead is an objective property of the policy that is known to some degree in the empirical research. In this situation, instrumental arguments based on better-quality research, all else being equal, will be more persuasive to others than those based on shoddy research.

Second, the accuracy and persuasiveness of an argument do not need to be self-evident. Groups can counteract their opponents' efforts at misrepresentation (Austen-Smith and Wright 1992; Milbrath 1963, 211). In an issue network, there will be not only a variety of other interest group advocates who can supply well-informed rebuttals but also a number of independent policy experts in think tanks, executive agencies, research centers, and so on, organizations that are familiar with the current research and can weigh in on the accuracy of various arguments (Hall 1996, 90–91). Because lobbyists attempt to counter the arguments of those with whom they disagree, debate in the aggregate can expose blind spots, biases, and falsehoods (Habermas 1998, 58; Johnson 1991, 184). The strength of ideas is tested in the adversarial processes of debate, and better arguments are revealed in a discursive test of competing arguments. Rather than being a painful necessity of politics, conflict and disagreement are essential to democratic politics, tending to expose weak or inaccurate arguments (Elster 1989, 112–13). Disagreement in advocacy processes has the aggregate effect of creating better causal understandings, exposing new perspectives, and allowing for learning (Knight and Johnson 1994, 286; Manin 1987, 351).

Third, Congress has the capacity to create added incentives for groups to provide accurate information in debate. Congressional staff and support agencies can verify lobbyists' claims and empirically based arguments (Rasmusen 1993; Wright 1996, 112). If a group becomes known to provide bad information, Congress can simply close off that group's access. With a number of groups competing to gain access to Congress, Congress can pick and choose when deciding on whom to confer access (Hansen 1991; Kingdon 1989, 82). Empirically, those lobbyists who have a reputation for having the best policy-relevant information are likely to receive special access (Hansen 1991; Schlozman and Tierney 1986, 97). As a result, credibility is lobbyists' most valued resource, and groups are reluctant to provide bad information to Congress or to use shoddy or hack policy analysis in an indiscriminate fashion (Schlozman and Tierney 1986, 104).

Through these mechanisms and under the idealized circumstances that the truth is knowable and demonstrable, Congress can learn about the objective qualities of policies from debate among interest groups. The assertion that a policy will causally lead to specific outcomes is a falsifiable claim and hence knowable as a fact accepted by the scientific research community. Public debate limits lobbyists' ability to make false objective or instrumental arguments, since the scrutiny of claims made in public debate exposes falsehoods and other inadequate arguments. In the adversarial setting of debate, where groups attempt to show the weaknesses in each other's arguments, objective information tends to get sorted out, and false arguments often are not worth making since they tend not to be persuasive and indeed can be costly to the group's credibility if the group is caught in a lie. If a group finds that the available instrumental arguments are not in its favor, given the state of research-based knowledge for the policy topic, it will be constrained to make normative or nonfalsifiable arguments regarding the intrinsic desirability of the policy or of possible outcomes.

When one side of the debate is constrained from making instrumental arguments, Congress can learn about the likely outcomes of a policy from debate among lobbyists—that is, Congress can learn whether the policy is likely to be welfare enhancing. If the supporters argue that the policy will be efficient and effective and opponents do not contradict the claim, or if opponents assert that the policy will not be efficient or effective and supporters do not contradict the claim, then Congress can learn about the causal framework and the likely outcomes of the policy from debate among lobbyists. In Habermas's terms, an argument is valid or "rational" if uncoerced agreement emerges from debate (Bohman 1990, 96; Habermas 1995, 127). If groups on each side disagree regarding whether the policy is likely to be efficient in a causal sense, then Congress cannot learn from debate about the likely outcomes of the policy. In this case, neither side's instrumental arguments are valid in Habermas's sense. Finally, in this simplified debate space, debate among lobbyists can provide Congress with information only about the truth of the relative effectiveness of the policy, not about its normative desirability. This simplification again assumes that expert debate cannot prioritize normative goals but can only state the best means to given ends.[8]

In the real world of politics, however, debate does not always clarify issues or lead to enlightened policies because the truth about a policy's future effectiveness often is not knowable or demonstrable as required in this idealized version of debate. Given bounded rationality, interest groups can know the likely outcomes of the policy only through the available expert-defined causal framework that links policies to outcomes. As I show in chapter 3, uncertainty and ambiguity are inherent in policy ideas and policy proposals, so the future effectiveness of policies, once put into practice, cannot ever be known with certainty. The likelihood a policy will fail in practice is a function of the degree of uncertainty in the causal framework. Uncertainty describes the degree of confidence experts have in the stated causal relationships, which is a function of the availability of research-based empirical evidence indicating whether the policy is likely to yield its expected outcomes. The prospects for divisiveness are a function of the degree of ambiguity in the causal framework. Ambiguity describes the degree of agreement among experts on the structure of the causal framework. In some cases, experts may hold contradictory or competing expectations regarding the likely impacts of a policy choice, possibly suggesting that the policy will succeed in some ways and fail in others.

Before enacting a new policy, Congress ideally would like to learn about these research-based informational properties of the causal framework regarding the chances of unintended consequences, such as failure or divisiveness. Chapter 3 shows that the motivation for groups to support or oppose a policy also depends critically on the informational properties of the causal framework. Relative certainty tends to mobilize supporting groups, uncertainty tends to mobilize opposing groups, and ambiguity has the potential to mobilize groups on both sides of the debate. As I show next, because groups' motiva-

---

8. Implicitly, this is to argue that social efficiency creates a bias against the ideological Left, since the Left prioritizes the equity of distributions and the Right prioritizes aggregate wealth. At the same time, the Left may favor socially efficient policies, since they facilitate government interventions into the economy. I discuss the political biases of expertise at greater length in the conclusion.

tions to support and oppose policies depend on the state of knowledge, and given the practical costs involved in using expert-based arguments, Congress makes inferences about the true state of knowledge (certainty, uncertainty, or ambiguity) based on the aggregate pressure from groups.[9]

Uncertainty

Assume that Congress is considering whether to develop a new program based on innovative, socially efficient incentive-based ideas. Groups that expect to benefit from the new, efficient program have an interest in telling Congress that the program will work as planned (that is, state that the true policy is B_1 in figure 1), and groups that expect to suffer some harm have an interest in telling Congress the program will be a disaster (state that the true policy is B_2 or worse). But there is uncertainty both for groups and for Congress about whether the truth is B_1 or B_2. When there is uncertainty about the likely effects of policies, groups do not already know the truth about the policy's effectiveness, which, in turn, implies that it is costly for groups to gather research-based information regarding the causal structure of policies because groups must conduct research to construct instrumental arguments that will survive the rigors of adversarial public debate. There is a cost to gathering high-quality research information that supports an instrumental argument regarding the relative efficacy of a policy, since doing so requires a search through journals and technical reports, and there is a cost to incorporating this technical information into a coherent argument that can be understood by those who are not familiar with the research. While instrumental arguments are costly, normative arguments need not be. To construct a normative argument, a group needs only to state the relative desirability of a policy or of its possible outcome.[10]

---

9. In the terms used by game theorists, groups can be one of three "types," certainty, uncertainty, and ambiguity. Evidence-based argumentation is a form of costly signaling, and so the messages groups send can reveal the group's type (Banks 1991).
10. I am maintaining the simplification set out previously to focus on the nature of instrumental arguments. To the that extent normative arguments are empirically based, they will be governed by the same truth-revealing properties of public debate as instrumental arguments.

Given the cost of including research in testimony under uncertainty, and given the amended Becker model of pressure set out in the previous chapter, I next show that for two reasons, interest groups that are more willing to invest resources to gather technical research information in order to construct their arguments want to tell Congress the truth about rather than misrepresent the research on the likely effectiveness of the policy.

First, consider those groups with purely extrinsic preferences regarding policy outcomes. These groups may confront two possible states of the world regarding the policy alternative: the case of strong evidence and the case of weak evidence. In the case of strong evidence, the empirical research shows that the innovative policy would work as planned. In the case of weak evidence, there is a relative dearth of information regarding the policy's likely effectiveness. In addition, there may be empirical research that demonstrates the policy is likely to fail in practice—and as will be clearer in a moment, this third state of the world can be subsumed under the weak evidence case. Among outcome-oriented groups, I show next that groups in favor of the policy alternative gain an advantage in debates when there is strong evidence to support the policy, and groups opposed to the policy alternative gain an advantage when there is weak evidence.

In the strong evidence case, when the research makes it clear that the policy should realize efficiencies (such as in B_1), then according to the amended Becker model predictions summarized in table 2, the supporters are most motivated to invest resources in a lobbying campaign. These supporting groups will be willing to invest scarce resources to dig up costly research in order to construct instrumental arguments to show Congress that the policy is likely to work in practice. As Becker (1983) shows, under relative certainty, groups that stand to benefit from efficiency tend to gain more per unit of lobbying resources expended. Conversely, in the weak evidence case, when the research cannot show that the policy will realize efficiencies (either showing that the policy is likely to fail, as in B_2, or that there is too much uncertainty about whether the policy is likely to succeed), then the opponents are most motivated to invest resources to show Congress that the policy is not likely to succeed or at least risks failure. The prospective beneficiaries are risk averse, so uncertainty tends to reduce their perceived benefits and increases their incentive to lobby against the policy. That is, an outcome-oriented group is motivated to invest resources to gather and assimilate research on the issue whenever the research-based state of knowledge happens to be in the group's favor (see Kollman 1998, 64). When the research supports a group's position, the group will be more willing than its opponents to invest resources to uncover the existing research to construct instrumental arguments for its testimony. That is, groups with positions supported by the published research tend to be the most willing to send "costly" research-based arguments in testimony to argue when the policy will or will not work in practice.

Second, consider all groups, including those with intrinsic preferences for or against socially efficient policies that would like to dig up empirically based research to legitimate their ideologically informed positions. Again fortuitously, interest groups that have interests consistent with the research or the state of knowledge should find scientific policy information that supports their position cheaper to gather, as scientific studies by their methods tend to produce unbiased estimates of the truth (see Kollman 1998, 64). When there is strong research-based evidence to show that the policy will likely succeed in practice, it is relatively cheap for groups who favor the policy to locate research to support their arguments, and relatively costly for opposition groups. Conversely, when there is only weak evidence available, it is relatively cheap for opposition groups to construct research-based arguments to show the policy courts disaster, and relatively expensive for supporting groups to construct favorable research-based arguments. At the extreme, groups could choose to fund hack "advocacy research" that mimics scientific research but is designed to produce particular results, and advocacy research potentially can be done very inexpensively. But it is very costly to mimic the high-quality research that is readily available in the peer-reviewed journals.[11] If the goal is to persuade Congress in an instrumental

---

11. This is by no means to deny the ready availability of advocacy analysis, but it is a fair presumption that Congress can distinguish hack social science from peer-reviewed quality social science. If advocacy analysis indeed indiscriminately informs the political process, this project's empirical results will demonstrate that fact: the state of knowledge simply will not constrain group testimony. See the null hypothesis of a "babbling" equilibrium that follows.

sense, then the costs of advocacy research often are prohibitive.[12] Scientific information is always cheaper to gather when the truth is in the group's favor.

In the context of uncertainty, the available policy research or the state of knowledge systematically constrains lobbyist testimony (see Kollman 1998, 26). Groups that find it overly costly to make instrumental arguments can fall back on normative or value-based arguments. If a group does not choose to expend resources to communicate technical information in testimony, its testimony will tend to be limited to low-cost, nonfalsifiable normative opinion statements that urge Congress to "do the right thing" in a nonconsequentialist style. Normative arguments are less persuasive to Congress than instrumental arguments about the efficacy of policies if Congress is assumed to be consequentialist—that is, if Congress is interested in enacting policies that are likely to create new benefits through efficiency. In this case, the group that would like to argue counter to research findings is placed at a competitive disadvantage in debates before Congress.

So, fortuitously for Congress, interest groups' willingness to invest in costly research and the cost of research both correlate to the true state of research-based knowledge for a given policy proposal. A group with a position that is supported by the empirical evaluation literature will gain a greater benefit in investing scarce group resources in communicating that research. Because they have a lesser intrinsic motivation and because it is costly to argue against research, groups that have positions not supported by research divert their resources to lobby on other issues where their efforts will be comparatively more productive. This coincidence between congressional preferences and groups' incentives to invest resources in lobbying campaigns is a sufficient condition for credibility to arise in testimony in a signaling framework, implying that the state of knowledge for a policy should constrain lobbyist speech. In technical terms, the result in the case of either weak or strong evidence is an informative separating equilibrium (see Ainsworth 1993, 52; Banks 1991; Koll-

---

12. This is not to say that groups do not conduct advocacy research, only that groups that do so would have an even greater advantage in politics if the research were in their favor. Imagine how much easier life would be for the Tobacco Institute if the peer-reviewed science did not indicate a link between smoking and cancer.

man 1998).[13] In particular, when research shows that the policy is likely to be efficient and effective, only the supporters will invest in research to make instrumental arguments, thereby showing Congress that the policy is likely to resolve the collective-action problem among groups through efficiency gains. These predictions are summarized in table 5.

Assuming that Congress wishes to enact policies that are both efficient and effective and not to enact policies that are not efficient and/or effective, under both certainty and uncertainty, interest groups in their self-interest provide the information Congress needs to make a correct decision. In particular, my model identifies a set of circumstances under which interest groups can be expected to lobby vigorously for efficient policy and Congress will incorporate efficiency into legislation. In my model, Congress does not have to understand all of the analytical consequences of policies for the full set of groups because interest groups credibly signal the quality of policies to Congress, both when the policy is likely to work and when the policy is likely to fail. That is, my model does not impose unrealistic assumptions on the analytical capacities of Congress or assume that Congress has full information on the implications of policy for the full set of interest groups. Finally, my model expects that groups will pressure Congress not to enact policies that lack empirical support. And to emphasize again, these optimistic expectations rest on assumptions that everyone involved is pursuing his or her self-interest.

TABLE 5.   Information Affects Style of Testimony: Uncertainty

	Supporters	Opponents
Strong Evidence		
Extrinsic Preferences	Not Constrained	Constrained
Intrinsic Preferences	Not Constrained	Constrained
Weak Evidence		
Extrinsic Preferences	Silent	Not Constrained
Intrinsic Preferences	Constrained	Not Constrained

Note: Not constrained = both instrumental and normative arguments, constrained = normative arguments only, silent = sits out debate.

---

13. While there are multiple equilibriums in signaling games, the most informative equilibrium is taken to be the behavioral prediction (Banks 1991, 25–26).

Ambiguity

As described in chapter 3, experts may propose several causal frameworks as a way to interpret a given policy proposal, each with potentially contradictory or competing expectations. Contradictory expectations suggest that the policy intervention may succeed on some dimensions yet at the same time fail on others. Competing expectations are the result of methodological disagreements. For example, experts using one method could assert that the research indicates that the policy will succeed, and other experts using a different method could assert that the policy will fail. Under these forms of ambiguity, supplying additional research-based expert information to debates will only worsen disagreements among debate participants.

First, consider the strong-evidence case, where there is little uncertainty about the likely efficacy of the innovative policy but conceptual or methodological ambiguity about the desirability of the policy. Among groups with extrinsic preferences, supporters will remain silent because information only increases their ambivalence (see table 3). Meanwhile, the opponents will not be constrained in their statements because whenever experts disagree, it is relatively easy to dig up research-based evidence that the policy will fail in practice or lead to further divisiveness. Groups with intrinsic preferences can choose to focus their attention strategically on a single outcome dimension: among these groups, stronger evaluation evidence will mobilize both sides because each side readily can demonstrate that the policy will yield results along the dimension on which they strategically focus. With strong evidence and ambiguity, groups on both sides of the debate can be expected to pool on the same message type, both effectively making instrumental arguments for and against the policy. Those in favor will say the policy will make society better off, and those against will say the policy will lead to disaster. In this case, information mobilizes both supporters and opponents and consequently only worsens disagreements. In the aggregate, Congress either hears persuasive instrumental arguments on both sides of the debate or hears only the opposition's instrumental claims that the policy will likely fail. Congress at best can infer only that the policy will be divisive if implemented.

Next, consider the weak-evidence case, where there is a relative dearth of evidence about the policy's likely effectiveness. When there is little evidence to show that the policy will work in practice, the incentives are identical to the weak-evidence case of table 5: groups opposed to the policy can be expected to highlight the relative dearth of research to show that the policy entails too many risks and is too uncertain in its results, and supporters will not attempt to counter these arguments. Among groups with extrinsic preferences, the supporters will remain silent because they are risk averse and not convinced policy will succeed, while the opponents will be mobilized to demonstrate that the evidence suggests that the policy is too risky or uncertain. Groups with intrinsic preferences that favor the policy will be constrained through the adversarial processes of debate to make normative arguments in favor of the policy, while opponents will exploit the lack of evidence to make instrumental arguments that the policy is too risky. Congress will hear the opponents' instrumental claims that the policy risks failure and will hear primarily normative arguments, if any, from the supporters. As in table 5, uncertainty gives the advantage to the opponents. The full set of predictions is set out in table 6.

If Congress wishes only to enact policies that are likely to be efficient and effective in practice, all else being equal, then it is likely not to favor policies with an ambiguous causal framework. With ambiguity, Congress will get a clear picture of the effect of evaluation research on groups' interests only when there is little information available and when the opponents are mobilized and so will not be inclined to support the policy. When there is strong evidence to show that the policy will succeed in some respects and fail in others, Congress will hear compelling empirical arguments from both sides.

TABLE 6.   Information Affects Style of Testimony: Ambiguity

	Supporters	Opponents
Strong Evidence		
Extrinsic Preferences	Silent	Not Constrained
Intrinsic Preferences	Not Constrained	Not Constrained
Weak Evidence		
Extrinsic Preferences	Silent	Not Constrained
Intrinsic Preferences	Constrained	Not Constrained

Note: Not constrained = both instrumental and normative arguments, constrained = normative arguments only, silent = sits out debate

Either way, the policy is not likely to resolve the collective-action problem among interest groups: information at best only worsens disagreements among groups. Again, these sorts of causal ambiguities for understanding the implications of policies may be common, but they are by no means a necessary description of a policy's state of knowledge. Consistent with most common descriptions of the legislative process, my model expects the process to display a bias against the use of research-based expertise and democratic failure to be perhaps more frequent than success. Inconsistent with the established view, however, my model expects democratic success to occur on occasion and under an identifiable set of circumstances.

Theories of Democratic Failure and Babbling Interest Groups

Tables 5 and 6 imply that efficiency should prevail in majoritarian politics under some—perhaps infrequent—circumstances. The established positive literature on Congress (e.g., Arnold 1990; Shepsle and Weingast 1984) in its starkest form argues that Congress almost never favors policies that are socially efficient; democracy fails to use expertise for unchanging structural incentives embedded in the electoral process. In this view, as summarized in chapter 2, legislative politics is driven only by symbols, intuitions, and opinion rather than by efforts to solve complex social problems; political actors have intrinsic preferences regarding policies and thus do not care about the expected consequences of government interventions. For example, Kelman's (1981) survey of interest groups on incentives-based regulation in environmental policy finds that interest groups often do not understand the complicated logic of socially efficient policy because it is based mostly on microeconomic theory. Instead, he finds that groups favor or oppose efficient policy primarily on ideological grounds, depending on whether the group is pro–free market or anti–free market. In this view, research-based information should be irrelevant to interest group behavior, whether pressuring for or against policies.

Similarly, in the traditional positive literature on legislatures, Congress does not care about policy outcomes and engages only in position taking, advertising, and credit claiming (Mayhew 1974, 124–25). And unfortunately for the democratic polity, because Congress never cares about truthful information regarding policy outcomes, interest groups will never invest scarce group resources in gathering scientific policy information to construct their arguments, and legislators learn nothing from debate among groups.

Either way, whether it is Congress or interest groups that refuse to concern themselves with the research on expert, socially efficient policy, the result is that all testimony will be uninformative. This implies a null hypothesis with respect to lobbyists' use of research-based information in public debates: interest groups will make any conceivable claim in testimony, perhaps relying heavily on hack advocacy analysis. Congress consequently does not listen to interest groups, so information does not constrain lobbyist speech. This is technically known as a "babbling" equilibrium (Banks 1991, 24): groups are never expected to use expertise, so Congress never learns from groups' testimony. The implication of the established literature is that interest groups will pool on the same type of claim in the sense that their messages are meaningless to Congress. This is the strong claim of the established literature on positive political economy and is set out in table 7 as the null expectation.

The Variety of Issues, Members, and Groups

A necessary condition for lobbyists' arguments to be credible is that Congress must want to learn about the likely outcomes of the policy, otherwise, groups will not have an incentive to invest resources in gathering costly, research-based technical information (Ainsworth 1993, 53). In practice, Congress considers policies for a variety of purposes. Sometimes, members of Congress indeed care only about their position or the slogan that accompanies a policy rather than the

TABLE 7. Null Predictions (all groups)

	Supporters	Opponents
Strong Evidence	Babble	Babble
Weak Evidence	Babble	Babble

consequences of enacted policy. On some occasions, members clearly will favor policies for uninformed "political" reasons. For example, legislators do not need degrees in rocket science to know that they favor pork-barrel projects for their districts irrespective of the projects' relative efficiency, or legislators may have moral or ideological reasons to favor or oppose a policy—perhaps on human cloning or embryonic stem cell research—irrespective of the policy's practical consequences.

In addition, there is likely to be a variety of interest group types, some with intrinsic preferences and some with extrinsic preferences regarding policies. In practice, some interest groups can be expected to be more ideologically driven then others for group maintenance and organizational reasons. Mass-membership groups may want to polarize debates and make inflammatory statements to create a sense of crisis to attract and retain members (Kelman 1981). In contrast, groups that do not depend on mass membership (such as business groups and trade associations) may be better able to focus on program outcomes. Groups, that is, may conform closer either to Weber's ethic of responsibility, where outcomes matter, or to the ethic of ultimate ends, where information about outcomes is irrelevant.

For these reasons, the effect of information on group activity and statements made in debate should vary across interest groups and issues. The empirical variety of groups, legislators, and issue types is important to keep in mind. The current literature generally casts debates about incentives in legislative politics in terms of what Congress "single-mindedly" seeks (for a refreshing contrast, see Whiteman 1995). In fact, informed debate is likely to be highly conditional, a relatively unexplored but obviously important area.

Conclusion

Congress can be expected to favor policies that have the prospect of increasing social efficiency, but since Congress has a hard time knowing the state of knowledge regarding a policy's likely effects, which would require reading lobbyists' minds and seeing into the future, Congress must rely on interest group statements about the likely effectiveness of policies. The processes of public debate often prevent lobbyists from exploiting this dependency, and Congress frequently can learn the information it needs to govern effectively, even in this age of complex policies and highly technical analyses. The overall pattern of expressed support for and opposition to a proposal from interest groups—both those that can expect to gain from the policy and those that can expect to be harmed by the policy—signals Congress about the program's likely success or the research community's relative confidence in the program. Because it is costlier to argue against the research, the groups that are placed at a disadvantage in a debate can be expected to divert resources to more productive uses.

The absence of pressure from interest groups to support a socially efficient policy signals to Congress that the policy is not likely to work. The demobilization of supporters and mobilization of opponents from uncertainty creates a bias in politics in favor of the regulatory status quo (Ritov and Baron 1992; Walker 1969, 890). Ambiguity leads only to intractable disagreements and tends to demobilize groups that truly desire efficient and informed policies. In contrast, making compelling evaluation information available should mobilize supporters and demobilize opponents, which, in turn, should signal to Congress that the socially efficient policy is likely to resolve the collective-action problem among interest groups. If enough prospectively gaining interest groups have confidence that a socially efficient intervention will succeed and actively advocate the policy to Congress, and if the opposition groups do not effectively contradict these claims then Congress will believe that the policy enhances welfare. In this situation, Congress should take the program under serious consideration as a possible solution to a complex collective problem among interest groups.

PART II

~

THE CASE STUDIES

5

Introduction to the Case Studies

Ordinary citizens and organized interest groups care deeply about many of the policy issues involving environmental quality, elementary and secondary education, and health care. Chapters 6–8 give case studies of a major effort in Congress to adopt an innovative, socially efficient policy in each of these areas. In each case, Congress seeks new, creative solutions to address a seemingly intractable policy problem that creates gridlock among interest groups and frustration among citizens. In each case, Congress tries to address a controversial problem by creating—or at least intending to create—greater efficiency through market-oriented regulatory policy. Chapter 6 examines an emissions trading program to address the acid rain environmental problem (proposed in 1989); chapter looks at 7 a school-choice voucher program as a means for education reform (1991 and again in 2001); and chapter 8 addresses a policy to promote the growth of health maintenance organizations (HMOs) as a means regulate quality and prices in health care delivery (1972).

Each case study gives a detailed explication of the first major set of hearings for each of these proposals, using the policy research available at the time to give an annotation and analysis of the proposal and the debate at the hearing. Committee hearings are the most prominent forum in the legislative process in which public debate among interest groups occurs.[1] While these policies remain very much in the headlines, I focus on the initial set of hearings in each case since, by necessity, the purpose of the initial hearings is to define

---

1. See the appendix to this book for an analysis of the validity of using hearings data for the study as well as an analysis of the reliability of the data coded in the hearings.

the nature of the policy problems and the proposed solutions. Even though some of these hearings are in the remote past, understanding the origins of these programs provides a context for current debates, as these policies are still under consideration as cutting-edge expert interventions.[2]

This chapter provides some useful background information for the case studies. It explains the basic logic of market-oriented regulation and provides the theoretical structure for the case study analyses to follow.

Market-Oriented Regulation as Socially Efficient Policy

The politics of market-oriented regulatory policies, along with the politics of nearly all expert-informed interventions, has been largely overlooked in the positive literature on American politics. This gap has occurred for a variety of reasons, but perhaps the most important is that even the possibility of creative government interventions in markets and social relations is often ruled out as a basic theoretical assumption. Implicit in many institutional analyses based on the spatial framework as well as theories that assume that all political issues can be reduced to some left-right ideological dimension is an assumption that politics involves only the zero sum redistribution of existing resources among groups in society. To maintain this limited focus, these theories implicitly assume that markets perform efficiently and create the greatest possible aggregate benefits to society without government interventions. By assumption, the only role available for government is to redistribute the bounty that markets produce, either for moral reasons such as reducing the inequalities that go hand in hand with capitalist production or for amoral reasons such as redistributing resources to the politically powerful or to localities as a way for legislators to secure reelection.

This assumption that markets produce the greatest aggregate benefits for society indeed has considerable merit. In the economic

2. Examining only the initial administration proposal for each program also enhances comparability between cases, since the politics of initiation are likely to differ from the politics of program renewal.

theory of perfect competition, competitive markets allocate resources efficiently.[3] Competitive markets give millions of people both the information and the incentives to do what an omniscient social planner would want them to do, and markets direct resources to the uses that society most highly values. People acting in their self-interest advance society's interests by using privately held resources to produce the greatest amount of wealth. Markets routinely perform a nearly infinite array of jobs and activities very effectively, a task that would be mind-boggling for some central authority to direct.

Markets can do so because they leverage people's worst shortcomings to society's advantage. First, people are often greedy and selfish. Markets align individuals' and business firms' private interests with society's collective interest in using resources in a way that most advantages society. Markets exploit gains from trade in the decentralized exchanges that occur through a system of prices. In a competitive market, the quantity of a good that is supplied equals the quantity that is demanded, given the opportunity costs of the factors used to produce the good. When this equilibrium occurs, the price at which the good is exchanged reflects the good's value to society,[4] and the good is used to its maximum advantage. Second, people are boundedly rational and generally can excel only if they focus on a particular narrow problem. In markets, people specialize to make the most effective use of their skills. Specialization leads to improved skills and to new advances in technology and thus increases overall production for a given amount of time, labor, and inputs.

Believing that politics exclusively involves the distribution of existing resources, however, requires the belief that markets necessarily result in a state of maximum efficiency and, therefore, that no improvements can be made by government intervention. For example, the neoliberal Chicago school economists argue that markets are everywhere and always efficient, so any government intervention can only create inefficiencies (Posner 1974; Stigler 1975). In practice, however, real-world markets do not always meet the conditions necessary for an ideal competitive market. When a market is not at a

---

3. For a good summary of markets, see Munger 2000.
4. More specifically, demand that is made effective among consumers with money and resources.

competitive equilibrium, the market allocation cannot be efficient or produce the best possible outcome for society.[5] Neoclassical economics focuses on the conditions where there is not a perfectly competitive market or the conditions for market failure, where the market processes do not use resources to society's greatest advantage. These conditions include externalities, public goods, and market power.

Externalities. With externalities, a resource that is valued by people who are not party to a market transaction is not priced or is available to firms for free, so the price does not take into account the true social cost of the resource. Because people are greedy, industry consumes the resource more than is socially optimal (Bator 1958). The problem of externalities lies at the heart of many environmental problems, where industry makes excessive use of the disposal capacity of the environment, and the result is harmful pollution. Chapter 6 examines a problem of externalities in environmental politics, the problem of acid rain caused by sulfur dioxide emissions from Midwest coal-burning electric utility plants.

Public goods. In the problem of public goods, the benefits of a good accrue to everyone in society or anyone who wants to consume the good, irrespective of each individual's or firm's contribution toward the production of the good. Public goods are not produced at optimal levels because, again, people are greedy and will not voluntarily spend money for a good that they can get for free. Instead, people will choose to free ride on the efforts of others (Olson 1965). Education is a classic public good; everyone in society benefits from the education of a child, but people ordinarily do not voluntarily pay for the education of someone else's child. Chapter 7 examines some of the politics behind the public production of elementary and secondary education.

Market power. When a firm controls either the supply or demand side of a market, that firm has the power to set prices. Since, once again, firms are greedy, they will use market power to set prices to charge more for a good they sell or produce and to pay less for a

---

5. The neoliberal belief in the unbridled efficiency of markets simply dismisses the empirical realities of market failure, so the assertion that government interventions produce only inefficiencies can be seen solely as an ideological belief rather than as a description of reality (Przeworski 1990, 22).

good they wish to purchase. One way that firms can manipulate demand is if information asymmetry exists and the producer can induce demand for a good (Arrow 1963). Health care markets are rife with information asymmetries. Doctors have the specialized expertise and the legal authority to prescribe tests, drugs, and procedures and thus can increase the demand for their services. As a result, consumers purchase too much health care service at too high a price. This problem of professionally induced demand is especially acute when insurance companies rather than consumers pay for physician services. Chapter 8 examines market power from information asymmetry in the politics of health care market reforms.

⌁

When there is a demonstrable failure of the market, society may aspire to do better and to improve on market outcomes. This suggests that Congress has the potential to develop creative policies as solutions to market failure, since the market cannot arguably be at an optimum state. These creative interventions can take many forms. All of the cases that follow consider a particular form of government intervention called market-oriented regulation (see Schultze 1977).

Like markets themselves, market-oriented regulations leverage people's worst weaknesses, greed and bounded rationality, for society's greatest advantage. First, consider greed. Market-oriented regulations develop some mechanism, using perhaps a tax or allowance system, to make the cost of using or purchasing a resource equal to its true social opportunity cost. The government-created market in essence prices the resource and in so doing creates private incentives for the regulated entities to use the resource in a way that advances socially desired or public-interested outcomes.[6]

Next, consider bounded rationality. Market-oriented regulations allow the regulated entities to gain from trade and from specialization, because under this form of regulation the central authority does not dictate how people are to respond to regulatory incentives. In

---

6. As Schultze (1977, 17–18) puts it, "Market-like arrangements not only minimize the need for coercion as a means of organizing society, they also reduce the need for compassion, patriotism, brotherly love, and cultural solidarity as a means of motivating forces behind social improvements."

essence, through decentralization of authority and an appropriate incentive mechanism, market-oriented regulations allow for beneficial exchanges and encourage experimentation in the means to respond to the newly created incentives. Market-oriented approaches allow firms and individuals to act on their own information regarding how best to respond to these incentives.

In contrast, central authority or command-and-control policies are a much more direct approach to addressing market failure and other social problems. When the government issues a direct command to industry to change its behavior, social responsibilities are clear and the dictate demonstrates the symbolic importance of the social goal. The central authority cannot have the full information needed to make each actor most efficiently reach desired goals, however, and generally lacks sufficient authority, monitoring capacity, or resources to force industry to comply with direct regulations through fines or through litigation. The result is that command-and-control regulation in practice is unduly expensive, burdensome, and inefficient; it does not create incentives to enter into exchanges or to experiment with new technologies; and it relies too much on good intentions of administrators and assumes that administrators avoid capture by the regulated industry. Market-oriented regulations are more likely than specific commands from a central authority to create efficient solutions for society's aspirations for public policy because they harness private incentives and private information to create a socially efficient outcome.

Three Market-Oriented Policy Proposals

Market-oriented solutions, at least in principle, can work as creative, innovative, efficient approaches to social problems, providing an expert-based causal framework where the gainers can expect to gain more than the losers lose. These policies can capture efficiencies in relation to an unregulated status quo under the conditions of market failure (externalities, public goods, or market power). These policies are also efficient relative to a command-and-control status quo through the use of decentralization and an incentive mechanism.

The acid rain and the school-choice cases describe policies where efficiencies may be gained relative to a command-and-control status quo. The intent in the policy in the HMO case is to create a competitive market where one simply does not exist in the absence of a government intervention.

An Emissions Trading Program to Control Acid Rain

By the early 1980s, as the problem of acid rain gained headlines, Congress felt the need to compel reductions in sulfur dioxide emissions from coal-fired electric utilities, which had been identified as the main precursor to acid rain. The original Clean Air Act used a command-and-control approach to limit sulfur dioxide emissions. Because of the inefficiencies in this regulatory approach, Congress was unable to find a means to increase the stringency of emissions standards without causing a noticeable increase in the costs of electricity for Midwest consumers as well as high costs and engineering problems for the electric utilities. To remedy this problem, many economists suggested that the government adopt an emissions trading program in which the government would issue a set of allowances to industry. Each allowance would permit the industry to emit a specific quantity of a pollutant. Some firms might clean their plants very cost-effectively, while others might find meeting their emissions limit very costly. Under an emissions trading system, firms that can clean up cheaply could exceed their control requirements and then sell their excess allowances to other firms. In this case, all firms have incentives to clean their emissions, since firms can either profit from selling excess allowances or minimize their costs from having to purchase allowances. And further, gains from trade ensure that the final distribution of allowances is the most cost-effective allocation of control responsibility where the marginal cost of control is equal across all emissions points. In essence, an emissions trading program promises to clean the environment more than under a command-and-control approach and to do so at less cost. Using this logic, in 1989 the George H. W. Bush administration proposed an emissions trading program as Title IV of the Clean Air Act Amendments.

A School-Choice Voucher Program to
Improve Public Education

Throughout the 1980s, it became increasingly clear that student per-formance in many public schools was substandard and that many students were poorly equipped for the knowledge-driven workplace of the information age. States and localities tried a long list of educa-tion reforms, none of which seemed to work and which even in con-cept did not seem to be related to student performance or effective schools. In light of the dismal record of local-level education reforms, many education reformers suggested the benefits of a national school-choice voucher program. In such a program, the school district allows each school complete freedom to experiment with its curriculum and teaching methods, with the proviso that all students participating in the voucher program can choose which school they would like to attend. Schools receive their funding as a function of their enrollment. Education-reform experts argue that in this decentralized and competitive system, all schools have incentives to become more effective in their teaching methods and thus more desirable to their consumers—students and their parents. In 1991, the Bush administration proposed the America 2000: Excellence in Education Act to amend what was then called chapter 1 of the Ele-mentary and Secondary Education Act to create school-choice voucher programs at the state level. For reasons set out in chapter 7, this school-choice voucher program made little headway in Con-gress. In 2001, the administration of George W. Bush proposed another school-choice voucher program entitled the Leave No Child Behind Act.

HMOs to Control the Costs of Health Care Delivery

In the late 1960s, shortly after the enactment and implementation of Medicare, the costs of health insurance and health care services in the United States began to increase at an alarming rate without any cor-responding dramatic improvement in the population's overall health. Third-party insurance payment and the professional domi-nance of health care delivery did not seem to offer any prospects for slowing the rate of increase. At the time, many health policy researchers were demonstrating the efficiencies gained in the prepaid group practice form of health care delivery, which came to be called HMOs, over the fee-for-service form of delivery. HMOs combined a more efficient organization for delivering health care services with an incentive system for physicians to control the number and costs of services and to emphasize ambulatory and preventative care that is relatively inexpensive and demonstrably more beneficial for patients' overall health. Presumably, when forced to compete with these cost-effective health care organizations, mainstream medical practices would also need to economize on costs. In 1971, President Richard M. Nixon used this efficiency logic to design his health strategy HMO initiative.

Case Study Overview

The cases seek to illustrate the conditions, set out in chapter 4, under which Congress can gain from groups the information it needs to govern effectively and to exercise its autonomy and construct creative solutions to social problems as well as the conditions under which Congress does not gain useful information from debate among interest groups. As in chapter 4, assume that it is relatively easy for Congress to know the expected outcomes from a given intervention; these are often the outcomes described in the policy proposal itself. It is much more difficult for Congress to learn about the state of knowledge that governs the proposal—in other words, the likelihood that the program will fail to work in practice or will have unintended consequences. The causal framework that states the hypothetical relationships between the proposed government intervention and potential outcomes will have a set of informational properties that are known to experts, in particular the degree of uncertainty and ambiguity inherent in the proposal's framework. Policies that entail too much uncertainty stand a good chance of failure, and those with ambiguous benefits may turn out to be too divisive in practice.

To learn about these informational properties, Congress would like to learn about the policy from debate among interest groups. As I show in chapter 4, there is a fortuitous coincidence that the propensity of interest groups to make instrumental arguments regarding the likely success or failure of the policy is also conditioned on the policy's informational properties—the degree of uncertainty and the degree of ambiguity. Congress can learn from debate among interest groups if one side of the debate makes instrumental arguments (for or against) the policy and the other side does not counter these instrumental assertions. The empirical research question for the case studies to follow is under what conditions Congress will get this sort of clear message from interest group debate. Technically, the cases seek to illustrate the conditions for informative separating equilibria and the conditions for uninformative pooling equilibria. Congress's ability to learn about the state of knowledge that governs a policy from interest group debate—in particular, the conditions where learning can and cannot occur—is the central question of the political economy of expertise.

The four cases I selected to study are very similar in their internal designs and expectations for a socially efficient outcome from a government intervention. Each proposal involves decentralization of authority and an incentive mechanism, but the debate for each policy is very different. The model set out in chapters 3 and 4 helps to explain why. That is, I selected the cases on the relevant conditions for debate shown in table 8 to illustrate and explain the debate pattern in each hearing.

TABLE 8.   Conditions for Debate

Certainty	The full information baseline. Technically, a high degree of confidence in the hypotheses that define the connections in a single, coherent causal framework.
Uncertainty	When the amount of research-based empirical evidence available to indicate whether the policy will yield its expected outcomes is limited or sparse. Technically, a low degree of confidence in the hypotheses that define the connections in the causal framework.
Ambiguity	When there is disagreement among experts on the definition of the causal framework. Conceptual ambiguities arise when experts have contradictory expectations regarding the likely effects of a policy. Methodological ambiguities arise when experts can confirm competing expectations regarding the effects of a policy.

The first two case studies focus on the effect of uncertainty in the political economy of expertise. These two cases illustrate the conditions for separating equilibria set out in table 5. The 1989 acid rain case study in chapter 6 examines the September–October 1989 hearings on H.R. 3030, Clean Air Act Reauthorization (parts 1 and 2, the emissions trading program of the Clean Air Act Amendments), before the House of Representatives Subcommittee on Energy and Power. Strong and unambiguous empirical evidence suggested that the emissions trading program would work well, so it fits the strong-evidence case of table 5. Here, the prospectively gaining groups should assert both normative and instrumental arguments regarding the program's effectiveness, and the prospectively harmed groups should be constrained to oppose the program with only normative arguments. For simplicity, I label the predictions for unambiguous and strong empirical evidence the *certainty predictions.*

Certainty predictions. Strong and clear evidence to show that the policy will work as expected will mobilize (risk-averse) prospective gainers; supporters make instrumental arguments in favor of the policy, and opponents do not try to disprove those instrumental arguments (separating equilibrium).

The 1991 school-choice voucher case study in the first half of chapter 7 examines the testimony given in the June–July 1991 hearings on H.R. 2460, the America 2000 Excellence in Education Act proposal, before the House Subcommittee on Elementary, Secondary, and Vocational Education. In contrast to the acid rain program, the 1991 school-choice voucher program had almost no evidence to support its effectiveness, so it fits the weak-evidence condition for both tables 5 and 6 (which yield identical predictions). In this case, the prospectively harmed groups make both instrumental and normative arguments, and the prospectively gaining groups are limited to normative arguments. Again for simplicity, I label the weak-evidence conditions from both of these tables the *uncertainty predictions.*

Uncertainty predictions. Uncertainty advantages groups that oppose the policy. In all cases, when there is considerable uncertainty, groups opposed to the policy can demonstrate that the policy is too risky to try through instrumental arguments, and supporters, including those with intrinsic preferences in favor of the policy, do not attempt to disprove this (separating equilibrium).

The remaining two case studies focus on the effects of ambiguity. In both cases, strong evidence existed to sharpen expectations about the likely outcomes of the policy. But with ambiguity in the causal relations, groups on both sides of the debate are free to exploit experts' ambiguous expectations and consequently pool on the same instrumental argument type. In these cases, groups on each side of the debate should effectively use of instrumental arguments for and against the policy.

The 2001 school-choice voucher case study in the second half of chapter 7 examines the March 29, 2001, hearings on H.R. 1, Transforming the Federal Role in Education (the Bush administration's Leave No Child Behind proposal), with testimony before the House Committee on Education and the Workforce. This case illustrates the effect on debate when experts hold contradictory expectations regarding the likely outcomes of a policy: in one view the program is expected to be a great success, while in another view it is expected to be a great failure. Finally, chapter 8 examines the testimony in the April–May 1972 hearings on H.R. 5615, Health Maintenance Organizations, before the House Subcommittee on Public Health and the Environment. The 1972 HMO case illustrates the effect on debate that comes from competing expert expectations, mostly resulting from methodological disputes. I group both the contradictory and competing expectations conditions under the *ambiguity predictions.*

> *Ambiguity predictions.* Ambiguity creates opportunities for groups to muddy the waters with expert arguments; when there is strong evidence to support the policy, groups with intrinsic preferences can pool on instrumental arguments (pooling equilibrium). Groups with extrinsic preferences about the full set of outcomes remain silent.

All four cases consider incentive regulatory programs that the established positive literature in its strongest claims asserts should be "politically repellant" to members of Congress (Arnold 1990, 79). To the extent members consider any of these policies, it is for ideological or political reasons only. In this view, lobbyist testimony should never be constrained by empirical evaluation information under any circumstances. Expert knowledge and the empirical research consequently should not matter to debates over these policies.

> *Null predictions.* Group testimony should not be responsive to the degree of uncertainty or ambiguity; in all cases, groups make any instrumental or normative argument that is convenient— whether true or false—in a "babbling equilibrium."

My expectations and those of the established literature depart dramatically on the 1989 acid rain case and the 1991 school-choice case, where I expect groups on each side of the debate to separate in their arguments. I explain why political actors both are and are not constrained by policy expertise, particularly the outcome of the 1989 acid rain and the 1991 school choice cases, while the established literature can explain only failures, such as those in the 2001 school-choice and the 1972 HMO cases. A correct theory should account for all of the case outcomes that I present in the next three chapters.

6

Emissions Trading and Confidence from EPA Experimentation

> I want to focus on something that most people go to sleep on the minute we talk about it but which is absolutely a major part of this proposal, the emissions trading system. We have got to find a way of making that work or getting rid of it. Yet it is something that is hard to get people to do more than snore through when we talk about it.
>
> —PHILIP SHARP (D-IN), Clean Air Act
> Reauthorization Hearings, 1989

The case study in this chapter examines the policy idea, program evidence, and politics behind the 1989 Bush administration proposal to adopt an innovative emissions trading program to control sulfur dioxide emissions, the main precursor to the scientific, policy, and political problem known as acid rain.[1] Congress saw the emissions trading program as a potential solution to this vexing and contentious environmental issue. The program promised in theory to clean the air at lower cost to industry. In this case, the expert community had relative certainty that the program would work well in practice, so groups in favor of the program pressured Congress to enact the program. These efforts resulted in the emissions trading program of the Clean Air Act Amendments of 1990, a significant legislative breakthrough with regard to the seemingly unsolvable political problem of acid rain politics.

---

1. The correct scientific term for this phenomenon is *acid deposition,* but in this book I use the term by which the political problem is and was known, *acid rain.*

The Acid Rain Controversy

The 1980s witnessed the rise of acid rain as a salient policy problem, and Congress struggled throughout the decade to act to limit sulfur dioxide emissions, the main precursor to acid rain and dry acidic deposition. As of 1988, Congress's command-and-control approaches to the problem had failed to resolve the complicated conflicts among interested parties. Major interest groups, electric utilities, environmentalists, and the United Mine Workers (UMW) "cycled" among different proposals, first to establish the original inefficient command-and-control policy and then to join together as odd-bedfellow coalitions to defeat any subsequent revisions.

During the 1977 reauthorization of the Clean Air Act, prior to the rise of acid rain as a salient policy problem, Congress enacted a regulatory program that in effect forced states to adopt highly inefficient uniform command-and-control technology standards to limit sulfur dioxide emissions. During the debate, eastern coal producers strongly opposed any Environmental Protection Agency (EPA) rules that would create incentives for Midwest utilities to switch from high-sulfur coal, mined primarily in the East and Midwest, to low-sulfur coal, mined primarily in the West. The UMW particularly opposed any such changes because the union is well organized in the East but not in the West (Ackerman and Hassler 1981, 31; Passell, 1989, 1). In what is now known as the "clean air, dirty coal" coalition, environmentalists joined these eastern high-sulfur coal producers basically to force all utilities to "scrub"[2] most all of the sulfur dioxide out of their emissions, irrespective of the amount of sulfur contained in the coal that the utilities burned.[3] The effect was to create a regulatory protection for the high-sulfur coal market, since scrubbing made the sulfur content of the coal burned irrelevant for compliance with environmental regulations (Ackerman and Hassler 1981, 27; Lave and Omenn 1981, 42).

---

2. The leading technology available at the time to reduce the rate of sulfur dioxide in utility plant emissions was a chemical emissions treatment known as flue gas desulfurization, or "scrubbing."

3. While the 1977 statutory language does not explicitly require all utilities to scrub their emissions (a uniform technology standard), in light of the committee report, §111 was widely read as a uniform-scrubbing standard (Bryner 1994, 170; "Clean Air Bill Stalled" 1984, 342; Lave and Omenn 1981, 41–42).

The equipment used to scrub emissions is expensive to install and use and is not reliable, and the scrubbing process produces a considerable amount of waste. The forced-scrubbing standards thus ensured opposition from the regulated electric utilities to sulfur dioxide emission controls (Ackerman and Hassler 1981, 22). Congressional debate and the House committee report, however, were "explicit in wanting to force utilities to burn local coal" (Lave and Omenn 1981, 42; see also Ackerman and Hassler 1981, 32), which was a deadweight economic loss, amounting to billions of dollars in higher utility rates,[4] enacted to preserve mining jobs in the Midwest. To Congress, prior to the acid rain controversy of the 1980s, "the fact that the air quality in the East might suffer was deemed less important than preserving local jobs and company investments" (Lave and Omenn 1981, 42). The fact that sulfur dioxide cleanup would not occur under forced scrubbing, in addition to the fact that a handful of jobs were being preserved at an extremely high cost, underscored the inefficiency of sulfur dioxide control program.

The 1977 authorization for the Clean Air Act ended in 1981, forcing clean air back onto Congress's agenda (Bryner 1994, 103). With the early 1980s, though, came the rise of acid rain as a newly salient political issue (Kraft 1994, 106). In the atmosphere, the sulfur dioxide and nitrogen oxides that are released when coal is burned become transformed into sulfuric and nitric acid and return to earth, often hundreds of miles away, in the form of acidic rain or dry particles (Bryner 1994, 79; S. E. Schwartz 1989, 753). Acid rain is believed to kill fish in freshwater lakes and streams, harm forests and crops, promote deterioration in building materials, and threaten human health (Shabecoff 1989a). As a result, the problem of acid rain gained headlines throughout the 1980s as a major controversy (S. E. Schwartz 1989, 753).

Midwest utilities' contribution to this problem comes not simply from the burning of high-sulfur coal;[5] between the 1950s and 1970s, these utilities also constructed tall smokestacks that aided in dispers-

---

4. The CBO estimated that forced scrubbing would cost $4.2 billion more per year than under a rights-trading program, with only between five and ten thousand jobs saved (Portney 1990, 76).

5. Coal-burning utilities accounted for about 75 percent of the 24 million tons of sulfur dioxide released each year in this time period.

ing these pollutants into the northeastern United States and Canada (Bryner 1994, 82; Lave and Omenn 1981, 43). This effect added a new layer of interregional and international conflict on top of the coal production rivalry between the Midwest and the West. As the *New York Times* reported, "The question of what to do about acid rain has pitted region against region and produced an angry stalemate in Congress" (Shabecoff 1989a, 5).

By many accounts, disagreements in Congress about how to deal with the acid rain problem became the main stumbling block to reauthorizing the Clean Air Act throughout the 1980s (Bryner 1994, 111; "Clean Air Bill Stalled" 1984, 339; R. E. Cohen 1992, 37; Kraft 1994, 106). Clean air bills in the Senate were reported out of committee but tended not to reach the floor, and bills in the House usually never left committee.[6] In 1984, a typical year for the decade's acid rain legislative effort, both houses of Congress fruitlessly tried to find a way to compel more stringent regulatory control. The Senate committee, dominated by members from the Northeast and West, marked up a bill that required utilities to reduce sulfur dioxide emissions by 10 million tons[7] and to bear the costs of doing so, a plan known as the "polluter pays" formula. These costs would fall disproportionately on the Midwest, which has by far the dirtiest utility plants. Midwestern members of the committee had called for spreading the costs nationwide, a plan that defines the cost-sharing formula ("Clean Air Bill Stalled" 1984, 340). The Senate leadership, however, never brought this bill to the floor (Bryner 1994, 111).[8] In the House, Henry Waxman (D-CA) proposed a bill that would have required the installation of scrubbers on the fifty dirtiest utility plants but spread the costs with a nationwide tax on electricity. He withdrew the bill in subcommittee, though, after his panel voted to strip sulfur dioxide controls from the legislation ("Clean Air Bill Stalled" 1984, 339), an

---

6. The Senate Environment and Public Works Committee at the time generally was seen as an advocate of the environment; midwestern members tended to avoid assignments to the committee. The House Energy and Commerce Committee had wide geographic representation, leaving the committee highly divided over acid rain (see Bryner 1994, 119–20; "Clean Air Bill Stalled" 1984, 340; R. E. Cohen 1992, 68–78).

7. From 1980 total levels, around 24 million tons. This cap was stricter than the one proposed in 1982 (Bryner 1994, 111).

8. The Senate majority leader at the time, Robert Byrd (D-WV), represents a high-sulfur state and worked closely with the UMW on all acid rain legislation.

effort engineered by midwestern committee members (Bryner 1994, 111).

Congress renewed its effort to revise the clean air law once again in 1988, trying new and different cost-sharing plans in an attempt to find a new basis for a winning coalition under the command-and-control approach. In the Senate, George Mitchell (D-ME), chair of the Subcommittee on Environmental Protection, worked closely with the UMW throughout 1988 since it was widely understood that Majority Leader Robert Byrd's (D-WV) approval of any plan hinged on UMW approval (R. E. Cohen 1992, 39).[9] Both Mitchell and the UMW agreed on a cost-sharing tax on fossil-fuel-produced electric power to subsidize the expensive and burdensome scrubbers on the most heavily polluting utilities ("Clean Air Bill Fails" 1988, 145; Paquette 1989). Together, Mitchell and Byrd devised an inefficient command-and-control regulatory plan as a means to protect jobs in the coal fields of Appalachia (R. E. Cohen 1992, 41; Paquette 1989).

At this time, the electric utilities' position on all acid rain legislation was to attempt to stall that report (Shabecoff 1989a) until after the publication of the final report of the National Acid Precipitation Assessment Program (NAPAP), the government's 10-year study of acid rain that was not due out until the following year. Utilities chose to delay because they objected to the highly inefficient and expensive scrubbing requirement. An executive of the American Electric Power Services Corporation, the largest privately owned utility that relies almost exclusively on high-sulfur coal for boiler fuel, said that Mitchell's bill would have forced the company to spend $1.3 billion on new scrubbers and would have raised electricity rates by 48 percent for industrial customers ("AEP Says" 1989, 10).

Environmentalists, for their part, objected to the legislation in the belief that the Mitchell bill was not stringent enough and was primarily intended to protect high-sulfur coal jobs. Majority Leader Byrd never called the bill to the floor (Bryner 1994, 112; "Clean Air Bill Fails" 1988, 143). The UMW's Richard L. Trumka wrote that "when a breakthrough seemed possible" with Mitchell's bill, "a truly strange pair of bedfellows—the electric utility industry and the envi-

---

9. Byrd knew he did not have the votes on the floor, and he wanted to work with the UMW to minimize political fallout (R. E. Cohen 1992, 39). Mitchell consequently worked closely with the UMW ("Clean Air Bill Fails" 1988, 145).

ronmental lobby—joined forces to kill a reasonable acid rain-control compromise" (1989, 19). Congress simply could not solve the acid rain problem given this cycling in coalitions among the electric utilities, environmentalists, and the UMW. Mitchell conceded defeat in an angry speech on the Senate floor, calling his opponents "'rigid and unyielding . . . even when faced with the certainty that their rigidity would result in no action this year'" (quoted in "Clean Air Bill Fails" 1988, 148).

Bush Emissions Trading Proposal

In June 1989, President George H. W. Bush outlined a permit-trading scheme for controlling sulfur dioxide emissions as a possible way out of the acid rain dilemma.[10] Table 9 summarizes the proposal's main provisions.[11] Under Bush's plan, the EPA was to allocate one allowance per ton of permissible emissions for each coal-fired electric utility facility covered in the program. These allowances were to be allocated among plants according to an initial baseline assessment. The baseline was to be calculated as the average number of tons per year of sulfur dioxide emissions a plant would have generated between 1985 and 1987 if it had been in compliance with permitted rates, based on the amount of fuel it consumed in that time.[12] During Phase 1 of the program (between 1995 and 2000), 107 Midwest electric utility plants would have to meet a moderately stringent per-plant standard of 2.5 pounds of sulfur dioxide per Mega British thermal unit (MBtu) of electricity generated but could choose any

---

10. The Bush administration made acid rain a top priority for several reasons: the issue's salience, the president's interest in foreign policy (regarding Canada), the compatibility of the market approach with Republican free-market ideology, the fact that utilities tended to be solid Republican supporters and were few in numbers (Bryner 1994, 115–16, 173; R. E. Cohen 1992, 56), and the utilities' intransigence after years of generous cost-sharing offers (Bryner 1994, 135).

11. C. Boyden Gray, one of the main proponents of the incentives approach in the Bush White House, first heard of the idea from the Project 88 report of Senators Tim Wirth (D-CO) and John Heinz (R-PA) (R. E. Cohen 1992, 58).

12. That is, the administration chose a grandfathering scheme to allocate permits as opposed to a zero-revenue auction or some other scheme. The administration chose the period from 1985 to 1987 because this was the most recent three-year period from which fuel consumption data were available, data generated by the NAPAP study.

TABLE 9.   Summary of Bush Emissions Trading Proposal (1989)

Allowance Definition	"Authorization, issued by the Administrator under this title, to emit, during a specified calendar year, a ton of sulfur dioxide or nitrogen oxides."
Baseline Definition	"For each steam-electric unit in operation prior to January 1, 1985, the baseline shall be the annual average quantity of mmBtu consumed in fuel during calendar years 1985, 1986, and 1987. . . ." multiplied by its emission rate in lbs/Mbtu, and divided by 2000.
Allowance System	"Allowances issued under this title may be transferred among the owners or operators of affected sources under this title, as provided by regulation. In phase I, transfers of allowances shall be limited to affected sources within a single State, except that an owner or operator of two or more affected sources may transfer allowances among those sources, irrespective of state boundaries. In phase II, allowances may be transferred among affected sources within each of the geographic regions of the country, as prescribed by regulation."
New Units	"The owner and operator of each new unit must hold allowances equal to the annual tonnage of sulfur dioxide emitted by the unit, after December 31, 2000. New units shall not be eligible for an allocation of sulfur dioxide allowances. . . . [N]ew units may obtain allowances from any unit allocated allowances under this title."
Excess Emissions Fee	"Shall be calculated on the basis of the number of tons emitted in excess of allowances multiplied by \$2,000. . . . The owner or operator of any affected source liable for payment of a fee . . . is also liable to offset the excess emissions by an equal tonnage amount in the following calendar year, or such longer period as the administrator shall prescribe."
Monitoring	"All sources subject to this title shall be required to install and operate CEMS [continuous emissions monitoring systems] and quality assure the data for sulfur dioxide, nitrogen oxides, opacity and volumetric flow for each unit subject to this title."

Source: Quoted from the administration proposal text.

means to do so, including purchasing or leasing allowances from other utilities. New units would have to obtain necessary allowances from the market. The market for allowances would be limited in Phase 1 to within-system or within-state transactions. In Phase 2 (beginning in 2000), the sulfur dioxide emission standard would be reduced to a more stringent control standard of 1.2 pounds per Mbtu, and coverage would be extended to 200 to 300 plants, with trading restrictions removed.[13] The proposal also included provisions for monitoring compliance and for a fee for noncompliance.

Emissions Trading Causal Theory

The Bush administration's proposal was not made from whole cloth. Instead, its design was based on a well-known model of emission-control policy known as "emissions trading." Under the plan, utilities could clean up emissions beyond their permit requirements and sell leftover allowances, or they could increase emissions beyond permitted levels if they purchased additional allowances. This market mechanism is intended to facilitate cost-efficiency in environmental control compared to a mandated standards approach. Under this scheme, the dirtiest utilities tend to have the greatest incentives to clean up the most because of their lower marginal costs and the relatively clean facilities with high marginal costs of control might find it cheaper to purchase allowances (see Bryner 1994, 207). Other buyers might be western utilities that wanted to expand production under a tight national emissions limit ("Clean Air Act Rewritten" 1990, 276). This form of regulation creates incentives for utilities to find the best means to control emissions since each utility has incentives to clean up as much as is economically feasible, and the industry-wide cap on emissions creates an impetus for the industry to reduce emissions overall.

The two basic factors affecting the cost and effectiveness of a pollution-control program are the varying marginal cost of controlling emissions between emission points and the asymmetry of information between firms and the government for what the marginal cost is

---

13. For a summary, see Hershey 1989. Utilities did not have total flexibility in Phase 1, however, because governors received the power to prevent plants from switching to low-sulfur coal.

at each point. The marginal cost of controlling emissions varies greatly among emission points, both within and between firms—as much as one hundred to one for sulfur dioxide. The marginal cost of control for an emission point is a function of, among other things, the age, size, and production technology of the plant and the availability of control technology and fuel substitutes (Dudek and Palmisano 1988, 220–21; Hahn and Stavins 1995, 180). An efficient allocation of control responsibility among firms will set the marginal cost of control as equal across emission points and among the firms. Because of this variation in the marginal cost of emission control between emission points, a uniform percentage reduction requirement in a command-and-control regulatory approach where the government establishes the specific emission-control requirements for each firm is likely to be an overly expensive means for an industry as a whole to meet the environmental target (Hahn and Stavins 1995, 180).

In principle, the government could set the emission-control responsibility for each emission point so that the marginal cost of control was the same for each. It is unlikely, however, that the government could employ a regulator who is sufficiently omniscient to make these price assignments efficiently, or at least cost to industry. Such an allocation would require that the regulator have full information about each plant's production process, the range of possible changes in production processes, the available control technology, and how each alternative method would perform at each emission point (see Liroff 1986, 21; Tietenberg 1985, 30). The regulator also would need to keep abreast of changes in pollution-control technology, the cost and availability of fuel substitutes, and design modifications to each plant's production process.

At any point in time, information about each plant's production process is private for each firm. Given the quantity of this private information required, the government could acquire this information only at great cost, if at all (Hahn and Stavins 1995, 181). Firms have few incentives to reveal the costs of alternative control methods or production process changes because new control requirements on the firm increase production costs relative to those of existing and potential competitors. In addition, firms have incentives to overstate their control costs to weaken their control requirements or to seek an exemption on the argument that the control technology is not feasible for the plant. Because of this fundamental mismatch between information and incentives to act on information, the command-and-control approach to pollution control can never be cost-effective (Tietenberg 1985, 16).

These two conditions affect the efficiency and likely effectiveness of an emission-control program. Emissions trading policy has been proposed as a general means for the government to efficiently control emissions without knowing the marginal cost of control at each emission point. Under the emissions permit trading system model, like the one in the Bush proposal, the regulatory agency does not need to decide what control technology firms must use; such a system shifts the control responsibility to the firm's management, which has access to better information about control options. This kind of system also provides a mechanism for achieving an efficient allocation of emission-control responsibility. The regulatory agency needs only to set a per-period cap on total emissions in the covered region, to establish the market institutions allowing for emissions trading, and to enforce compliance with the terms of each trade (Hahn and Noll 1982, 120; Hahn and Noll 1983, 64; Hahn and Stavins 1995, 182; NAPA 1994, 18).

To start the program, the government allocates emission permits that add up to the industry-wide emission cap.[14] Each permit, or allowance, gives a facility the right to emit one unit (e.g., one ton) of emissions in a specified time period.[15] The initial permit allocation establishes each facility's emission-control requirement. As in the Bush proposal, when a firm controls more emissions than it needs, it may sell or lease its excess permits to another firm, reallocate the right to another emission point within the firm, or bank the right to use in another time period (Dudek and Palmisano 1988, 221; Hahn and Stavins 1995, 182). Firms that have difficulty reaching their target control level or that can reach their permitted level only at great expense may choose to buy rights to emit more then their allowance.

---

14. In the Bush proposal, the baseline distribution is a function of each plant's 1985–87 three-year average energy consumption and actual or permitted emission rate, whichever is lesser.
15. In the Bush plan, a permit entitles the holder to emit one ton of sulfur dioxide in a given year.

A government agency enforces the terms of trades by monitoring to ensure that the firm in fact reduces emissions beyond its allocation and maintains this level of control and by imposing fines or other penalties for noncompliance (Hahn and Noll 1982, 120).[16]

Under this system, the allocation of permits among firms and thus the equilibrium distribution of emission-control responsibility under the program is determined by the set of trades in each time period rather than by the central control authority.[17] If the government sets the overall emissions cap to be lower than the current emissions for the industry, or if there is the potential for economic growth among firms that emit the pollutant, then emissions allowances will be scarce and so will be bid up in price (NAPA 1994, 18). In this case, firms that can control emissions beyond their permitted level relatively inexpensively have an incentive to reduce emissions because they may sell their allowances to firms with high cleanup costs (Hahn and Stavins 1995, 181). In theory, firms have an incentive to exchange permits up to the point where the marginal cost to control emissions is equal across firms (Hahn and Stavins 1995, 180). At this equilibrium distribution of permits, no firm will have allowances to sell at a price less than the marginal cost of controlling emissions (Hahn and Stavins 1995, 183; Tietenberg 1985, 16). That is, under this program, the equilibrium distribution of permits will be, at least in theory, the most cost-efficient distribution for any given level of pollution control the government sets. Table 10 provides a summary of the emissions trading causal framework.

Theoretical Efficiency in the Causal Framework

The emissions trading model is carefully tailored to the set of conditions underlying pollution-control problems. In its causal frame-

---

16. The Bush plan requires firms to continuously monitor their emissions and penalizes firms for emitting more sulfur dioxide than is permitted.

17. Trades may be restricted (either by administrative review or by geographic limits to the market) to minimize the possibility of "hot spots," and there may be other forms of administrative review to ensure compliance. As I explain later in this volume, the equilibrium efficiency of the market is a function, among other things, of the amount of regulatory review of trades. The Bush program limits trading in the first phase of the program mostly to plants within a state and then removes this restriction in the second phase. These restrictions were relaxed somewhat in the final legislation.

work, an emissions trading program promises the greatest amount of environmental cleanup at the least cost to industry. Under a tradable permit program, environmental cleanup is harnessed to the entre-preneurial energy of the private sector (Dudek and Palmisano 1988, 223). Next I list a census of the expected benefits from emissions trading identified in the environmental economics literature.

An emissions trading program can be expected to have a variety of socially efficient benefits beyond those achievable under a com-mand-and-control emissions control program. First, emissions trad-ing reduces the costs of pollution control for all of the regulated firms compared to a uniform percentage reduction requirement, a least-cost solution that could not be achieved in a regulatory program where the government specifies the control technology or require-ments for each emission point (CBO 1985, 86; Hahn and Noll 1982, 121; Hahn and Stavins 1995, 183; Liroff 1986, 3; NAPA 1994, 18; Tietenberg 1985, 22). This result not only improves market compet-itiveness for the regulated industry but also benefits industry down the product stream and consumers in general since some fraction of

TABLE 10. Emissions Trading: Causal Framework

- The principle behind emissions trading is this: A group of dischargers is faced with meeting a common regulatory standard, but some sources in the group can reduce pollution at less cost than others. The group then devises a scheme for dischargers with high control costs to purchase additional reductions from the dischargers with low control costs, providing protection equal to the original standards but at less expense (CBO 1985, 84–85).

- The rationale for market-based approaches is straightforward. Direct or indirect price or cost signals aimed at pollution are used to encourage individual deci-sion-makers to determine what action is best, given their unique circumstances. Some sources may prefer to pay the governmentally imposed market costs and continue to pollute, or they may choose to install equipment instead of buying marketable permits. Others may find it cheaper to modify their production processes or input products in ways that eliminate or reduce the pollution, thus avoiding or minimizing the external costs associated with the pollution. The totality of the individual responses to the incentives should result in a reduction in pollution at a cost that is lower than the alternative, since only those polluters that find it cheaper to do so will undertake abatement. The higher the price for polluting (ceteris paribus), the greater the incentive to reduce pollution is, and therefore the greater the reduction is likely to be (NAPA 1994, 10).

Note: All are full quotations from the cited texts.

the savings from efficient regulation will get passed on to consumers. Second, this sort of program gives firms flexibility in how to meet their emission-reduction requirements, reduces the transaction costs that go along with this form of regulatory oversight, and gives firms flexibility in designing their production processes.

Third, this form of regulation creates demand for innovations in cost-effective control technology.[18] Under uniform technology standards, firms have little incentive to reduce emissions beyond their initial control obligations, so firms are reluctant to experiment with new forms of technology.[19] Technology standards cement in place the officially endorsed means of emission control because any new technology must obtain regulatory approval (with the attendant delay and uncertainties) before firms may switch (Hahn and Noll 1983, 65; NAPA 1994, 11). In addition, the firm bears the risk if new technology fails to function properly but bears no risk if the officially sanctioned technology fails.

Fourth, a permit market reduces (but does not eliminate) the barriers to entry into the product market of the regulated industry compared to command-and-control approaches, which benefits firms in high-growth areas. To make command-and-control regulatory requirements more palatable to the regulated industry, given the excessive cost and burden, these regulatory standards often are stricter for new sources (such as the New Source Performance Standards, or NSPS, in the Clean Air Act) than for existing sources. Hahn and Noll point out that "the winning political coalition behind the NSPS for power plants included Northeastern and Midwestern interests that were trying to slow the growth of the Sunbelt states" (1983, 71). More stringent control requirements for new sources help to preserve existing facilities, thereby inhibiting structural change in the

---

18. Tietenberg (1985, 33) gives the formal statement for this phenomenon. Assume that a new method of emission control reduces the marginal cost of control for a firm for all levels of emission reductions. Without trading, the firm will capture only the difference from meeting the current control requirement. With trading, the firm captures this gain as well as all gains up to where the new marginal cost of control equals the permit price. The greater savings under trading makes it more likely that firms will experiment with new technology, helping to stimulate demand for innovations.

19. This bias against experimentation is explicit with technology standards but also occurs under performance standards because firms have no incentive to exceed control requirements (Hahn and Stavins 1995, 180).

economy and harming regions with the potential for high economic and population growth (Hahn and Noll 1982, 121; Hahn and Noll 1983, 65; Tietenberg 1985, 95).

Fifth, not only are control costs unnecessarily large under uniform standards, but the burden of these costs is not shared equitably. To the extent that environmental cleanup costs are passed onto consumers, the cleanup costs regressively impact low-income households (Tietenberg 1985, 96). Stringent new-source emissions standards under a command-and-control regulatory scheme will disproportionately impact high-growth regions (Tietenberg 1985, 95). Also, given the high variance in the marginal cost of controlling emissions among emission points, the costs of a uniform percentage reduction falls disproportionately on a subset of firms within an industry (Tietenberg 1985, 97).

Finally, a tradable permit program has lower administrative regulatory costs than command-and-control approaches do, benefiting both regulators and environmentalists. Regulators do not have to expend resources investigating optimal technology for diverse pollution sources or undertake the political and legal struggles that accompany establishing or changing costly control standards (Hahn and Noll 1983, 66).[20] Because of the high cost of compliance and the fertile soil for litigation, it is often more cost-effective for firms to engage in protracted litigation about command-and-control standards than to comply, and these challenges often succeed (Tietenberg 1985, 32). Firms may assert that onerous standards will put them out of business or that the standard is not feasible as an engineering matter for their specific production processes. Under a well-functioning tradable permit system, in contrast, the availability of relatively inexpensive emission allowances may make it cheaper for high-cost sources to purchase allowances from another firm than to litigate and will reduce the firms' prospects for relief from the courts based on claims that complying is too costly or infeasible (Tietenberg 1985, 32). With emissions trading, firms should find it cheaper and easier to meet control requirements than to litigate. Reducing the technical

---

20. Instead, in the basic form of permit markets, the agency needs only to ensure that trades are recorded and enforced. For some substances, especially those where the locational impacts are concentrated, the agency needs to exercise some oversight of trades (NAPA 1994, 19).

control information burden on regulators also makes it easier for the government to regulate new or diverse types of pollution (NAPA 1994, 11).

Prospectively Gaining Groups Are Diverse

The Bush proposal reflected the basic program model in the emissions trading literature. In its causal framing, the proposal promised social efficiency as an analytical matter, and so in theory could be expected to yield considerable benefits that would appeal to a variety of political actors. Because of the potential for gains from emission trading as well as the built-in flexibility in choosing the means of control, individual firms' cost-minimizing strategies for emission control lower the costs of control for all firms collectively. As Tietenberg writes, "Self-interest in this case coincides with cost-effectiveness" (1985, 16). Firms may favor a tradable permit program because it lowers production costs and entails less governmental regulatory control of production and emission-control processes; firms appreciate this added flexibility (Dudek and Palmisano 1988, 221–23). Environmentalists should, at least in principle,[21] favor this form of regulation because it reduces firms' incentives for litigation and delay and stimulates new control innovations and because the reduced costs lessen business opposition to environmental cleanup. In addition, under command-and-control regulation, new sources lead to a deterioration of environmental quality. Under tradable permits, new sources simply shift the permit demand curve to the right, which, because of the fixed number of allowances, increases the cost of allowances but not the total amount of emissions (Tietenberg 1985, 34). As Tietenberg summarizes,

> All parties have something to gain from this flexibility. Control authorities are relieved of the need to stop growth or to decide how much additional control each existing source should bear. Existing sources are compensated for further reductions under the permit system; with more stringent emissions standards they would bear the financial burden themselves. New sources would have an

---

21. I discuss environmentalists' concerns with emissions trading later in this chapter.

option to move into regions which under the command-and-control policy would be closed to future growth. (1985, 34)

Or as Dudek and Palmisano write, "The dreaded trade-off between economic well-being and environmental quality is improved and environmental objectives cease to be a barrier to entry" (1988, 223).

At the time of the Bush proposal, the list of active interest groups that theoretically could gain from the program was relatively extensive and diverse. Utilities appreciate the flexibility permitted in the means to achieve reductions, and both dirty and clean plants could benefit from allowance trades, "as the seller would receive income for its ingenuity and the buyer could pay less for the credit than for the cost of equivalent emissions control technology or a shutdown of its facility" ("Bush's Clean Air Proposals" 1989, 7). The bill made "concessions to utilities by giving them freedom to choose the control strategy, to sell or purchase pollution credits" ("Bush Acid Rain Plan" 1989, 8). In addition, natural gas producers (a potential fuel source that does not contain sulfur), manufacturers of scrubbers and other emissions-cleaning technology, and low-sulfur coal producers all could benefit from the program. "The potential changes in the regulatory picture offer a fairly wide range of opportunities, and companies in areas as different as gas turbine manufacturing and coal and lime production [for use in scrubbers] are positioned to benefit from new regulations" (Hylton 1989, 6). I show later in this chapter that environmental groups, consumer groups, and organizations representing state regulators also came out in favor of the Bush proposal.

Opposition

The clear losing groups under the proposal were the high-sulfur coal producers and in particular the UMW, which would no longer enjoy the economic rents gained from the forced-scrubbing requirements of the existing Clean Air Act or the regulatory protection for high-sulfur coal. At the time, the *New York Times* noted "Many utilities . . . would meet the standard by switching from high-sulfur coal extracted by members of the United Mine Workers in the East and Midwest to low-sulfur coal from the West, coal largely mined by nonunion workers" (Passell 1989, 1). Low-sulfur western coal is more expensive for Midwest utilities than local high-sulfur coal but is still cheaper than installing scrubbers ("Acid Rain Study" 7).[22] As the *Chicago Tribune* reported, "'There's no question that Illinois coal is in jeopardy under this measure,' said Taylor Pensoneau, vice president of the Illinois Coal Association" (Arndt 1989, 1).

In the terms of chapter 3, the emissions trading concept provides a socially efficient causal framework for the problem of how to control sulfur dioxide emissions. Emissions trading held the promise of improving aggregate welfare relative to the existing acid rain program: the UMW would lose its regulatory protection for high-sulfur coal, but the rest of the set of active interest groups in principle could benefit enormously from the program. Because it was in theory a welfare improvement, the program had the prospects of creating positive-sum benefits that could appeal to a diverse set of interest groups. In addition, regulatory protection for an industry has not been seen as a legitimate social goal in the United States, at least since the onset of the Great Depression (J. Goldstein 1993). Any command-and-control program to regulate emissions is likely to be overly costly as well as environmentally ineffective relative to an emissions trading program, where firms can buy permits up to the point where it is equally costly to install technological or process controls. Because the Bush proposal was based on a socially efficient causal framework, it could in principle attract the political support of diverse interest groups and other political actors and thus help to resolve the complex politics surrounding the acid rain problem.

The State of Knowledge in 1989: Confidence from the EPA Demonstrations

Of course, the emissions trading concept was only hypothetical, or could be expected to produce these broad benefits only in theory.

---

22. The study also showed that under a more stringent reduction of 13 million tons or more would make scrubbers the least-cost approach because only scrubbers can drastically reduce sulfur from emissions.

Chapter 3 shows that the groups that could expect to benefit from the program had to be convinced that the program would indeed work in practice. If groups have too much uncertainty or believe the program is too risky to try, they will not pressure Congress to enact the innovative program. In the emissions trading case, strong research-based evidence existed and could inform debates on environmental emissions trading. The EPA had experimented with the emissions trading concept for more than a decade, and these programs had been extensively evaluated in the environmental economics literature. As of 1989, the research-based state of knowledge strongly suggested that the emissions trading concept as proposed by the Bush administration would work well in practice.

The EPA began experimenting with emissions trading programs in the mid-1970s, and by the time of the Bush proposal these programs had a long track record of demonstrable success.[23] Overall, despite some built-in limitations described subsequently in this chapter, the evaluation literature gave the EPA demonstrations very high marks. Evaluation results from the EPA's experiments with the offset, bubble, netting, and banking programs as well as results from a lead trading program among refiners showed that even limited emissions trading programs could allow industry to reduce emissions at a substantial cost savings compared to command-and-control regulation.

The EPA's programs were the first—and, until Title IV was enacted, the most ambitious—set of attempts in the United States to use market incentives as a way to control emissions (Hahn and Hester 1989b, 368).[24] Each program established a set of rules under which emissions reduction credits (ERCs) could be traded within a firm or among firms on a very limited basis (Tietenberg 1985, 7).

The environmental economics evaluation literature gives a clear consensus that these early EPA emissions trading experiments, despite the limitations described later in this chapter, offered indus-

23. For details and systematic evaluations of the early EPA programs, see CBO 1985; Hahn and Hester 1989a, 1989b; Liroff 1986; Roberts 1982. For an evaluation of the EPA lead-trading program among refineries, see Hahn and Hester 1989b; Hahn and McGartland 1989.

24. The EPA consolidated the four emissions trading programs under its December 1986 Final Emissions Trading Policy Statement (51 Fed. Reg. 43,814 [1986]), which codified the definition of emission reduction credits (surplus, enforceable, permanent, and quantifiable [51 Fed. Reg. 43,814, 43,831 (1986)]) and conceptually links the four emissions trading programs into a theoretical whole as incentive-based regulation (Dudek and Palmisano 1988, 228).

try cost-efficient flexibility while doing little if any harm to environmental progress (see table 11 for representative quotations). In general, the flexibility from emissions trading "has resulted in significant aggregate cost savings—in the billions of dollars—without significantly affecting environmental quality" (Hahn and Hester 1989b, 376). Tietenberg sums up his evaluation study by stating that the available data from the EPA "leave no doubt that a substantial cost savings is being achieved by the current emissions trading program" and that "the existence of any emissions trading transactions . . . implies that the command-and-control allocation was not cost effective" (1985, 52). According to Dudek and Palmisano, "There is no dispute in any quarter regarding the cost savings due to emissions trading. There may be some dispute over the exact size of the cost

TABLE 11. Emissions Trading: Research Community Assessment (as of 1989)

- The picture of the lead rights trading and banking program that emerges . . . is that of a well-designed program that gave rise to a vigorous market in lead rights. Trading in this market enabled refiners to achieve large cost savings. Moreover, the introduction of trading probably enabled some refiners to make the transition to lower lead content standards when they would otherwise have been unable to do so and remain in business. The environmental effect of the program as planned was neutral, since it did not allow any increase in the total amount of lead added to gasoline. In short, trading and banking of lead rights is an example of a successful marketable permits program (Hahn and Hester 1989b, 389).

- There have been no extraordinary enforcement problems encountered by regulators; and the system has been "debugged" to the point that manuals, procedures, and human capital pertaining to offset trading exist in virtually all regulatory agencies (Dudek and Palmisano 1988, 225).

- By asking new sources in nonattainment areas to secure tradeoffs, the potential for a market in pollution rights had been created (Roberts 1982, 97).

- Bubbles can reduce emissions below levels otherwise required by RACT, produce earlier compliance because fewer new controls must be planned and installed, and simplify enforcement because the state can focus its attention on the few sources where the most reductions are expected (Liroff 1986, 69).

- The willingness of firms to go to the expense of obtaining offsets indicates that they derive some net gain from doing so, but the extent of this gain cannot be estimated (Hahn and Hester 1989b, 374).

Note: Quotations are from the cited texts.

savings. Yet by any measure, the cost savings to date are impressive"
(1988, 233). The National Association of Public Administrators
asserted that "the cost-effective properties of economic incentive systems have been widely accepted in theory and in practice" (1994,
10–11).

While these programs produced substantial aggregate savings
without harming environmental progress, economists Hahn and
Hester (1989a, 110; 1989b, 376) emphasize that as a result of design
limits, these programs did not realize all of their potential benefits.
The early EPA emissions trading programs did not even closely
approximate a competitive, efficient market for ERCS. One principal
indicator that this is the case is the relatively small number of
interfirm trades, where the marginal cost of control varies the most.
Hahn and Hester (1989b, 373; see also Tietenberg 1985, 56) report
that only about 10 percent of offset program trades were external,
and only two bubble transactions occurred between firms. In addition, ERC banking institutions did not emerge in most localities,
which would have facilitated interfirm trades (Hahn and Hester
1989b, 373). Finally, the EPA and state programs maintained a high
degree of regulatory oversight and required lengthy reviews for each
trade. They conclude, "The general failure of active markets in emissions reduction credits to develop is the greatest disappointment of
emissions trading. Until such markets exist, the full potential of
emissions trading to reduce pollution control costs will go unreal-
ized" (Hahn and Hester 1989a, 151).

The early EPA emissions trading programs controlled emissions at
less cost than command-and-control regulation, but because of limitations in the program designs the successes were not as great as they
could have been (see, e.g., Dudek and Palmisano 1988, 218; NAPA
1994, 20). Several authors have argued that the programs could have
had greater success if they had more fully embraced market mechanisms. These researchers uniformly advocate a more comprehensive
permit trading market design, such as that found in the Bush proposal. Hahn and Noll, for example, wrote, "A next logical step in
reforming air pollution regulation is to adopt a more comprehensive
marketable permits system by eliminating the requirements that
trades be reviewed on a case-by-case basis by regulators, that a source
be in compliance with standards prior to trading, and that new facil-

ities remain in compliance with new source performance standards" (1983, 64). In Roberts's words, "Ironically, many of our current difficulties are rooted in our unwillingness to more wholeheartedly embrace the marketable discharge permit idea" (1982, 108). The Bush proposal more fully embraced the market regulatory model than did the EPA experiments, so by the claims of the evaluation literature, participating groups could expect the acid rain program to more closely approximate the efficiency promises than even the relatively successful EPA experiments.

Agreement on a Causal Framework

As the certainty prediction in chapter 5 states, when there is strong evidence to show that the program would work or little uncertainty in the causal logic behind the program, supporting groups should be motivated to support it with research-based instrumental arguments, and opposition groups lack credible instrumental or research-based arguments to attack the program. Consequently, pressure from the supporting groups should be more effective than pressure from the opposition. An implicit assumption in the certainty predictions, however, is that there is no ambiguity in the causal framework—in other words, multiple explanations were not available to link the emissions trading concept to expected outcomes. When there is ambiguity in the form of contradictory or competing expectations among experts, empirical evaluation evidence can confuse as much as clarify decision making and heighten disagreements among groups.

In the emissions trading case, very little ambiguity existed among interested experts, in particular among environmental economists. Regulatory protection for high-sulfur coal was not seen as a legitimate goal of an environmental protection program. And perhaps more importantly, there has traditionally been very little dissent among economists in the benefits of a well-functioning market. This level of agreement is perhaps due to several factors, including the nature of training in graduate economics departments and the self-selection of intellectually compatible scholars into the discipline. One can see this degree of agreement in the evaluation literature on

emissions trading that I cite above, where the consensus was that the
EPA demonstrations would be improved by expanding the market
principles embedded in the programs.

As a possible consequence of this agreement on a causal framework among experts for the emissions trading program, by the late
1980s, environmentalists and the electric utilities also had converged
on a consensus that a well-functioning emissions trading program
would be the best way to address the acid rain problem. So, in effect,
the only question for these groups and for Congress was whether the
market would operate efficiently. By 1989, the evaluations of the EPA
programs were published, and the regulated utilities and environmental groups came to support the Bush emissions trading proposal.

When the emissions trading concept was first introduced in the
1960s, many in the environmental movement were skeptical for both
ideological and practical reasons. Many environmentalists felt (and
still feel) strongly that the ability to enjoy a clean environment is a
fundamental right for citizens that morally cannot be bought or sold
at a profit (Kelman 1981). Hahn and Hester note, "Environmentalists balk at the idea that 'unused' rights could be sold to another firm,
which could then increase its emissions and further deprive the public of its right to environmental quality" (Hahn and Hester 1989b,
397). From this perspective, regulation instead ought to "squeeze
every emission reduction out of industry at every opportunity"
(Dudek and Palmisano 1988, 237). Some environmental groups were
uncomfortable with leaving cleanup decisions to the polluting industries, which most environmentalists did not trust (Dudek and
Palmisano 1988, 237). For these reasons, prior to 1989, "environmentalists have been almost unanimous in their opposition to emissions trading" (Hahn and Hester 1989a, 142).

This idea that environmental groups opposed emissions trading
for purely ideological or intrinsic reasons amounts to a folk wisdom
in some of the literature, providing a complete explanation for why
environmentalists oppose emission trading (e.g., Kelman 1981).
Environmentalists, however, had very practical and programmatic
reasons to be skeptical of the early EPA emissions trading programs
in practice, and these concerns guided environmentalists' opposition
to the early EPA programs and largely explain their program-design
limitations. When the experiments succeeded, environmentalists

came to more fully embrace the market-based concept. And perhaps ironically, removing the design limitations made emissions trading program more effective, increasing environmentalists' support for the concept.

The early EPA emissions trading programs were all grafted onto the existing command-and-control structure of the Clean Air Act and consequently inherited the allocation of legal control responsibility among firms that were permitted under the act's existing State Implementation Plans (SIPS). For any emissions trading program to operate without (at minimum) causing harm to the environment, the program must have a clear definition of the control responsibility baseline from which firms may count reductions as surplus, or calculate ERCS (Tietenberg 1985, 120).[25] If firms' initial baseline control responsibility is sufficiently lax, then emissions trading can worsen environmental quality (Hahn and Hester 1989a, 150–51). Unfortunately, states developed the allocation of responsibilities among firms in their SIPS in short time and with incomplete information, and so in several ways the SIPS could not serve as a clear baseline from which to calculate trades in the EPA experiments. To set standards, local control authorities had to rely on simplifying assumptions, such as setting reasonably available control technology (RACT) standards for whole industries rather than for individual firms (Liroff 1986, 25–26). As a result, local control authorities set relatively loose RACT standards to avoid imposing an unattainable standard on the dirtiest sources (Hahn and Hester 1989a, 117; Tietenberg 1985, 114).

In practice, many covered facilities' emissions already were below their permitted limits prior to participating in the EPA's experimental programs (Tietenberg 1985, 114). These sources subsequently sought to trade away emissions reduction credits in the EPA experimental programs for reductions they had already achieved rather than those that were made to participate in the programs; they sought to receive a credit without reducing their emissions from their

25. I discuss firms' concerns regarding the baseline control assignment later in this chapter. Cost-efficiency is not sensitive to the initial allocation of responsibility, although assigning some firms too much or too little responsibility can confer market power. Firms have a strong interest in the baseline control responsibility distribution for equity reasons, since surplus emission control in a permit trading plan has value.

actual levels.[26] Or a firm might seek to receive tradable credits for shutting down facilities for economic reasons rather than environmental reasons, shutdowns that would have occurred even without emissions trading incentives. In this way, a firm could trade away "rights" to pollution it never intended to emit. To environmentalists this appeared to be simply exploiting loopholes in these programs, a practice that came to be labeled "paper trades" (Dudek and Palmisano 1988, 239; Hahn and Hester 1989a, 117; Hahn and Hester 1989b, 397; Liroff 1986, 11).[27]

Even if control baselines were firmly established, the emissions trading concept requires that regulators monitor firms' emissions to ensure that firms produce and maintain their stated reductions (Tietenberg 1985, 169). This monitoring information is particularly difficult for regulators to gather with certainty, and regulators often had to estimate emission reductions based on samples of emissions or fuels (Roberts 1982, 105). In addition, many firms used participation in the emissions programs simply to delay compliance with legal requirements during the time-consuming proposal development and review processes (Liroff 1986, 14–15). Finally, environmentalists argued that reviewing emissions trades took administrative resources away from the traditional enforcement programs (Liroff 1986, 39). As Tietenberg notes, "Environmentalists feared, and no doubt some industrialists hoped, the program would open a large number of loopholes, leaving a legacy of reduced compliance" (1985, 11–12).

Overall, throughout the 1980s, environmentalists were concerned with whether the baseline control responsibility among firms in the EPA programs was sufficient to achieve actual emission reductions (instead of merely paper trades) and that the complexity of these new programs allowed firms simply to delay emission reductions and to

---

26. For example, a firm may have installed control equipment in the past to meet its legal RACT requirements, so the plant may have been below its permitted RACT limits prior to participating in an emissions trading program, or a plant's permit may assume that a plant of its type operates at full capacity, but the firm historically may never have operated its plant at greater than some percentage (Liroff 1986, 15).

27. Of course, the problem of paper trades was not inherent to emissions trading programs but instead was a result of inadequate emissions inventories in SIPS. These inadequacies were an equal problem for the command-and-control approach, and emissions trading only helped to expose the "fictional nature" of SIPS (Hahn and Hester 1989a, 117).

stretch agency enforcement capacity to the point of ineffectiveness. In response, the EPA required firms to apply the most stringent control technology before they could participate in these early experimental programs, limited the durability of property rights inherent in ERCS, and employed extended review for any trades that did occur. These design features in the EPA experiments with emissions trading reduced the efficiency of the programs and caused industry groups initially to be wary of emissions trading as well. Overall, however, the evaluations of the early EPA experimental programs showed that emissions trading could achieve environmental goals at relatively low cost despite the worst fears of both industry and environmentalists. If anything, the EPA experiments demonstrated the importance of a firm control baseline, of free trade among firms, and of the transparency of exchanges and enforcement, all design features that were addressed in the Bush proposal. Because the Bush proposal embraced the market concept more completely than did the early EPA programs, it received the support of both the regulated electric utilities and environmentalists—to Congress, a very powerful consensus.

Analysis of Arguments in the 1989 Hearings Testimony

Emissions trading promises enormous benefits to a variety of groups, and such a program is, in principle, consistent with society's interests in cleaning the environment at least cost. The benefits from the program were only hypothetical, however, and Congress had a strong interest in knowing whether the program could be expected to work in practice, particularly in the assessments of interest groups. Congress would not want to enact a program that, for example, would be both overly costly to industry and an environmental disaster. Given the consensus among a diverse set of interest groups, including environmentalists, electric utilities, and others, including consumer groups and natural gas producers, the only real question facing Congress was whether the emissions trading program would or would not meet its stated goals. In this case, as I have shown, extensive research-based evaluations of the EPA experiments were available at the time of the hearings to inform the decision. And as a result, I expect debate at the 1989 acid rain hearings to conform to the certainty predictions of chapter 5. Under certainty, the supporting groups are most motivated to include empirically based research in their testimony, and opposing groups do not make instrumental arguments as a way to support their position. Under the certainty predictions, the prospectively gaining groups (the supporters) will use instrumental arguments to endorse the program, and the groups that expect to suffer a harm (the opponents) will not counter with their own instrumental arguments. For Congress, the effect of debate in this case is to clarify the quality and strength of the empirical research favoring the program.

Table 12 lists the arguments made in the primary hearings on the administration proposal in the House Commerce subcommittee.[28] As the table shows, groups make a variety of types of claims in testimony. Some of these arguments focused on the normative dimensions to the emissions trading program, and others focused on instrumental arguments regarding the likely efficacy or causal logic of the Bush emissions trading proposal (see table 4 for the definition of argument types). The normative arguments considered the effects of the program on employment for certain sectors (particularly coal miners) and whether the costs of acid rain cleanup should be spread nationally. The instrumental arguments considered the causal efficacy of the program, including issues surrounding barriers to entry from the initial allocation of credits, whether the program should be expanded to include industrial producers of sulfur dioxide emissions, and other specific provisions.

Separating Equilibrium Indicating Efficiency

Table 12 shows that, as an empirical matter, groups on the two sides of the debate do separate in their arguments, and they do so in the pattern expected in the certainty predictions. The opposition groups, and the umw in particular, limited themselves to normative arguments, while the supporting groups that could expect a benefit from the program made both instrumental and normative arguments.

---

28. All citations to testimony in this section are to U.S. House of Representatives, *HR 3030 Clean Air Act Reauthorization Hearings*, pts. 1–3, September–October 1989.

TABLE 12. Testimony: Clean Air Act Reauthorization (Parts 1 to 3)

Arguments	Supporters	Opponents
Normative		
Economic effects on coal industry and mining jobs	OOCC, NCAC, WFA	NCA, UMW
Regional share of emissions reduction costs unfair	APPA, EEI, CFA, ELCON, PSCI, OOCC	UMW
Favors regional cost sharing	OOCC, PUCT, PSCI, CFA, ELCON, APPA, NCAC	UMW
Opposed to regional cost sharing	AGA/INGAA, NARUC, NRECA, NCAC	—
Any acid rain program leads to higher energy costs for consumers; lowers overall economic growth; creates dependence on foreign oil	EEI, AEP, WFA, OOCC, ELCON, NCAC, NCA, WPPI	UMW
Instrumental		
Emissions trading is cost effective and economically efficient	OOCC, ELCON, NARUC, EEI, AGA/INGAA, AEP, NRECA	—
Emissions trading gives firms needed flexibility	CFA, EEI, AGA/INGAA, ELCON, NCAC, NARUC, NRECA	—
Allowances create barriers to entry to product market (credit hoarding, cap too tight for trades)	CFA, ELCON, APPA, AES, NIEP, AEP, PUCT, NRECA, EEI, WPPI	—
Program should include industrials	PUCT, CFA, NARUC, PSCI, NCAC, OOCC	—
Program should not include industrials	AES	—
Does not promote conservation or clean coal technology	CFA, EEI, NCA, NARUC, WFA, OOCC	—
Regulate allowances in the public interest	CFA, NARUC, NIEP	—
Favors emissions tax over emissions trading	PUCT, AGA/INGAA, CFA, APPA, WFA, PCSI	—
Discusses specific provisions (cap, offsets, permiting, misc. regulation).	VEPCO, AEP, EEI, APPA, NARUC, ELCON, NCA	—
Other		
Inadequacy of data on acid rain effects, wait for NAPAP	EEI	NCA
Effects of acid rain are known	NCAC	—
Adequacy of current act	ELCON, EEI	NCA

Opposition Groups Constrained to
Normative Arguments

High-sulfur coal interests, the groups that could be expected to lose the benefit of regulatory protection from the command-and-control regime, are never observed to make an instrumental attack on the quality of the design of the program in testimony. In particular, the UMW focuses its attack by saying that the program would work so well that many high-sulfur coal miners would lose their jobs, a normative or "nondesign" claim.[29] Trumka, the UMW president, simply concedes that the program is likely to have the efficient results promised in theory. He argues, for example, that "permanent unemployment for tens of thousands of [high sulfur coal] miners . . . would surely follow from the passage of . . . H.R. 3030" (UMW 1:456).[30]

Rather than claiming that the program would fail, Trumka argues in favor of the preservation eastern coal-mining jobs:

> Most control advocates . . . continue to ignore the fact that the leading bills in Congress . . . will also result in massive, long-term unemployment in the high sulfur coal industry and economic catastrophe for communities throughout northern Appalachia and the Midwest. What Congress has yet to come to grips with then is not whether to pass legislation to reduce acid rain, but how to achieve significant and lasting reductions while at the same time minimizing the impact on coal State economies. (UMW 1:455–56)

Trumka explicitly states that he is arguing on normative rather than on design grounds, focusing on the policy's effect rather than its

---

29. The arguments these groups made in hearings are representative of the arguments groups make in the media: representatives of high-sulfur coal interests were steadfast in their opposition to the market-trading plan but also stuck to normative arguments. These groups focused on the potential mining jobs lost and disruptions in the coal market. For example, "The Ohio Mining & Reclamation Association blasted the Bush proposal, saying it drastically cuts the state's already diminishing coal production" ("Midwest Threatened" 1989, 8), or, "NCA President Richard Lawson said Bush was 'seeking to accomplish too much, too soon,' and elements were 'unnecessarily, unduly harsh and economically onerous'" ("Shortage"1989, 1).

30. Trumka also argues that H.R. 3030 would lead to double-digit increases in electrical rates, but he later argues that the command-and-control approach would increase rates even more (UMW 1:457), which again only concedes the cost efficiency of the emissions trading program.

internal design: "When you talk of least cost . . . you have to talk not only least cost of the solution but least cost of the solution and the effects of the solution" (UMW 1:456).

The UMW pushes instead for bills that contain cost-sharing plans along with inefficient engineering controls. To support this policy alternative, Trumka argues that although forced scrubbing is overly costly, the inefficiency is not so large as to be socially unbearable. "Despite the hysterical opposition cost sharing has engendered, it is important to note that the cost sharing proposals contained in [the competing bills mandating technology standards] would cost the average ratepayer only 25 to 75 cents a month" (UMW 1:457). Unfortunately for the UMW, while regulatory protections for industry abound in environmental politics, these protections are a difficult sell in public debates; in this debate, the other parties did not view regulatory protection for high-sulfur coal as a legitimate goal of the sulfur dioxide emissions program.

The National Coal Association (NCA) represents both high- and low-sulfur coal producers and consequently announces at the hearing that it cannot take a strong stand on the acid rain issue (NCA 1:695). The high-sulfur wing of the association strongly opposes the bill, and the low-sulfur wing has issues with some of the bill's provisions. As a result, the NCA announces its opposition to the administration bill as introduced but, like the UMW, at no point argues that the emissions trading concept will fail if implemented. The NCA's testimony is consistent with the expectations set out in the certainty predictions.

The NCA asserts four basic points in its testimony (NCA 2:607–8). First, that strict acid rain controls will limit the use of coal in power generation and thus in effect will establish national energy policy. This is simply an attempt to change the focus or dimension of debate away from environmental policy. Second, the NCA concedes that the administration's emissions trading bill will work as planned, but when reductions from nonutility sources are taken into account, the overall effect will exceed the administration's emissions reduction goals of 10 million tons. Third, the NCA argues that the total cap on emissions will increase the cost of compliance for utilities, since utilities would have to obtain emissions credits if they wanted to increase production or build new capacity. This is an argument that the administration's bill is more costly than the status quo rather than a claim that increased restriction through command-and-control is in any way preferable. Finally, the NCA argues that the bill should have greater incentives for utilities to adopt clean coal technologies, an argument that is independent of the emissions trading concept. The NCA somewhat opposes the administration bill but does not fabricate evidence or use hack social science to argue that emissions trading is a failed concept. Instead, the NCA attempts to shift the focus of the debate to the problems of national energy policy in general, arguments independent of the emissions trading program that is under consideration.

Prospectively Gaining Groups Make Both Instrumental and Normative Arguments

A variety of interest groups can expect to benefit from efficiency gains if Congress chooses to switch from command-and-control regulation to a well-designed emissions trading program. In particular, environmental groups favor emissions trading because it has the prospect of reducing sulfur dioxide emissions, and the regulated electric utilities favor the program because it promises to reduce the costs of and other regulatory burdens from command-and-control regulation. Indeed, in the hearings, utilities (the Edison Electric Institute, or EEI), consumer groups (the Consumer Federation of America [CFA] and the Electricity Consumers Resource Council [ELCON]), regulators (the National Association of Regulatory Utility Commissioners, or NARUC), environmental groups (the National Clean Air Coalition, or NCAC), natural gas producers (the American Gas Association and Interstate Natural Gas Association of America [AGA/INGAA]), and others make a variety of instrumental arguments regarding the program's likely effectiveness. They argue that the allowance trading program would be efficient, effective, and flexible.

At the hearing, both environmental groups and the regulated industry groups strongly endorse the causal logic of the emissions trading program. EEI, representing large investor-owned electric utility companies, states, "We believe that, in theory, a market based approach that provides for trading permits and allowances would be far more effective than a command and control approach" (EEI 1:563). American Electric Power (AEP), one of the largest high-sulfur coal-burning utilities in the United States, argues, "To the extent that emissions trading takes place, compliance costs can only go in one direction, and that is down" (AEP 2:380). The representative of the Public Service Commission of Indiana (PSCI), another coal-burning utility, contends, "I applaud the idea of taking a market approach to deal with this issue. I think the administration is being creative" (PSCI 3:70).

Contrary to the folk wisdom about environmentalists' supposed knee-jerk ideological opposition to emissions trading, Richard Ayres of the NCAC and Natural Resources Defense Council (NRDC) applauds the emissions trading proposal: "One of the things that is often cited is flexibility. The argument is made that if individual sources get allowances and are free to trade them, that they will, by the operation of the market, find the most cost effective way to achieve reductions. That is certainly a strong argument" (NCAC 1:531).[31] In the transcript of its written testimony, the NCAC states, "The emission 'allowance' trading scheme in H.R. 3030, an approach we have supported in concept, could foster partial cost sharing" (NCAC 1:471).

Organizations representing consumers also speak on behalf of the program's causal logic and internal design. According to the CFA, "We think that the system, if it is put under public interest regulation, could act as an important flexible and balancing mechanism to decrease costs" (CFA 1:545). Representing, ELCON, John E. Barker, Armco's assistant vice president for energy affairs, states, "We strongly support a market-based approach because we think the marketplace disciplines the least cost compliance strategy" (ELCON 1:491).

Other groups also lend support to the internal mechanism of the policy design. The lobbyist for clean-burning natural gas (AGA/INGAA) need only state the program's theory and the expectations for efficiency:

---

31. Ayres finishes the sentence by saying, "although I think some of the proponents have forgotten that in the Sikorski-Conte bill there is also a provision for trading of emissions reduction obligations" (NCAC 1:531).

Basically, what we are trying to do . . . is to internalize a social and economic cost to the country. We decided that acid rain is a very expensive problem, a health problem, and an economic problem, and we are trying to solve that in such a way, again, within the market system and the freedom of choice of the various participants so that we can more nearly reflect the true costs of emitting that sulfur and those nitrogen oxides. (NGAA/AGA 1:525)

NARUC states that its membership favors "trading within a utility system as well as intra and interstate trading, and this position, we believe, is consistent with the major principle underlying our total position that we have flexibility and cost effectiveness be a feature of the program" (NARUC 1:642).

Example: Debate about Market Competition and Program Efficacy

One way to see the effect of research on testimony is to examine the responses from a panel of lobbyists representing groups with diverse interests, where a member of Congress directly poses an analytical design question to the panel. This helps to illustrate the appeal of the concept itself to a variety of groups and the contrast between the instrumental and empirical statements of supporters and negative but normative responses of opponents (1:547–49). In addition, the example shows how a representative is very willing to engage the panel in analytical discussion in a way that simply contradicts the established literature's belief that members of Congress are simply interested in position taking, since the analytical debate that follows almost certainly would be inaccessible to constituents.

The example begins with a question from Representative Jim Bates (D-CA), who is from San Diego, an area with relatively clean electric utilities. Bates is interested in lessening the burden of sulfur dioxide control on the Midwest ratepayers and utilities to reduce midwestern committee members' opposition to sulfur dioxide control and to reduce the need for a national cost-sharing plan. To reduce the overall cost for controlling emissions, Bates asks the panel about market competitiveness, a basic principle from textbook price theory. Bates's idea is to modify the Bush program to include other sources of sulfur dioxide emissions, such as industrial plants. Economic price theory shows that increasing the number of participants makes the market more competitive. Competitiveness would drive down the cost of the program by minimizing costs and also would make regional cost sharing less of a political roadblock in the committee to enacting acid rain controls. The question and responses, editing out extraneous points, are as follows:

BATES: I am just curious if each of you could respond with regard to your views on whether broadening the base, bringing in the industrialists, or finding other sources that might lighten the load so that we could then afford to engage in cost sharing?

JOHN HUGHES [ELCON]: If cost sharing is being used as an excuse to have a less than least cost bill, then it will impose an unduly expensive burden on the ratepayers and consumers who will ultimately have to pay for that.

JOHN BARKER [ELCON]: The position of ELCON is, we ought to develop the least cost program as a fundamental principle, and if that least cost involves market trades and the market principle, that is where we are coming from to totally support that.

KENNETH LAY [AGA/INGAA]: Too often we talk in terms of cost sharing as another term for protecting high sulfur coal jobs and mandating scrubbers on Midwest utilities. . . . [T]hat is not a least cost solution to achieving the goal of reducing sulfur and nitrogen oxide emissions by some targeted amount. The whole economy suffers if, in fact, we don't go for the least cost, most efficient solution. It seems to me that the two are quite different.

Our position is, again, let's go for the least cost solution which, in fact, should be achieved through a flexible, market oriented approach, including the trading of units.

But, having said that, from the standpoint of the committee, if, in fact, it is determined that the current proposal is not fair to certain regions, and we need to have more fairness, then probably expanding the network so, in fact, some of the large industrial users also have to either reduce emissions or buy units that are generated as part of the whole process would make economic efficiency sense.

RICHARD AYRES: In terms of cost sharing, I think I would agree with Mr. Lay that it is important for a way to be found that requires allowances to be in hand on the part of the industrial users or some other method to spread the costs away from the utility sector directly.

MARK COOPER [CFA]: One argument you can argue, if you want to turn it around, is suggest that the administration has proposed an artificially distorted market because it has excluded some people from the market, the industrials, and one way to achieve more equitable cost sharing is to bring those industrials, given the administrative nightmare of getting them all and having to draw some lines, and that will create a much more vigorous market in permits. . . . That is one way to keep the philosophy of free market approaches and simply note that the market is distorted by administrative fiat at the outset and we could balance the problem in that fashion.

RICHARD TRUMKA: When you talk of least cost—some people use that term—you have to talk of not only least cost of the solution but least cost of the solution and the effects of the solution, and I think they are two different figures.

If you are looking at the economy, the country, and what is best policy, you have to look at not only least cost of solution but least cost of solution and effect of solution. The only way to do that is to have the type of cost sharing fee that has been brought about or suggested by the [command-and-control bills], I believe.

This panel illustrates how a diverse group of lobbyists, with the exception of the UMW, can support the efficient program using instrumental arguments regarding the program's causal logic. Although the lobbyists make similar assertions, each does so for radically different reasons. Consumer representatives (CFA and ELCON) support the program since it expected to cost the least. The AGA/INGAA lobbyist supports the program because if it worked as designed, it would produce a windfall for his industry. The environmental lobbyist (NCAC) favors strengthening the program to increase its benefits to the environment. All of these groups favor the program on the expectation that it would produce its socially efficient results. All groups grasp the economics price theory concept that increasing the number of market participants would drive the equilibrium distribution closer to an efficient solution, and this is particularly clear for Cooper's and Lay's testimony.[32] In contrast, Trumka's testimony does not deny the economic principle behind the legislation and instead appeals to the normative value of preserving high-sulfur coal-mining jobs.

Congress Embraces Emissions Trading Approach

The central question for this book is whether this sort of separating equilibrium in debate helps to inform the committee members regarding the likely efficacy of the environmental policy that is so appealing in concept. Viewed from above, the debate as summarized in table 12 is informative in the sense that the committee heard a coherent and informed message regarding the policy's instrumental effectiveness. On normative questions regarding the desirability of the outcomes, the debate is less clear, and committee members would have to make a judgment call on the relative value of aggregate efficiency versus the harms to an identified group of miners.

The basic political issue regarding sulfur dioxide cleanup for the committee members was the distribution of the cost of cleanup across geographic regions. These costs are passed on to consumers—that is, constituents—in the form of higher electricity rates. The midwestern members argued in the hearing that the bill required their region to bear a disproportionate share of the cleanup costs. Consequently, midwestern members pushed for a general sharing of the costs, similar to the savings-and-loan bailout or the national financing of hydropower in the West. Members from western states argued in response that their utilities had already cleaned up and should not be required to pay a second time to help midwestern utilities to clean up their excessive emissions. These distributional issues, however, are largely independent of the mechanism chosen to control emissions. Indeed, many committee members were interested in the emissions trading program precisely because if it worked in practice it could minimize costs and thus reduce but not eliminate the inter-

---

32. This is indeed Kenneth Lay, later best known as a central figure in the Enron scandal.

regional dispute on cost sharing. Therefore, committee members' only question about the emissions trading program was whether it would work in practice and thereby help to resolve this interregional dispute.

While the debate sent a clear message regarding the efficacy of the program, the question remains whether committee members listened to and learned from the instrumental arguments made in debate. I show that the committee indeed "received" the message in two ways. First, the committee and subcommittee chairs directly engaged lobbyists in technical questions to help refine the program's design; second, the committee devoted a considerable amount of its scarce time to ironing out the specific details of the program design and implementation.

Committee Chairs Engaged in Technical Issues

The committee and subcommittee chairs used the hearing as a way to improve on the program to ensure its effectiveness—in particular, to ensure that the market for emissions would be competitive and hence socially efficient. The importance of the quality of the program's design and of instrumental arguments to the committee chairs can be directly seen through their questioning and behavior.

At the hearing, many lobbyists expressed the concern that the permit-trading market would be imposed on a locally monopolistic industry, the utilities, that is not likely to trade according to the principles of free competition; thus, the program might not reach the cost-effective distribution of control responsibility. This concern is expressed by both large public utilities and independent utilities—that is, participants prospectively on both the supply and demand sides of the permit market. AEP is a large investor-owned utility that would be expected to produce surplus permits. The subcommittee chair, Philip Sharp (D-IN), engages the AEP lobbyist, A. Joseph Dowd, on this point.

SHARP: If I am correct, your system could potentially be the largest creator and, therefore, largest seller of allowances. Would you review with us why it is you think your system will not perform the way the Council of Economic Advisers would like for you to and believes that you will?

DOWD: First, I think I might like to second some things that were said earlier regarding theoretical economists. My understanding is that their view of the world is that if there is a buck to be made out there, that everyone will move heaven and Earth to make that buck. That is not necessarily so; that is not necessarily the way that it works out.

Would we put a scrubber on a unit when we otherwise wouldn't have to for our own operations solely for the purpose of selling emissions credits to other regions of the country, and would we live for 30 or 40 years with the headaches, the operational headaches, the sludge disposal headaches that would be created by that scrubber?

Let me put it another way. If we scrub as we will in Phase 1 very heavily and continue to burn our local high sulfur coal in Ohio and possibly in Indiana, yes, we could get further emissions reductions if we switched in addition to scrubbing, if we switched to a low sulfur coal. Would we do that solely for the purpose of selling emission credits to other regions of the county? Would we put miners out of work in Ohio or Indiana or northern Kentucky simply in order to be able to sell emissions credits to the Southwest or other parts of the country?

These are the practical problems that we foresee that, unfortunately, I don't believe that the theoretical economists fully appreciate. (AEP 2:409)

In this example, the subcommittee chair is raising a red flag about how the program could fail. In the next example, Sharp listens to the constructive comments of a consumer group lobbyist on how to address this design limitation and learns that there are potential "fixes to a part of the problem."

At the hearing, the lobbyist from the Office of the Ohio Consumer's Counsel (OOCC) first illustrates the empirically proven success of the EPA lead trading program among refiners, remarking, "I believe it is possible to structure a trading system where you can have sufficient liquidity. . . . If you look at what happens in the refinery industry with the trading system for lead rights, about three-quarters of the potential participants in that market have in fact participated in that market, with very substantial savings" (OOCC 3:71). The oocc lobbyist then argues that the limitations in the market for allowances could be addressed by improving the proposal's design by establishing a futures-trading mechanism to help establish predictability in allowance prices, changing the authority of state regulators to give them incentives to make the market work, and holding auctions so that independent power producers do not get shut out of the electricity generation market (oocc 3:71). In response to these points, Sharp states, "Obviously there are some fixes to a part of the problem. In theory we could in our legislation forbid the interference in that market place, potentially" (Sharp 3:71).

Likewise, the full committee chair, John Dingell (D-MI), engages lobbyists in discussion on highly analytical, instrumental design issues. For example, several lobbyists—a state regulator, a consumer advocate, and utilities—argue that local public utility commissions might limit transactions for political rather than economic reasons. Dingell presses the CFA's Mark Cooper on this point.

DINGELL: Dr. Cooper, will you tell us about any problems you
    see with the allowance trading system. [Especially,] will there
    be hoarding of these allowances to serve the purposes of the
    particular State, or the particular [utility] acting under perhaps
    the guidance and the control of the State public utilities com-
    mission?
COOPER: Hoarding is a serious threat both to the existing diversity
    within the industry and the entry of new independent power pro-
    ducers. . . . At the same time, we think that the system, if it is put
    under public interest regulation, could act as an important flexi-
    ble and balancing mechanism to decrease costs. (CFA 1:545)

The following exchange between Dingell and Cooper provides a second example of the role of analytical reasoning in the discussion.

DINGELL: Do you have any idea what the worth of [the tradable
    allowances] is or will be?
COOPER: I don't have any dollar worth, but one suspects if the plan
    is implemented that I have advocated in which industrial sources
    are also tapped, at least to purchase allowances, it would be at the
    marginal cost perhaps of cleaning up an industrial plant.

DINGELL: It might be very much higher, might it not?
COOPER: It might be higher, but it is certainly going to be a
  significantly valuable commodity. (CFA 1:545–46)

In both examples, both representative and lobbyist are struggling with
the best way to design the program so that it may reach its socially
efficient promises. The second exchange specifically occurs in terms
of the expected permit price relative to the marginal cost of controlling plant emissions, and so the participants are speaking directly to
the basic price theory causal logic behind the program. Again, this
analytical exchange would be inaccessible to ordinary citizens in the
district and thus was not engineered for public consumption. Instead,
the discussion is a clear attempt to iron out the details of the program
design to help ensure the program meets its goals.

Committee Devotes Scarce Hearing Time
to Ironing Out Technical Details

In addition to this direct observation of the importance of program
design to the committee chairs, the importance of these design issues
to the committee can also be seen in the quantity of scarce hearing time
devoted to ironing out technical details to ensure that the program
operates effectively. In their instrumental arguments, the prospectively
gaining groups were not overzealous in their support of these programs and would not be expected to be overzealous since prior experience has demonstrated their limited ability to produce all of their theoretical benefits. The specific design issues include questions of
transaction costs and restrictions on trades, barriers to entry into the
product market, the stringency of the overall emissions cap, and
interfirm equity in the allocation of baseline control responsibility.

The debate on the program's technical details among the prospective beneficiaries of the program is more in the spirit of refining or
improving on an already well designed program. This discussion is
nearly identical to the issues and concerns that were addressed in the
environmental economics literature. I show next that lobbyists' arguments on these topics very closely parallel the research evidence set
out in this academic literature. The prospectively gaining groups'
concerns regarding the Bush proposal are the same concerns

reflected in the literature about the limitations of—and ideas for improvements for—market plans in general. These hearings give the committee the information it needs to make the program socially efficient, consistent with the public interest, and to make an appropriate decision about whether to adopt the program.

Restrictions on Trades

One of the main barriers to industry participation in the early EPA experiments identified in the environmental economics literature was the transaction costs involved in EPA review of individual trades. The production and control decisions of public utilities are heavily regulated at the local level, and lengthy reviews would prevent some utilities from participating in the program at a socially efficient level (Hahn and Noll, 1983, 68). If public utilities do not respond to market incentives, the market simply will not get off the ground. At the hearings, EEI expresses concern that certain provisions in the permitting title of the Bush proposal will unintentionally limit trading, similar in effect to EPA review in the existing emissions trading programs:[33] "Unfortunately, H.R. 3030 would create regulatory barriers and prevent the full realization of benefits from such a program. By imposing cumbersome requirements, the bill would, in effect, restrict our ability to engage in emission trading" (EEI 1:563).

In addition to regulatory oversight at the national level, utilities are also regulated by state public utility commissions, which could restrict and increase transaction costs for trades. A PSCI lobbyist states, "We are regulated by a State commission and it is unclear to us whether the commission will allow us to build, to generate the

---

33. In the trade press, EEI charged that the permit program "raises obstacles to orderly trading" because utilities would have to "identify all trades ahead of time in a compliance plan based on a five-year permit program. Any additional trades would require amendment of the plan"; "even trades outlined in a compliance plan would be difficult to transact" since "they would have to be approved through the permit system by the EPA administrator" ("Acid Rain Battle" 1989). A spokesperson for EEI said, "The electric utility industry favors a market-based system of emissions trading where utilities and third parties could buy, lease, or trade emission permits" ("Acid Rain Battle" 1989). EEI representatives declared that the permit system is "unflexible, not workable, and an administrative nightmare" ("FERC Staff" 1989) and that "without the ability to trade, buy, or lease allowances quickly and easily—similar to stock market trading . . . utilities would not take advantage of trading to meet emission goals in the most economical and efficient way" ("EEI" 1989).

allowances in the first instance, and second, once we have generated the allowances whether they will let us turn them loose to trade them" (PSCI 3:71). The National Rural Electric Cooperative Association (NRECA) also testifies, "We question how this free market concept could operate in a market that is not truly free. State public utilities representing State and local interests could and would likely dictate alternatives for the regulated utilities other than those following the free market behavior" (NRECA 3:43).

Barriers to Entry to Product Market
In addition, firms may hoard permits to create a barrier to entry into the firm's product market or refuse to sell allowances to competitors that wish to locate or expand in the region covered by the emissions trading market (Tietenberg 1985, 138). The Hahn and Hester study suggests that this form of market power can create significant economic problems (1989b, 364). Because only major Midwest utilities received permits in the initial (Phase 1) distribution, it is likely that representatives of interests from other regions and smaller, independent utilities would object to the this lopsided distribution's effects on their ability to enter electricity markets.

Consistent with the evaluation literature, by far the greatest concern stated at the hearing was with the effect of market power creating barriers to entry into the electricity generation market.[34] Sounding this theme from the demand side of the market, a lobbyist for Wisconsin Public Power Inc. (WPPI), a smaller publicly held utility, argues,

---

34. Independent, nonutility generators (NUGS), which would be covered in Phase 2 of the Bush plan, also express concern about possible unfair competition in the trade press: "Since most independent generators are new and hence meet all new environmental standards, they are unlikely to own any allowances or be able to generate any. Utilities would have most of the allowances, and independents worry this situation will lead to unfair competition" ("Independents" 1989, 15). In addition, NUGS fear that "utilities see NUGS as competitors, and now have a route in which to block selling NUGS needed credits" ("Analyst Says" 1989, 3). The Electricity Consumers Resource Council also expresses concern that the plan "gives existing sources perpetual rights to the allowances . . . and new sources absolutely no rights" (quoted in "Industrials" 1989, 8). Representatives of the relatively clean utilities in the West express the same concern about eastern utilities' market power (see "Utilities Hit" 1989c, 3; "Clean Air and Coal" 1989, 5; "Western Fuels Coop" 1989d, 4; for the FERC response to this line of attack, see "FERC Staff" 1989, 13; "Hoarding" 1989, 8).

> At the risk of offending certain fellow economists of mine, neo-classical incentive schemes like these emission trading provisions may be attractive on the academic drawing boards but they have little value in the future of the electric utility industry. The very simple reason is that the electric utility industry does not match up well with the free-flowing competitive market conditions of the textbooks. Rather, it is [rife] with monopoly power vested in firms with significant economic political power and might. Entry is restricted and the highways are not open in nondiscriminatory fashion to bring together buyers and sellers. (WPPI/APPA 2:388)

The National Independent Energy Producers (NIEP), representing smaller nonutility producers, testifies, "Whether the excess allowances which are created will be available to independent generators under fair terms and conditions is unique to independent generators who are both supplier and competitor to the utilities from whom we must obtain offsets. No other industry is required to depend upon its direct competitors to obtain the right to do business" (NIEP 2:358). Finally, A. E. Staley Manufacturing, speaking for industrial producers of power, testifies, "The emissions cap and allowance system . . . would erect barriers to market entry for non-utilities and grant utilities a competitive advantage" (AES 2:393).[35]

Consumer groups are concerned not about the equity among utilities in the initial distribution of permits but about the effect of these potential noncompetitive practices on electricity rates. The CFA testifies that "permits create flexibility, and that is good, but they create a new strategic resource that could be used by the largest utilities to foil competition, which is rapidly growing in the industry. By vesting rights in the incumbents, the permit system may create an insurmountable barrier to entry" (CFA 1:462–63). ELCON states, "The existing utilities owning the allowance rights, if you will, are going to be a virtual monopoly and impose a zero growth on any new power producers, because those rights will either not be available or will be extremely expensive and prohibitive" (ELCON 1:491).

---

35. AES also opposed including industrials on the argument that these producers have already reduced emissions, so further reductions would be overly costly (AES 2:393).

Total Emissions Cap Too Tight

Some early emissions trading studies showed that a too stringent total emissions cap will prevent trading from occurring, so the program will provide no gains from trade. One study, done by Energy Ventures Analysis, showed that the utilities under the cap were likely to hoard their credits to facilitate future growth. The researcher states, "The bill is so stringent it is almost impossible [for utilities] to generate significant amounts of credits to sell" (quoted in "Shortage" 1989, 2).

At the hearing, many lobbyists express concern that the 8.9 million ton reduction under the emissions cap Bush proposed would require such a great reduction that no credits would be available for trade.[36] AEP argues that after meeting its legal requirements under Phase 2, the company will have only 14,000 tons of overcontrol, a "minuscule amount" for a system the size of AEP and enough only to serve as a buffer if a nuclear or low-sulfur plant were to go down unexpectedly (AEP 2:380–81). AEP concludes,

> Our concern is that much less emissions trading will occur under H.R. 3030 than is projected by U.S. EPA and economists generally, with the results that compliance costs will be greater than anticipated. Most simply put, allowable emissions rates will be driven so low by the Phase 2 emission requirements that there will not be a great deal of over control left in the system to form the basis for

---

36. The offset requirement, where new plants would have to purchase allowances from scratch to cover all emissions, is directly connected to the emission caps issue, since caps "require new units built after enactment to have zero emissions, at least on paper, because it requires them—in addition to meeting New Source Performance Standards . . .—to offset any emissions by acquiring 'allowances' for polluting from other sources" ("President's Clean Air Bill" 1989, 15). EEI charged that offsets are "extremely punitive to utilities operating the cleanest plants," which "will have trouble reducing their already low level of emissions" and may "also find it difficult to purchase permits from the east where the demand for growth is the highest"; this requirement will "result in retarding growth in large portions of the nation" ("Acid Rain Battle" 1989). An AEP spokesman said that "emissions offsets would gradually be used up, and 'it may become impossible to find additional offsets at any price'" (Wald 1989, 1). According to a study done for EEI, the offset requirement would hinder trading among utilities by making "excess allowances valuable for utilities to keep for future use for new sources and/or increased utilization of existing sources" ("EEI" 1989). A representative of the Electricity Consumers Resource Council said that "there is not enough flexibility in the bill to generate enough of a marketplace for allowances" ("President's Clean Air Bill" 1989).

emissions trading. The lower allowable emissions rates are driven,
the less that will be left over for trading. (AEP 2:380)

Equity in the Baseline Permit Distribution

The environmental economics literature showed that the initial control and permit assignments in an emissions trading program affect
wealth distributions among participating firms (Hahn and Noll
1983, 67). The most common distribution rule is to grandfather
existing sources' permits, as was done in the Bush plan, and to
require new sources to obtain permits to cover all new emissions.
Using the command-and-control permit allocation as the baseline
allows all firms with existing facilities to be at least as well off in the
emissions trading program as they were under the command-and-
control system, since only firms with an incentive to trade will trade
(Tietenberg 1985, 111). "Both individually and collectively, existing
sources would prefer a permit approach using this distribution rule
to the command-and-control approach" (Tietenberg 1985, 111). A
grandfather rule that takes actual current emissions as the baseline
will tend to favor larger over smaller polluters and dirtier over
cleaner plants, however, since large and dirty sources typically can
control emissions at less marginal cost than small and clean sources
(Tietenberg 1985, 110).[37]

At the same time, assuming sources as price takers and a
sufficiently competitive market, the distribution of control responsibility does not affect the program's overall cost-effectiveness and
does not affect the amount of aggregate control (Tietenberg 1985,
97). Environmental groups therefore have little reason to be concerned about the initial distribution of control responsibility
between firms and thus have no reason to contest allocation decision
rules in their testimony.

The initial allocation of permits indeed was a major equity concern for the utilities at the hearing. The allocation of permits does not
affect the program efficiency, however, so the only groups that were

37. Hahn and Noll (1983, 90) propose a "zero revenue auction" as a means to distribute permits efficiently and to minimize the possibility of disproportionate allo-
cations in the initial control responsibility. The EPA proposed an auction to allocate
permits in its CFC trading program, and industry was almost universal in its opposition to it, which Hahn and McGartland (1989, 608) attribute to the increasing
uncertainty from the unfamiliar process.

concerned about the allocation in the Bush program's baseline were the utilities shut out of the initial distribution under the proposal.[38] APPA gives an example of a member utility that is deprived of initial emission credits under the Bush proposal's 1985–87 three-year average-allocation scheme.

> We have a member utility in Nebraska which had a 1985 emission rate of 1.3 pounds. . . . It also operated a 12 percent capacity factor in the base years because there was a big capacity surplus in the region at that time and they could buy some cheap economy power. . . . Now it could scrub the plant to get the emissions rate way down . . . to 0.39 pounds, but the plant could then never operate at a capacity factor higher than 37 percent. This is fully scrubbed and extremely clean and expensive. . . . It is simply an irrational and a wasteful result, and it shouldn't be permitted in this legislation. (APPA 1:673–74)

The Dog That Didn't Bark
Groups that in principle support the emissions trading program make these instrumental arguments in their testimony in an attempt to improve the program's design. High-sulfur coal interests, the true losing groups, are not observed to make instrumental attacks on the design of the program in response and instead concede that the program itself will work as claimed. An array of conceivable instrumental attacks on the program existed and had been articulated over the years; these attacks were available but not credible given the state of the evaluations of the EPA programs. For example, the UMW and the NCA do not try to get mileage out of (self-serving) arguments that the utility industry would simply exploit paper trades within the emis-

---

38. In his June announcement, Bush proposed that "all plants above a certain size should meet the same emission standard," but the draft legislation imposed a plant-by-plant cap on emissions using the plant's emissions during 1985–87 as a baseline ("Acid Rain Battle" 1989). Utilities' comments in the trade press reflect those they made in testimony. "Utilities' problems with the baseline stem from the fact that if, for example, a plant was used little during those years for any reason, it would be barred from using it more in the future. 'It caps our capacity . . . ,' said an Edison Electric Institute official" ("Utilities Give Draft" 1989). "The Edison Electric Institute . . . said the ceiling on individual pollution sources sharply reduced the flexibility industry had expected and might require some plants to curtail the output of electricity or to install expensive equipment to capture smokestack emissions" (Shabecoff 1989, sec. 1, p. 9).

sions trading program. In addition, these groups do not devise misleading instrumental attacks that focus on the peculiarities of the early EPA programs that were not incorporated into the Bush proposal, such as unreasonably high negotiation and transaction costs for locating ERCs, the durability of property rights in the tradable permits, and the potential number of trades in the Bush program. In this case, without misleading instrumental attacks from the opposition, Congress receives a clear message that the program, if refined to remedy its design limitations, will be efficient and effective.

Not long after this hearing, Congress embraced a modified version of the emissions trading program as a means to solve the acid rain deadlock.

Conclusion

This chapter shows how the availability of evaluation information helped to reduce opposition to an efficient policy proposal to attack the acid rain problem. The Bush administration's 1989 proposal used an innovative emissions trading program to control sulfur dioxide emissions in a socially efficient and effective manner. In addition, by 1989, a large body of empirical literature on EPA programs evaluated how emissions trading works in practice, unambiguously showing these programs' successes and limitations. A wide variety of prospectively gaining groups expressed support for the program through instrumental arguments in their testimony, although in all cases they qualified their support for the program design with limitations in emissions trading identified in the evaluation literature. The prospectively harmed group—the UMW—did not contradict the basic claim of the evaluation literature that these programs were empirically sound. Instead, the UMW focused its testimony on normative claims for why the inefficient regulatory status quo ought to be preserved, focusing on the likely hardships miners in the East would suffer if Congress removed the regulatory protection for high-sulfur coal from the Clean Air Act.

What is empirically most interesting in this case is a nonoccurrence: that the UMW did not attack the design or causal logic of the emissions trading program, which it strongly opposed. Also striking is the almost textbook airing of the strengths and weaknesses of the program by prospective gainers in their instrumental arguments. Noted economist Robert Hahn could have written much of the testimony. Contrary to much of the discussion in the established literature on Congress, the hearings were quite informative on the issue of emissions trading, and the debate closely reflected the state of knowledge on emissions trading available at the time in the peer-reviewed literature on environmental economics.

7

School Choice, Uncertainty, and Conceptual Ambiguities

Is there any sound evidence in our research which shows that . . . school choice works to improve academic achievement? Is there any sound evidence?

—CHARLES HAYES, America 2000
hearings, 1991

This chapter examines two cases of school-choice voucher program proposals. In 1991, the first Bush administration included a voucher program to reform elementary and secondary education in the America 2000 proposal. Education policy experts had great uncertainty, however, about how the program would work in practice since at the time there had never been a successful example of a voucher program implemented or studied. Because of this uncertainty, opposition groups pressured the Democratic-controlled committee to shelve the proposal. The second half of the chapter examines the second Bush administration's similar 2001 Leave No Child Behind proposal. In between these two proposals, information came to light from state-level experiments in school choice, and the differences between the cases illustrate the effect of increasing information on debates on this policy topic. Despite this new information, however, experts had contradictory expectations about the policy's likely benefits, and this ambiguity in the state of knowledge caused groups to use the research to speak past each other; consequently, neither side was able to make its pressure effective, and the Republican-controlled committee chose to shelve the voucher proposal.

The Need for Education Reforms

The publication of the National Commission on Excellence in Education's *A Nation at Risk* (1983) was a watershed event in the field of education reform. The report documented the steady decline in standardized test scores and American children's poor performance on international tests, forcefully demonstrating the dangers to the American economy from the poor education of its citizens in an increasingly global market. The book sparked a number of state- and local-level reform efforts during the 1980s (Chubb and Moe 1990, 6–8), but the end of the decade saw little noticeable improvement from these reforms, and Congress entered the fray to see if more significant reforms could be promoted from the national level.

Big business in particular was (and is) concerned about the supply of skilled labor in an increasingly technology-driven, global economy (Cross 1993, 56–57). Business is concerned that even as test scores decline, the technology in many workplaces makes greater demands on workers' ability to reason (Chubb and Moe 1990, 9; Cross 1993, 56; O'Day 1995, 100; Ravitch 1995, 2). Motorola, for example, spends about $5 million a year on basic training, much of it remedial education (Stanfield 1991, 1863). A trade association representative estimates that business spends $20–40 billion a year to train workers, making it harder for American business to be internationally competitive (Steinbach 1990, 853). The Business Roundtable devoted its entire 1989 annual meeting to the topic of K–12 education (Cross 1993, 55).

The initial reform efforts at the state and local level during the 1980s, aimed at improving the overall quality of education, amounted to a laundry list of top-down command-and-control approaches, such as raising graduation requirements, raising teacher salaries, toughening teacher certification standards, and lengthening school days or years (Chubb and Moe 1990, 10; Chubb 1988). The items on this list were all relatively obvious policy dimensions for states to manipulate. These reforms, however, did little to change average test scores, tended to help students who were already succeeding, and did not address curriculum issues aimed at promoting higher-order thinking, such as the ability to reason creatively or to solve problems, that many reformers wanted schools to promote. As

Chubb and Moe point out, in these more straightforward, top-down reform efforts, "the wrong puzzle is being solved. The standard view . . . is that these profile variables are the causes of ineffective performance and thus are the quantities that need to be manipulated in the interests of school effectiveness" (1990, 19). But unfortunately, most of the 1980s reform efforts arguably were not even related to school excellence and in practice had little effectiveness.

When George H. W. Bush's administration took up the issue of school reform in early 1991, the national government faced an education system that was underperforming in important ways that neither the states nor individual businesses had been able effectively to change and in which all of the obvious top-down reforms had already been shown to be ineffective. By the late 1980s, school reformers began to argue that schools needed the national government to help all students gain a first-rate education (Ambach 1993, 37). Leaders from both ends of Pennsylvania Avenue and from both parties began to look into ways for the federal government to go beyond its traditional role to promote improved elementary and secondary education.

First Bush Administration School Voucher Proposal

The George H. W. Bush administration's main effort at school reform, entitled America 2000, provided incentives to free up the demand side of elementary and secondary schools by allowing states to use the Elementary and Secondary Education Act (ESEA) chapter 1 funding to establish a school-choice voucher program under which students and parents would receive a voucher to cover some or all of a school's tuition and be free to choose any school in the district. As a consequence, each school's funding would be a function of its enrollment. Importantly, the administration's plan would permit parents to use vouchers at private and parochial as well as public schools. This dramatic proposal was a seemingly inexpensive way for Bush to become the "education president" without raising taxes or increasing expenditures (Dougherty and Sostre 1992, 165). Table 13 summarizes the Bush proposal. The plan also provided for grants for local districts to devise choice programs and offered waivers from federal regulations to permit greater innovation in school organizational structure and curriculum. The proposal provided funding for 535 new "break-the-mold" schools that could demonstrate innovative best practices for localities.

School-Choice Vouchers Causal Theory

The Bush proposal did not come out of thin air. A relatively extensive education policy literature describes the potential benefits to schools from the theoretical causal framework embedded in a school-choice voucher proposal. The program seeks to improve school effectiveness, which researchers believe requires teachers to exercise professional discretion and innovation, acting as a team with sense of purpose. The main barrier to school reform and improvement, according to choice proponents, is the heavy bureaucratization of school administration arising from top-down control of the schools and from collective bargaining with teachers unions. The policy research on school choice argues that efficiency gains will be realized

TABLE 13.   Summary of Bush School-Choice Proposal (1991)

- Parental Choice and Chapter 1. To provide for chapter 1 services for children participating in educational choice programs. Requires the local education agency (LEA) to provide . . . payments to parents of a per-child share of the LEA's basic chapter 1 grant. Allows parents to use such funds only for: (1) purchase of supplementary compensatory education services that meet the child's special educational needs from any elementary or secondary school, or any other public or private agency, organization, or institution that the LEA designates; and/or (2) transportation costs related to the child's participation in the choice program. . . . Allows an LEA to use chapter 1 funds for the additional transportation costs of children receiving chapter 1 services who are in an educational choice program.

- Assistance for Parental Choice Programs. Directs the Secretary to make one-year grants to LEAs that carry out educational choice programs. . . . Defines an educational choice program as one adopted by a State or an LEA under which: (1) parents select the school, including private schools, in which their children will be enrolled; and (2) sufficient financial support is provided to enable a significant number or percentage of parents to enroll their children in a variety of schools and educational programs, including private schools.

Note: Quoted from the administration proposal text.

if schools are simply allowed to compete in a marketplace for education (see, e.g., Chubb and Moe 1990; Coleman 1981; Greene, Peterson, and Du 1996).

Reformers identified a set of characteristics associated with effective schools that might be fostered in a school-choice voucher program, including teacher professionalism, coherence and a sense of mission within a school, and curriculum diversity among schools. Reformers wished to foster greater teacher professionalism and collegiality because the technology of teaching is bottom-heavy. Teachers with subject matter and instructional expertise need professional autonomy to adapt curriculum and teaching style to the varying and unpredictable circumstances in the classroom (Heid and Leak 1991, 223). Increased professionalism among teachers would make them more collaborative and collegial as well as more autonomous and able to adapt curricula to students' particular needs and interests (Raywid 1992, 107–8). Treating teachers as professionals and giving them more control over their working conditions also is likely to encourage the best and brightest to become teachers (Martin and Burke 1990, 77).

In addition, reformers sought to instill a sense of mission and commonality among teachers as colleagues and intellectual coherence in the curriculum (Raywid 1984, 73). Principals might receive the managerial capacity to build a coherent and dynamic teaching team and the authority to link reward with merit (Chubb and Moe 1990, 48–50, 57). Finally, reformers sought to increase diversity among schools and curricula for both pedagogical and normative reasons. Parents should be able to select among a variety of types of schools, using such criteria as school size, curriculum, and pedagogical approach to best match their children's interests and learning styles (Biggs and Porter 1994, 38; Raywid 1992, 107). Having a wide variety of schools and curricula helps to ensure a better fit to a diverse society (Martin and Burke 1990, 77), thereby giving parents more control over the education of their children and avoiding the democratic danger of establishing a single public orthodoxy (Raywid 1992, 112–24).

According to voucher proponents, government control of the schools through an administrative bureaucracy does not permit or encourage professionalism, leadership, coherence, and curricular diversity for a variety of reasons, so reforms that increase the top-down control of the bureaucracy are by their nature inefficient and ineffective in promoting educational excellence. A central bureaucracy cannot promote teacher professionalism because it is difficult for bureaucrats to measure and reward professional behavior in an objective or quantifiable manner. Bureaucratic authority does not allow teachers discretion to exercise their expertise and professional judgment (Chubb and Moe 1990, 36, 187). With the top-down control of schools, administrators at all levels of government require teachers to conform to particular teaching practices and procedures, not all of which are related to excellence, and administrators often impose time-consuming information-gathering requirements to monitor teachers' conformity to these rules. This hierarchical control of the classroom stifles teacher creativity needed to teach students in the way reformers envision and constrains teachers' choice of curriculum and textbooks, instructional methods, and emphases (Chubb and Moe 1990, 59). As Chubb and Moe put it, "It is impossible to hand down a set of rules from on high that will somehow transform bad teachers into good ones—and it is organizationally counterproductive to reward and sanction teachers on these grounds" (1990, 36).

Reformers argue that the current means of controlling education through the public, bureaucratic control of school policy and through collective bargaining causes this inefficient administration of education. The top-down control of schools not only promotes bureaucratization but also imposes contradictory educational goals on schools. In addition, unions foster bureaucratization as a way of enforcing school district concessions made during collective bargaining. Unions use collective bargaining to limit principals' discretion in contracts and through formal agreements regarding promotion, tenure, hiring, job requirements, participation in extracurricular activities, and so on.

Taken together, the effect of these forces, in the view of voucher proponents, is a type of governmental failure. According to Chubb and Moe, "This social outcome is the product of countless individual decisions, but it is not an outcome that any of the major players would want or intend if acting alone. It is truly a product of the system as a whole, an unintended consequence of the way the system works" (1990, 71).

Choice as a Mechanism for School Reform

Some reformers have suggested the use of voucher programs as a mechanism to make schools more effective and to reduce centralized control.[1] In such a system, schools receive complete control over their curriculum, teaching methods, terms of employment, and organization. Parents and students in turn control which school the students attend and receive a voucher for a set amount of money that may be used for tuition. As a consequence, parents and students decide where public school funding goes. Table 14 describes the basic outline of the school-choice reform causal framework, where authority is decentralized to the school and parents and students control which school students attend.

The basic assumption of the voucher causal model is that competition in the market setting would give schools incentives to organize themselves effectively as a way to satisfy parents as customers. This is

TABLE 14.   Voucher Program: Causal Framework

• The educational improvement rationale assumes that voucher systems would create markets and that, as a result of competition, the better schools would achieve a growing share of these markets. The inferior schools would have to improve or lose their clientele (Lieberman 1989, 152).

• Prochoice arguments: choice would require less bureaucracy and more school-level autonomy; staff motivation, leadership, and morale would improve with educational choice; parental involvement will be greater under choice; schools will be more diverse, innovative, and flexible. As a result of the preceding four arguments, student achievement will increase under choice; competition and market forces will reduce costs and increase efficiency under choice (Witte 1992, 208).

Note: Quotataions from the cited texts.

---

1. Voucher programs differ significantly from "controlled-choice" plans, where the district establishes a wide variety of magnet programs or specialized schools, perhaps using surveys of parental interests. Under controlled choice, parents are allowed to choose any school in the district but within the constraints of space and desegregation goals so that no school is threatened with extinction (Armor 1989, 31).

because the funding for students in a voucher program would follow them to their chosen schools. Those schools that fail to organize effectively would get weeded out of the market (Chubb and Moe 1990, 190; Raywid 1992, 108–9). An unrestricted voucher program would enable students to attend any school that met minimal criteria, including private and parochial schools. Power would be decentralized to schools in a voucher system to create an institutional environment similar to that currently enjoyed by private schools, the kind of school many reformers feel is most effective (Chubb and Moe 1990, 29). Accountability would be built into the program from the aggregation of parents' and students' choices rather than from the top-down control of public bureaucracies.

In a well-designed choice program, parents get clear and accurate information about the educational missions and the relative merits of different schools from a central location as well as assistance and counseling to interpret that information (Biggs and Porter 1994, 45). Because schools would have incentives to organize most effectively, the effect in theory would be to promote school-level autonomy from the central bureaucracy (Martin and Burke 1990, 75; Witte 1992, 208) and to give greater accountability to parents (Raywid 1992, 112–14). The intended effect of decentralization and market-based incentives is to foster systemwide reforms and to produce effective publicly funded schools.

Theoretical Efficiency in the Causal Framework

The school-choice model, assuming its causal framework is empirically sound, suggests several potential benefits for public education. In this market for education, there is the potential for gains from trade for both parents and schools—schools will have a better fit with parents' educational values and will gain greater sense of purpose (Chubb and Moe 1990, 30; Steinbach and Peirce 1989, 1692). Each school individually will be more coherent because students, teachers, and administrators select themselves into the school's mission and environment (Chubb and Moe 1990, 55; Raywid 1984, 73; Steinbach and Peirce 1989, 1694). At the same time, the school system as a whole will offer more diverse curricula and teaching methods and will be more innovative (Witte 1992, 208). Teachers presumably will be more motivated and enthusiastic when they can exercise their best professional judgment and creativity, and better-quality teachers will enter the profession when they have greater control over their working conditions and performance (Heid and Leak 1991, 222; Martin and Burke 1990, 77). The net result of these changes should be improved student achievement, more efficient use of resources, and overall more effective schools.

As in the emissions trading model, researchers do not present school choice as a panacea, and there are potential limitations even in theory to the effectiveness of the model. Schools might engage in anticompetitive practices such as price-fixing or territorial agreements that would limit the competitiveness of the market for schools and limit the available choices to parents. Parents may not have access to information or may have trouble understanding information available to them to select the best-fitting school, or the information may be inaccurate or incomplete. In some areas, transportation costs could increase substantially, and its availability will limit options. Income, education, and other advantages are unequally distributed in society, which may bias markets in favor of the rich. "To the extent that these and other imperfections are serious, markets are less likely to generate the diversity, quality, and levels of services that consumers want, and prices are likely to be higher than they otherwise would be" (Chubb and Moe 1990, 34). These market imperfections may be reduced by incorporating information agencies and counseling programs, subsidizing transportation, creating state-level subsidies for students from poorer districts, applying antitrust laws, and so on (Chubb and Moe 1990, 34).

Prospectively Gaining Groups Are Diverse

As in the emissions trading example, the voucher program's potential for increased efficiency and effectiveness in public education can appeal to a wide variety of interests in society. As Raywid notes, "One of the logically interesting things about choice is that it is espoused for contradictory reasons" (1992, 115). Vouchers in theory could garner wide political support for a variety of reasons. Both liberals and conservatives have espoused vouchers (D. Cohen and Farrar 1977, 72–73; Coleman 1981, 19). For liberals, vouchers promise to extend the opportunity to choose private schools to poor parents, similar to the opportunities currently enjoyed only by the rich, thereby enabling poor students to escape bad neighborhood schools (D. Cohen and Farrar 1977, 72; Martin and Burke 1990, 77; Raywid 1992, 112; Coleman 1981, 20). In addition, a uniform curriculum does not represent the values of the diverse subcultures in American society and instead tends to socialize students into the dominant culture (Biggs and Porter 1994, 37). On both of these counts, there has been support for vouchers in the African American community (Dougherty and Sostre 1992, 167–68). At the same time, market-oriented conservative politicians and activists support school choice, often for ideological reasons. The diversity in curricula that would occur in a school choice program appeals to social conservatives and the religious Right (Dougherty and Sostre 1992, 163).

The Catholic Church strongly favors school voucher programs as long as the vouchers can be redeemed at parochial schools. A voucher program would clearly boost attendance at Catholic parochial schools, which were suffering from declining enrollment and financial difficulties (D. Cohen and Farrar 1977, 72; Dougherty and Sostre 1992, 169). In November 1990, the U.S. Catholic bishops earmarked $2 million to establish a national office on school choice and to establish a lobbying organization for Catholic parents.

Business also has much to gain from a voucher program, but only if the program indeed makes schools more effective. Chubb and Moe note that "the business community has strong incentives to take a coldly analytical approach to the problem, and . . . to acquire the best possible knowledge about why the problem exists and what can be done about it—and to evaluate . . . the full range of policy and institutional options, however unsettling they may be to defenders of the status quo" (1990, 13). Around the time of the Bush proposal, however, national business groups—certainly an ideological constituency for school choice proposals—did not endorse school choice (Dougherty and Sostre 1992, 174 n.3).[2] "Ironically, three big business organizations, the Committee for Economic Development,

2. Throughout the 1970s and 1980s, business groups and ideological conservatives pushed for private school tuition tax credits as part of the general deregulatory fervor, but these were not explicitly tied to public school reform (Dougherty and Sostre 1992, 163).

the Business Roundtable and the National Alliance of Business, have
expressed reservations about choice" (Stanfield 1991, 1141). For
example, the president of the National Alliance of Business stated,
"There are those who believe that choice is the only thing we need to
do, an ideological panacea. We do not believe that. Our attitude at
this stage is that choice needs to have a lot more experimentation
done" (quoted in Dougherty and Sostre 1992, 174 n.3). The Committee for Economic Development in 1985 issued a policy position in
favor of choice limited only to public schools (Dougherty and Sostre
1992, 174 n.3).

Opposition

Teachers' unions, such as the National Education Association and its
local affiliates and the American Federation of Teachers (AFT),
adamantly oppose any choice reform that is based on vouchers
(Armor 1989, 35–36).[3] The intent of a voucher program is to weaken
the power of teachers' unions. Voucher proponents Chubb and Moe
argue that unions' achievements in collective bargaining raise costs
and decrease flexibility, thereby leaving unionized schools at a disadvantage in a competitive market: "Unions do best in noncompetitive,
protected, regulated settings—like government—where costs can
simply be passed on and ineffectiveness has almost nothing to do
with organizational survival" (1990, 53). Teachers' unions probably
could not guarantee their members benefits gained from collective
bargaining in a market environment; the idea of choice is to disrupt
these guarantees by giving principals greater discretion to impose
coherence on each school's school teaching and curriculum. Thus,
teachers' unions see *school choice* as a euphemism for *union busting*
(D. Cohen and Farrar 1977, 73).

Also opposed to unrestricted voucher programs are national edu-
cation associations that represent school administrators, such as the
American Association of School Administrators, the National School
Boards Association (NSBA), the Council of Chief State School

---

3. The late Albert Shanker, former president of the AFT, and Adam Urbanski, president of the Rochester Teachers Association, were among some prominent teachers'
union leaders who endorsed choice among public schools (Chubb and Moe 1990,
207; Heid and Leak 1991, 224).

Officers (CCSSO), and the national Parent-Teacher Association (PTA). School boards not only want to maintain their control of district funds but also express concern about the effect of choice on their ability to plan school budgets and hiring (D. Cohen and Farrar 1977, 73). In addition, civil libertarians are concerned about the entanglement of church and state in a voucher plan, and some civil rights activists worry about the effect of a private school voucher program on desegregation progress (D. Cohen and Farrar 1977, 73).

～

As in the emissions trading case in chapter 6, school choice has potential efficiency gains that could appeal to a diverse set of groups—the promise of effective schools and improved achievement, decreased costs from reduced bureaucratization, a close match to parents' and students' preferences, increased parental involvement in and sense of ownership of schools, greater opportunities for the poor, and increased diversity in school curriculum. But as I show next, unlike the emissions trading case, in 1991 a considerable amount of uncertainty existed over how a true voucher program would work in practice, since there had been only very limited local-level experience with voucher programs and a relative dearth of empirical research on the topic.

The State of Knowledge in 1991: Uncertainty about the Effectiveness of School Choice

That school reform based on choice envisions such disruption in educational institutions suggests that information about the likelihood of success should be at a particular premium. Historically, both teachers' unions and local school board organizations have opposed school-choice voucher programs whenever they are proposed.[4] Because of the political efforts of organized education associations, very few local-level experiments with school-choice voucher programs had been tried or evaluated prior to 1991 (Chubb and Moe

---

4. For example, the California Teachers Association mounted a $12 million campaign against a major California choice proposition (Peirce 1989, 2901; see also Lieberman 1994; Zuckman 1992, 471).

1990, 11–12). According to voucher proponents Chubb and Moe, "In order to show that institutions have important consequences for schools, one needs to show that institutional variation leads to a variation in schools—yet American public schools are all governed through highly uniform institutions of direct democratic control. There is no significant variation in institutions on which to base an enlightening analysis" (Chubb and Moe 1990, 27; see also 216). As table 15 summarizes, at the time of the 1991 Bush proposal, the education policy research community had great uncertainty about how a school-choice voucher program would work in practice.

Some evidence about how a voucher program would work in practice may be gleaned, however, from the districts and states that adopted controlled choice, from two very small voucher experiments, and by econometric models that include private schools (Chubb and Moe 1990).[5] The evidence from the studies of controlled choice and comparisons to private schools were equivocal at best, and the former in some ways suggested that choice in practice would be more costly than expected.[6] By 1991, the only large-scale choice plan, in Minnesota, allowed choice only among public schools. The only markedly successful decentralized choice plan was one in East Harlem, New York, which was on a small scale, centrally controlled,

---

5. Chubb and Moe (1990) claim to demonstrate the link between vouchers and school effectiveness in their comparison of test scores between students in private and in public schools. I do not discuss their results for two reasons. First, in general, compelling information in politics must come from actual demonstrations and social experiments, not from theoretical models. Political actors are very unlikely to rely exclusively on modeling results to determine their beliefs about a policy's effectiveness. Equally important, the Chubb and Moe models have several profound methodological problems. First, Chubb and Moe are unable to control for the self-selection of both students and teachers into private schools. The authors claim to control for nonrandom assignment of students by modeling the yearly change in test scores, but the rate of improvement will be correlated with the unobserved selection factors just as much as absolute test scores. Second, Chubb and Moe do not model the endogeneity of educational outcomes and school autonomy and so build in the causal direction between these two variables as a modeling assumption rather than as a result. And third, the total effect of autonomy produced a minuscule substantive improvement in test scores.
6. For details on and evaluations of the intradistrict controlled-choice programs in East Harlem, New York; Cambridge, Massachusetts; and Montclair, New Jersey, see Armor 1989; F. Brown and Contreras 1991; the Carnegie Foundation report (*School Choice* 1992); Cookson 1994; Martin and Burke 1990. For evaluations of interdistrict controlled choice, see the Carnegie Foundation report (*School Choice* 1992). On magnet schools, see Raywid 1984.

TABLE 15.   Voucher Program: Research Community Assessment (as of 1991)

- Despite all the political rhetoric concerning the benefits of parental and student choice, there is *virtually no evidence* to support the position that markets in and of themselves lead to school improvement. Although no one can reasonably claim to know exactly what does lead to school improvement, we can say that sweeping assertions that are based on virtually no evidence are a form of what might be called culpable naïveté (Cookson 1992, 101).

- The brute reality of American educational practice is that there is just one institutional form by which the public schools are governed. . . . *A comparative analysis of alternative institutional forms is generally not possible,* therefore, unless attention is restricted to relatively minor institutional details. . . . There is essentially nothing out there to study (Chubb and Moe 1990, 14).

- Although policy debates over educational choice are numerous, *experience with actual experiments in choice is very limited* (Witte 1992, 212).

- Because so few schools of choice plans include private schools, there is *very little empirical evidence* as to the consequences of including private schools in choice programs (Cookson 1994, 95).

- Because vouchers would radically change school organization and financing, it is hard for the average citizen—or expert, for that matter—to foresee all the consequences of a voucher plan. This *uncertainty,* coupled with concerns about loss of local control, makes voucher systems a very hard sell indeed (Armor 1989, 36).

- Thus far, *little evidence exists* that increasing choices for families causes educational improvement, greater parental involvement, or increased pupil learning (Martin 1991, 124).

- One of the most interesting features of the choice debate involves the position of researchers on the matter. The question arises in connection with the issue of the research base for choice. A recent publication of the Association for Supervisions and Curricular Development (1990) argued that there is *virtually none,* and at the last American Educational Research Association (AERA) meeting, it was striking how many presenters in the several sessions on choice began their presentations with some such statement as "Of course, *there is very little empirical research in support of choice.*" Whether one agrees with the claim or not, the frequency with which it was asserted was both marked and unusual (Raywid 1992, 115–16).

- There is *no systematic research* to support choice plans as an effective means of improving urban schools and reducing social class stratification in those schools. The much publicized choice plan in Minnesota has yet to yield meaningful results (Brown and Contreras 1991, 151).

Note: All are full quotations from the cited texts; emphasis added. The author encountered no assertions to the contrary in the literature.

and located in a nonrepresentative school district (Armor 1989, 32). The two uncontrolled voucher programs that had been tried by 1991 also both failed to shed much light on vouchers generally. One in Alum Rock, California, in the early 1970s showed no effects on test scores and generally did not produce much useful evaluation information (Martin and Burke 1990). The other was in Milwaukee, but this program was on a very small scale and had not been in existence long enough by the time of the 1991 Bush proposal to produce meaningful results.[7]

Perhaps more important, deciding whether a voucher program works well is far more complicated than answering a simple question of whether the program will or will not work as planned, since the outcomes of a voucher program can be evaluated in several different ways. Opponents to school choice have a powerful claim that democratic government should be in the business of educating all students and that the inevitable effect of school choice is to worsen inequalities in education. While individual students who participate in the program may benefit, the school system as a whole could become worse off. In this argument, bureaucratization is a necessary component of education in a democracy. And disagreement on this dimension will not be reduced solely by evaluation information showing that students who participate in a school voucher program improve their test scores. In other words, there are important conceptual ambiguities in the prospective benefits that may or may not come from a school-choice voucher proposal.

Analysis of the 1991 Hearings Testimony

Table 16 presents a classification of testimony given before the House Subcommittee on Elementary and Secondary Education regarding the 1991 Bush proposal.[8] I compare the claims made in testimony to the findings in the education research literature available at the time

---

7. On the Alum Rock experiment, see D. Cohen and Farrar 1977; Cookson 1994; Martin and Burke 1990; Witte 1992. On the Milwaukee program, see the Carnegie Foundation report (*School Choice* 1992); Witte 1992.
8. All citations to testimony in this section are to U.S. House of Representatives, *Hearings on H.R. 2460, America 2000 Excellence in Education Act,* June 18, 27, July 11, 1989.

TABLE 16. Testimony: America 2000 Excellence in Education Act

Arguments	Opponents	Supporters
Normative		
Opposed to regulatory waivers	PTA, LDF, CCSSO, AFT	—
Importance of public control of schools	PTA	—
Choice is divisive, fruitless debate	PTA, LDF	—
Harm to private schools	LDF	—
Parents have a right to choose child's education	—	USCC
Opposed to NAEP disclosure	NSBA	—
Instrumental		
Choice works only if limited to public schools	NSBA, CCSSO, AFT	—
Preference for national goals, standards and assessment approach, instructional technology, R&D, credentialing, etc.	CCSSO, AFT, NSBA, PTA	—
Need to provide teacher incentives, reward effective schools	AFT, CCSSO, NSBA	—
Vouchers lead to private school "creaming," won't help needy children	PTA, AFT, LDF	—
No information to support unrestricted voucher program, contrary evidence	PTA, AFT, NSBA, LDF, CCSSO	—
Parents don't have information to choose	LDF	—
New American schools won't help	NSBA, AFT	—
Other		
Opposes unrestricted voucher program	PTA, CCSSO, NSBA, AFT	—
Favors unrestricted voucher program	—	USCC

of the proposal. The 1991 proposal illustrates the kinds of claims lobbyists make in the absence of evaluation information, so the uncertainty predictions of chapter 5 should govern the debate. In this case,
I expect the opponents to make effective instrumental arguments
that a voucher program would be too risky to try, and the supporters
will not counter with instrumental arguments (see table 4 for a
definition of argument types). In this case, a clear message emerges
from debate on the 1991 proposal is that an uncontrolled school-
choice voucher program was too risky to try.

Separating Equilibrium in 1991 Hearings

As in chapter 6, the arguments shown in table 16 demonstrate that
empirically, supporters and opponents separate in the types of claims
they make in testimony. In this case, however, the supporters are
constrained to make only normative claims, and the opponents make
both normative and instrumental claims. In contrast to the emissions
trading example, the supporters are limited to normative arguments.
The U.S. Catholic Conference (uscc) speaks strongly in favor of the
voucher program but claims only that free choice is normatively preferred in American culture; the conference never claims that choice
would improve public education as a whole. In contrast, the opponents to school choice—teachers' organizations such as the AFT and
the PTA and school administration organizations such as the ccsso
and the NSBA—make a variety of empirical, research-based instrumental claims as well as normative or opinion-based arguments
against the school-choice voucher proposal.

Prospectively Gaining Group
In general, only parochial schools have tuition low enough for parents to use vouchers that have limited funding. The Catholic Church
schools expect an economic windfall under an unrestricted voucher
program, which would increase enrollment and financial support for
parochial schools. In her testimony, Sister Lourdes Sheehan of the
uscc asserts only that parental choice is normatively good in a free
society:

We believe that the time has come for all citizens of the United States, especially those like yourselves who govern in our names, to fortify the right and responsibility of all parents. Now, private schools, that is schools which provide quality education, have a clear mission, are accountable and have local autonomy, are available to those parents who both choose them and who can pay for them. I'm here today to ask you to provide that same option for all of America's children, especially the poor and disadvantaged. . . .

We believe strongly that all of America's children have a right to quality education and that parents are the first and foremost educators of their children. It follows logically that giving parents the means to exercise this right is in the best interests of parents, children, and the nation as a whole. (USCC 212, 213)

This rights-based argument asserts that the policy itself has intrinsic desirable properties, independent of its actual outcomes. The USCC does not argue that choice will somehow improve public education or make systemwide improvements, only that the policy itself has a superior fit with the American political culture, which prioritizes free choice in an individualist perspective, including the idea that the freedom of choice should not depend on economic circumstances.

Prospectively Harmed Groups
In response to the Bush proposal, the AFT and school board organizations send a clear message in the committee hearings that an uncontrolled school-choice voucher program is too risky to try. These opposition groups relied heavily on instrumental arguments that were based on the evaluation research literature on school choice, which in 1991 suggests that the benefits to public education from a school-choice program are ambiguous at best. The list of instrumental attacks these groups make on the voucher design corresponds closely to the limitations and questions identified in the literature.

For example, Representative Charles Hayes (D-IL) asks a panel, "Is there any sound evidence in our research which shows that . . . school choice works to improve academic achievement?" (Hayes 150). The panel responds that controlled choice and magnet schools have shown positive results but that the improvements likely result from the decentralization of authority to the schools rather than from market incentives. Phyllis McClure, representing the National

Association for the Advancement of Colored People's Legal Defense Fund (LDF), states, "There have been some good results in places like Community District 4 [East Harlem] in New York; but it wasn't just choice alone that did it" (LDF 150). This argument is consistent with the available evidence, which shows that decentralization efforts lead to innovation and tend to improve school performance but that these improvements do not come from the choice component that often accompanies these reforms (Cookson 1992, 102–3). Similarly, Gordon Ambach of the CCSSO states that voucher programs themselves have little evidence to support their effectiveness.

> When you ask the question about evidence for choice where we're talking about the possibility of using public resources to fund children in private institutions and to determine whether that yields any change in academic performance, my answer would be that we do not have evidence as to whether that does or does not change the level of performance. (CCSSO 151)

Lobbyists also question whether a voucher program can be expected to create incentives for effective schools and educational excellence. The PTA points out that survey data from Minnesota show that many parents do not choose schools based on educational excellence, a basic assumption embedded in the incentives behind choice plans: "Few parents choose schools on the basis of schools that are restructured. In Minnesota, over 40 percent of the parents who applied for Minnesota's Open Enrollment plan in 1989–1990 said they did so for convenience factors. Only 20 percent of the parents who transferred said it was for academic opportunity of a specific program" (PTA 74–75). NSBA states that choice is the wrong mechanism for systematically improving 16,000 school districts or improving the achievement of the nation's almost 3 million teachers and 40 million students; the bill is "flawed" because it relies on choice as the engine of reform (NSBA 225). "I think that there are many . . . ways the system can and will improve, but I don't see that Choice will drive that improvement either positively or negatively. Choice exists in most of our States to some extent now in many, many different ways but not in a voucher system that I'm aware of" (NSBA 252). Albert Shanker of the AFT argues in favor of controlled public school choice but does not do so for the reformist reasons of voucher proponents: "I would certainly give parents the right to choose among public schools but not because that's going to make the schools better, it's because its going to allow the schools to do things that they couldn't otherwise do that might be unpopular with parents" (AFT 260).

Another assumption of the voucher program was that the funding mechanism would make public schools similar to private schools, which are assumed to be more effective at educating students. Several opposition lobbyists cited results from a government-funded study, the National Assessment of Education Progress (NAEP), that shed doubt on the idea that private schools were organized more effectively and thus worth reproducing with public funds. The national PTA states,

> There is little relationship between vouchers and pursuing educational restructuring and reform. There's no evidence that choice boosts student achievement. In fact the results of a report released several weeks ago by the National Assessment of Education Progress showed that even though private schools can select their students, and their students are better at the earlier ages, the differences in the math scores of the older students tested is surprisingly small. Five percent of the 17 year olds in public school and 4 percent in private schools reached the level of mathematics required for college entry in other countries. (PTA 74)

Shanker cites the same NAEP results, giving more detail about private school students' social advantages relative to public school students, stating, "I think this ought to lead us to question the Choice issue" (AFT 186).

In sum, the lobbyist for the NSBA states, "Current research evidence does not justify a Federal investment of $200 million in Choice as a school improvement strategy" (NSBA 227).

Lingering Conceptual Ambiguities in the Causal Framework

In addition to the raw empirical uncertainty behind the voucher program, many education research experts at the time argue that quite a few unintended consequences could arise from a school voucher program. In essence, the researchers caution that a voucher program could endanger the ability of school systems as a whole to function and to educate all students. They argue that vouchers could permit resegregation along economic and racial lines, that the incentives from vouchers would not lead schools to prioritize educational excellence, and that a voucher program could worsen private schools. Again, the lobbyists discuss these issues at the hearing in a manner exactly paralleled in the education policy literature available at the time.

Sorting and Resegregation

A number of education researchers express the concern that uncontrolled voucher programs create a program that "sorts" students by several criteria. Here the concern is that the decentralized choices made by parents and schools, in the aggregate, will lead to additional social stratification and racial separation. First, some schools would use their selection processes to skim off the most talented, least disruptive, and least needy students, with the rest "dumped" into problem schools, worsening social stratification (F. Brown 1991, 117; Cookson 1991, 195; Martin 1991, 125). Having a few selective schools improve services to some children while other schools worsen services runs counter to norms of equity Americans hold in education and to mainstreaming efforts to achieve academic and social integration (Martin and Burke 1990, 75). This form of stratification would be reinforced by the unequal distribution of information on schools in society and by differences in parental involvement across social strata (Martin and Burke 1990, 75).

In this vein, the AFT lobbyist asks, "What would be the effect if private schools select students from public schools who are admitted, how many additional underclass schools does that create?" (AFT 187). The national PTA focuses its testimony on this point, arguing that a voucher program would benefit some students but play a cruel hoax on others, threatening "the concept of free, universal and equally accessible public schools for all children, no matter what the child's religion, disablement, intelligence level or language" (PTA 73). The PTA states,

Public school A loses a student and loses resources, which may have already been budgeted. If enough students move from public school A, programs must be reduced and the ability to compete diminished. The students who are left behind may be students who were denied access to the private school for whatever reasons. The winners in this case are certainly the non-public schools. The losers become the schools who lose the ability to compete as the result of student and financial loss and the students left in the public school system could be the children of the lowest income families and/or the most difficult children to educate—who are the fastest growing population of students in our schools today. (PTA 74)

In addition, the literature suggests that uncontrolled choice has the potential to increase racial and ethnic segregation (F. Brown 1991, 117; Carter and Sandler 1991, 176; Cookson 1991, 196; Witte 1992, 208, 222), for a variety of reasons. Students of particular races and classes are geographically clustered, and the cumulative effect of discrimination, residential segregation, low concentration of jobs, skills, educational attainment, poor self-esteem, lack of language skills and nonacademic distractions and social dislocation would shape patterns of parent and school choices. Many education researchers argue that district control over choice is necessary to prevent further segregation in the schools (Carter and Sandler 1991, 181; Cookson 1994, 93–94; Heid and Leak 1991, 223).

On racial stratification, citing a published article and a report, the PTA argues,

Vouchers will not provide increased educational opportunities for most needy children. A study conducted by the Chicago-based Design for Change, in their report entitled "Questioning the New Improved Sorting Machine," found that choice in the public schools sorted and selected children by income, color, and achievement. The selective schools were whiter, had fewer students with attendance problems, had fewer lower achieving students, fewer handicapped students and fewer at-risk children. Dennis Seeley in his article: "Is Choice Alone the Best Solution for Public Education?" warns that unlimited free market choice could lead to dangers of segregation, not only by race, but by socioeconomic class, region and clique, the further ghettoization of American society that is already too ghettoized. (PTA 75)

Vouchers Do Not Cause Schools to Prioritize Educational Excellence

Many educational researchers argue that schools are not market actors or good profit maximizers and consequently will simply not respond to the incentives in a school-choice plan to reorganize. Because schools are not-for-profit, public-service organizations, they do not have incentives to maximize profits, seek out bigger markets, or minimize production costs (F. Brown 1991, 118; F. Brown and Contreras 1991, 154). Further, because Americans do not accept the idea of winners and losers when it comes to education, available resources will tend to flow to those schools that are least viable, which in practice tends to minimize the market incentives that proponents contend in theory will be built into choice systems (F. Brown and Contreras 1991, 154). Finally, because education is a highly developed profession, parents can never have the kind of accountability idealized in choice reform proposals; education inherently conforms to the professional rather than the competitive market model of social control, and decentralization efforts tend only to enhance the power of those who already have it (D. Cohen and Farrar 1977, 92–93).

Along these lines, the CCSSO argues—clearly in its self-interest—that school reforms will not succeed unless the reform keeps the control of public schools in the hands of professional education establishment: "If you want to change an enormous public enterprise, you have got to craft the strategy which genuinely uses the people who are in that enterprise to help craft it" (CCSSO 148).

In addition, education researchers argue that schools maximizing student enrollment may not necessarily do so by raising academic standards. For example, a school might boost enrollment by emphasizing extracurricular activities or by extending the school day until seven o'clock at night to accommodate working parents, reallocations of resources that might come at the cost of academics. Instead of boosting morale among teacher professionals, competition may lead only to speeding-up practices, increased monitoring of performance, larger class size, or reduced salaries (Witte 1992, 208–9).

Instead of diversifying to capture specialized markets, schools may choose to standardize to a least common denominator standardize— like McDonald's fast food—to increase market share (Witte 1992, 208–9). Uncontrolled choice may lead to undesirable schools such as Nazi-based or ethnic nationalist curricula (Cookson 1991, 195; Martin and Burke 1990, 75). And while school choice may boost the self-esteem of students who are admitted to their preferred schools, it may dishearten and send the wrong signal to students who are not admitted (Martin 1991, 135).

Paralleling these arguments at the hearing, the AFT argues, "If you reward Choice you will essentially reward any school that's able to find anything that attracts people; it doesn't have to be higher academic standards. It could be anything else. If you really believe that our Nation is at risk because we are not achieving then don't reward attracting students, reward achievement" (AFT 258). The AFT continues by arguing that without district supervision, "there's nothing that prevents a Louis Farrakhan or a Ku Klux Klan or some group that—I mean there's no provision that says that you've got to teach anything in the English language, and it won't be the choice of a majority of parents but I don't want 3 percent of the kids in this country educated in that sort of way, not with taxpayers' dollars" (AFT 261).

Harm to Private Schools
One concern raised in the literature is that entangling private schools with public funding will cause participating private schools to lose their distinctiveness, certainly an unintended consequence of a voucher program. Private schools receiving public money from a voucher program may be subject to increased state and local oversight, such as increased accreditation requirements, affirmative action, insurance, health and safety, accountability reporting, and so on (Cookson 1991, 196; Martin 1991, 128). Essentially, implementing a voucher program could make private schools look more like the current public schools than the reverse. Echoing this issue at the hearing, the CCSSO's Ambach states, "I would urge upon the committee . . . a provision of a test for private school choice, which does in fact include all of the elements of being under public authority . . . namely, that the conditions of the Civil Rights Act, admissions of

children with limited English proficiency, admissions of children with handicapped conditions, and so on, are in fact built in" (ccsso 118).

Normative Arguments in Opposition

Finally, these opposition groups also make effective use of normative arguments.[9] For example, they argue that school choice harms the ideal of public education. The state governments have traditionally taken responsibility for educating future citizens in the democracy. The image of the local common school has long stood as a symbol of our shared democratic ideals (Cookson 1991, 196). School choice contradicts the Founding Fathers' purposes in establishing public education—to ensure a common commitment to democracy and the American purpose and to assimilate young citizens into the system of self-government (Martin and Burke 1990, 78). In this view, contrary to the voucher concept, society rather than parents is the "buyer" of children's education (Martin and Burke 1990, 78). Along these lines, at the hearing the pta witness states, "The more students . . . transfer to the private schools, the more parents will lobby for costlier vouchers while decreasing their political support of public schools" (pta 74).

The committee quickly shelved the Bush voucher idea. Soon thereafter, the committee embraced the Clinton administration's alternative approach to education reform, which was based on the concept of rigorous school standards, and Congress eventually enacted a standards-based reform in the Goals 2000 legislation. At this time, Democrats controlled the House Committee on Education and Labor, and it is likely that much of its decision was a political response to the pressure from unions, one of its main constituencies. It is certainly a counterfactual thought exercise to say what the com-

---

9. One important normative argument that often comes up in the context of choice was not raised at this particular set of hearings. This is the argument that voucher plans that include or have the potential to include parochial schools may entangle the state too much with religion, contrary to the Establishment clause ("Education" 1972).

mittee would have done had there been clear and compelling evidence to show that vouchers improve educational opportunities for all students. As I show next, however, the voucher idea did not fare much better in a Republican-controlled committee in 2001, even though by this time the voucher idea had accumulated new evaluation information from a decade of experience with local-level experiments.

Post-Milwaukee Research and the 2001 Testimony

In the 1990s, a variety of states and localities experimented with unrestricted school voucher programs, most notably in Milwaukee and in Cleveland, and these experiments produced new information to enlighten school-choice debates. Within the evaluation literature there was debate—particularly between John Witte of the University of Wisconsin and Paul Peterson of Harvard—about the correct statistical methods required to analyze the data from Milwaukee, the most prominent program. The Peterson study of the Milwaukee program used a randomized experimental design and found strong evidence that participants in the choice program had improved educational outcomes and test scores. Because the differences Peterson and his colleagues found occurred between two randomly assigned groups, the results were certainly compelling and difficult to assail. Peterson also notes, however, that the small-scale choice programs currently implemented are not large enough to allow tests of the institutional-level argument that school choice improves all schools. Because these larger, community-level concerns could not be ruled out, opponents of school choice could still argue that school choice would worsen public schools as a whole, even as it helps the few students who participate in the program.

Summary of Evaluations from Milwaukee

In his fifth-year report on the Milwaukee program, Witte found that participating parents' reported attitude toward choice schools tended to be better than toward their previous public schools (in terms of faculty and staff, curriculum and discipline), and choice parents also showed greater involvement in their children's schools. At the same time, Witte found that student achievement on standardized tests in reading and math was statistically no different between the choice students and low-income public school students as a whole (Witte, Sterr, and Thorn 1995, 2). Witte consequently concludes that school choice did not improve student achievement in Milwaukee. Because this was the first study of the Milwaukee data, it fueled attacks by opponents, who used the study to bolster claims that school choice is a poor mechanism for school reform (see Greene, Peterson, and Du 1996, 4).

Upon the release of this study, Paul Peterson and Jay Greene launched a critique arguing that the Witte study was contaminated by selection bias—that students who participated in the school choice program selected themselves into the program, and they did so on important unobserved characteristics that are negatively correlated with achievement. These researchers argued that the Witte evaluation compared apples and oranges: students from low-income families that participated in the choice program with students in the population of all Milwaukee public schools. Because it compared incomparable groups, it was not possible to rule out that selection is driving the null findings within Witte's methodological framework.

Peterson and Greene reanalyzed the Milwaukee data, taking advantage of a feature of the Milwaukee program, which by chance contained a true randomized experiment that enabled a test of educational achievement in the program. By law, if more students wished to enroll into a school than spaces were available, the school had to select randomly among the applicants. Students not selected into the program would simply reenroll in the public school system. Because of this random selection, Peterson and Greene could compare the gains for the program participants to those that were randomly not selected to participate, two groups roughly comparable except for the intervention of the program (Greene, Peterson, and Du 1996, 5).

Greene, Peterson, and Du found that the differences between the two groups in both reading and math achievement were trivial in the first two years of the program. After the third year, however, the choice students scored 5 percentile points higher on average than the nonchoice students on a mathematics achievement test, and after the fourth year, choice students scored nearly 11 points higher, differences that are statistically significant. Similarly, after the fourth year, choice students scored nearly 6 percentile points higher than nonchoice students on a reading achievement test, a difference that is also statistically significant. These differences are substantively large. Comparing the national average scores between black and white students, "if the results from Milwaukee can be generalized and extrapolated to twelve years, a large part of between-group reading differences and all of between-group math differences could be erased" (Greene, Peterson, and Du 1996, 5).

The Milwaukee program limited participation to only 1 percent of public school students and restricted the types of schools that could participate. In addition, the program required that no more than 65 percent of students in a school could be choice students, making it very unlikely that the program would foster entry of new private schools. Because of these restrictions, the Milwaukee program could not be expected to restructure public education in the city's school district as a whole—that is, the data from Milwaukee could not speak to the institutional argument of choice proponents. There is no way to gauge how many and what kinds of new schools would emerge in response to the program. As Witte notes, "It is impossible to predict the answers to these questions. There are no dynamic equilibrium models to simulate even estimates of new school creation" (Witte, Thorn, and Pritchard 1995, 6). The Milwaukee data could hardly be used to claim that competition among schools would improve all schools.

Nor could the results from Greene, Peterson, and Du's evaluation of the Milwaukee program rule out opponents' arguments that choice would worsen inequalities systemwide. Milwaukee's choice program was designed to provide an opportunity for poor families to send their children to private schools. In a separate evaluation, Witte used the data from the Milwaukee program, as well as a privately funded voucher program in Milwaukee that did not place similar restrictions on which students could participate, to show that broadening participation in the choice program—by dropping income limits, allowing schools to select among applicants, and allowing students currently enrolled in private schools to participate—would benefit the more affluent, and private schools would become even more selective (Witte, Thorn, and Pritchard 1995). The implication is that a large-scale unrestricted-choice program in Milwaukee would simply worsen inequalities.

In the terms of chapter 3, the evaluation literature on school choice contained a conceptual ambiguity in the causal framework by which school-choice evaluation information could be interpreted. Here, the experts offered contradictory expectations, where choice could arguably both help some students and hurt the school system as a whole. Proponents could argue that school choice in Milwaukee succeeded by improving the educational outcomes of those students who participated in the program. At the same time, opponents could use the same results to argue that school choice would benefit some students at the expense of the public education system as a whole. With this ambiguity, groups on both sides can be expected simply to muddy the waters in debates before Congress, making it difficult for Congress to learn about the true overall effects of the program.

The Bush Proposal: H.R. 1, No Child Left Behind

George W. Bush's administration revisited the issue of school choice despite these disagreements among experts when it made its proposal for the reauthorization of the ESEA in 2001. Principally, the administration proposed to allow students in persistently failing public schools to take their Title I funds either to another public school or to a private school. In addition, the Bush bill proposed funding school-choice demonstration research projects, with the idea that generating more information on how school choice works in practice would increase subsequent support. Table 17 summarizes the Bush bill's provisions.

Testimony Summary

The House Committee on Education and the Workforce held a hearing on the Bush proposal, "Transforming the Federal Role in Education for the 21st Century: Hearing on H.R. 1, H.R. 340, and H.R. 345" (March 29, 2001).[10] In the terms of chapter 4, given the multiple legitimate goals of an educational reform, groups could use the same evidence to support contradictory claims; as expected in the

---

10. All citations to testimony in this section are to this hearing.

ambiguity predictions, groups on both sides can pool on the same instrumental message type. And indeed, the hearing well illustrates how groups can use research-based claims to speak past each other.

～

Prospectively gaining groups. At these hearings, lobbyists from different ends of the ideological spectrum—a socially conservative group and a group that supports enhanced civil rights for minorities—spoke in support of school choice. Kenneth Connor of the socially conservative Family Research Council indicates that the group supports choice for ideological rather than programmatic reasons, calling choice a "profamily" provision. The group justifies its support in empirical instrumental terms in light of the positive results from the school-choice experiments for individual student achievement. Connor states, "We are pleased that H.R. 1 recognizes our current educational crisis and seeks to provide children a way out of an environment that is failing them. Students need to be able to pursue a quality education. We can provide resources and remove barriers to achievement. We must ensure that we leave no child behind" (75). Gail Foster of the Black Alliance for Educational Options supports choice as means of improving opportunities for

TABLE 17.   Bush School-Choice Provisions (2001)

- Disadvantaged students in Title I schools that fail to make adequate progress for three consecutive years would be able to use federal dollars to pay for tuition at another public or a private school, or to receive supplemental educational services from a provider of choice.

- The bill establishes an Educational Opportunity Fund to set up a limited number of demonstration projects in order to research the effectiveness of school choice programs in improving the academic performance of low-income students.

- Students attending unsafe schools or who are victims of violent crime would be able to transfer to a safe alternative, or to private school if space is not available in a safe school.

- Innovative Program funds could be used for public school choice, or private school choice for disadvantaged students in failing schools.

Source: From the bill proposal text.

low-income families. Here again, she justifies her support in instrumental terms regarding the benefits for individual students' achievement: "School Choice won't solve all of this nation's sociological contradictions. But it will save my child the way it saved yours, if you'll give me a chance" (84). In neither case does the lobbyist argue that school choice would improve public education as a whole; instead, perhaps strategically, both lobbyists focus on the outcome dimension that supports their intrinsic preferences: individual students in the program could be made better off.

⌒

Prospectively harmed groups. As with the 1991 proposal, both teachers' unions and school board associations oppose school choice. Both of these groups argue that school choice is likely to worsen the inequalities among schools and to worsen the school system as a whole, as this claim cannot be ruled out with the available evidence. For example, Randi Weingarten of the AFT argues that school choice could worsen public schools as a whole: "The AFT believes that the Administration bill is fatally flawed . . . with its incorporation of vouchers and block grants. It is indeed ironic that the otherwise strong focus of the bill on accountability is totally undermined by its incorporation of these two elements—two of the most unaccountable policies" (AFT 95). Similarly, Paul Houston of the American Association of School Administrators states, "Every single school we could find that had been defined as failing by state authority serves a concentration of high need students. . . . Permitting some students to use scarce federal funds to attend private or parochial schools and then imposing huge new administrative costs [on] public schools to track such students is an idea whose time has passed" (114). Again, in this case, the opposition lobbyists attack the program by strategically focusing on the outcome dimension of the performance of the school system as a whole, by which the program perhaps could be expected to fail.

⌒

Business is ambivalent. Given the ambiguities in the evaluation literature, the groups representing big business understandably continued to withhold support for the school-choice concept. Business is a natural constituent for school choice but has a direct stake in the quality of public education and approaches the question pragmatically. In the language of chapter 3, given business's wholly extrinsic preference for whichever policy will lead to better educational outcomes, business groups were like a deer in the headlights given the contradictory expectations among experts. The evaluation information that came to light in the 1990s in effect only increased their ambivalence.

Keith Bailey, representing the Business Coalition for Excellence in Education and the National Alliance of Business (NAB), does not argue on behalf of school choice. Instead, contradicting the market incentives logic of school choice the business groups support the use of standardized testing to funnel additional resources to schools that underperform. "To be held accountable, school officials and teachers must be supported by aligned systems of assessments and standards for academic content. . . . The Business Coalition calls for supplemental support to be provided to students who do not meet these standards" (60). Although a natural constituent of the school-choice idea, the NAB does not state its support for school choice. A lack of support from groups that would benefit from the efficiency improvements is understandable given the limitations and ambiguities in the current empirical research on school choice.

Perhaps as a consequence, the House Education and the Workforce Committee, now controlled by Republicans, again shelved the voucher idea in favor of less extreme accountability measures for public schools.

Conclusion

This chapter demonstrates, in contrast to the previous chapter, that the raw availability of program information is not sufficient to enable socially efficient policy reform. School-choice programs seek to make the public school system more effective through market incentives from parents' choices. The effect of a successful school-choice plan would be to reduce or eliminate the power of teachers' unions and school boards at the local level. In 1991, there existed little empirical evidence on whether disrupting the local-level school bureaucracy with private school vouchers would in fact improve education outcomes by any standard of evaluation. The idea simply had not been tried. As a consequence, business organizations—a natural constituency for the program—failed to support the 1991 Bush choice plan. Teachers' unions and school board organizations vigorously attacked the proposed program design but used instrumental arguments drawn from the evaluation research literature. The clear gaining group, the Catholic Church, argued only that choice is normatively good in American society. In the language of chapter 4, in the 1991 hearings the groups separated in their testimony, and only opposition groups give instrumental, empirically based arguments. The House committee, controlled by Democrats, eventually stripped the legislation of its school-choice components.

New information about the workings of school-choice programs came to light in the late 1990s but did not drive the system toward a consensus. Here supporters and opponents used the same information to talk past each other. Given the apparent increase in participants' test scores, supporters argued in an instrumental manner that school choice improved educational outcomes for participants. But because the programs were on a relatively small scale, opponents equally well argued that the students who did not participate were particularly disadvantaged and that the effect of school choice was likely to be increased inequality in educational outcomes across schools, to the detriment of the system as a whole. Although it could be argued that the opponents of school choice—teachers' unions and school administrators—were merely pursuing their self-interests in preserving the bureaucratic structure of public education, opponents tapped into very general values regarding a democratic government's obligation to all students. In this case, supporters and opponents pooled on the same type of instrumental, research-based testimony. Perhaps as a consequence, the House committee, controlled by Republicans, stripped the legislation of its provisions to allow parents to send their children to private schools with Title 1 money, limiting choice instead to public schools.

8

HMOs and Methodological Ambiguities

I hope you understand that some of our questions are directed in order to bring out the whole picture. Even though some of us may have authored bills, we like to know what we are doing as we proceed.

—Archer Nelson (r-mn), hmo hearings, 1972

This chapter examines the debates about the Nixon administration's health strategy, first introduced in 1971, which relied on the concept of health maintenance organizations (hmos) to help establish a competitive market for health care delivery. The Nixon administration felt the need to respond to the rapid escalation in health care costs brought on largely by the Medicare and Medicaid programs implemented in 1966. In this case study, I compare testimony by the American Medical Association (ama), an established medical professional group, to that of other groups in the 1972 hearings on the Nixon proposal. I show that the ama tried to rely on its professional authority in interpreting data from health research as a way to create methodological ambiguities. This strategy had limited effectiveness, however, especially since at this same time the long-standing authority of organized medicine was beginning its decline, and Congress's efforts eventually resulted in the hmo Act of 1973.

The Health Care Crisis and National Health Initiatives, 1969–1970

When the federal government enacted the Medicare and Medicaid programs in 1965, they focused exclusively on providing financing for health services for the elderly and poor rather than on changing the underlying organization for health care delivery (Mott 1971, 504; Newman 1972). Given organized medicine's political clout, this focus on financing was less a lack of understanding of the underlying structural problems in the market for health care, since the increase in demand would have a clear inflationary effect, than a political compromise to get the Medicare bill through Congress (Wolkstein 1970, 699).[1] As a consequence, the financing provisions simply preserved the predominant fee-for-service system with third-party financing, delegating the administration of the program to private insurance companies and state agencies (Newman 1972, 120; "Role" 1971, 988–89; Social Security Act, title XVIII, sec. 1801; Wolkstein 1970, 698). The inflationary effect of these programs changed mere inefficiency in health care delivery into a crisis, and this crisis put the organization and delivery of health care onto the federal government's agenda for the first time (Morone 1995, 186).

Simply identifying inefficiencies in the market for some service generally is insufficient to place an issue on the government agenda. In the late 1960s and early 1970s, however, the full set of efficiencies in the delivery of health care, combined with new demand from Medicare and Medicaid recipients, drove health care prices rapidly upward. The unexpectedly large costs of the new federal financing programs for health care assured that government would reconsider their design: "The result has been fiscal near-disaster in the public programs, expressed in anguished outcries from legislators entrapped into supporting levels of tax appropriations far beyond their expectations" (Falk 1970, 673; see also "Behind the Rising Cost" 1970, 63). This exigency put the organization and delivery of health care on the federal agenda for the first time (Morone 1995, 186).

Congress's initial response was to push either for catastrophic coverage or for the comprehensive financing of health care services

---

1. There is some debate about whether this compromise was merely pragmatic, shortsighted, or strategic. The pragmatic theory held that these programs would simply redistribute current financing from covered patients, to whom the costs of the medically indigent are passed, to the general population through government financing. This would imply no new inflationary pressures. The strategic theory held that national health insurance supporters thought Medicare's inflationary potential would serve as a lever for more general government financing of health care down the road.

through some form of national health insurance. A consensus soon developed among policy analysts and politicians alike, however, that in light of recent experience, the health care crisis could not be solved through financing alone, since the effect of financing programs proved inflationary in the absence of any competitive market for health care delivery (Arrow 1963). It became clear to the health care policy community that the federal government would have to get into the business of promoting the efficient organization of the health care delivery system. The Nixon administration devised its health care proposal against this political and analytical backdrop.

The Nixon Health Strategy: HMOs as Policy

The inflationary experience with the new federal health care financing programs helped to create a consensus among policymakers that the federal government needed to take responsibility for rationalizing the organization of health care delivery. Consequently, proposals for reform began to incorporate either direct or indirect means for the regulation of the health care sector. The Nixon administration ideologically was reluctant to impose direct regulation on the health care sector, however. The president's health policy advisers convinced him that they had found market-based means of controlling health care costs through HMOS, which were based on existing prepaid group practice models like Kaiser-Permanente and the Health Improvement Plan of Greater New York (HIP).[2] If the government could promote these rational forms of health care delivery, the argument went, the resulting competition in the health care market would help to control costs and allocate resources more rationally.

Nixon's health strategy, first introduced as legislation in February 1971, had both a financing component and a market-based regulatory component. The financing component of the Nixon health strategy relied exclusively on improving individuals' and families' access to private health insurance. Employers would be required to provide and partially subsidize the costs of private health insurance

---

2. The story of how Department of Health, Education, and Welfare officials came to advocate HMOS, on advice from Dr. Paul Ellwood, as the heart of the health strategy has been told repeatedly (see Bauman 1976; L. D. Brown 1983; Falkson 1980).

coverage that met minimum standards. Insurance carriers would have to set up insurance pools to cover small employers, the self-employed, and others not covered in the workplace. A Family Health Insurance Plan would cover the eligible unemployed, Medicaid would be limited to the needy aged, blind, and disabled, and Medicare would be improved and extended (see Falk 1970, 685; Wolkstein 1970, 706). But the Nixon health strategy did not impose any form of direct cost control on health services through direct regulation of prices. Instead, the Nixon administration put its analytical faith in indirect regulatory controls from a newly constituted health care market driven by competition from HMOs, both by incorporating an HMO-financing provision into Medicare and by providing grants and loans to subsidize the start-up of new HMOs (Flash 1971, 509; Havighurst 1970, 716; "President Nixon's Health Proposals" 1971).

The intent of the HMO component of the health strategy was to allocate scarce health system resources by creating an efficient, competitive market for health care. The federal government would subsidize the development of newly emerging HMOs, which would create self-regulating incentives for the industry to control costs and provide quality care (Bauman 1976, 130; Flash 1971, 512). Under Nixon's strategy, the federal government would only lend support through start-up grants, direct loans, and loan guarantees, along with additional support for HMOs that would locate in medically underserved areas. The proposal allocated $23 million for planning grants and $300 million in guarantees of private loans to HMO sponsors, along with $22 million in subsidies to induce HMOs to locate in inner cities and in rural areas (Havighurst 1970, 725). The strategy also would encourage HMO development by requiring employers to give their covered employees an HMO option where available as well as through changes to the Medicare law (a new part C) that would allow recipients to choose prepaid coverage. These provisions would provide further incentive for HMO development by opening up markets for HMOs among populations otherwise locked into traditional fee-for-service insurance (Havighurst 1970, 725).

Since the administration emphasized encouraging a new market for health care, the proposal left the definition of an eligible HMO purposefully vague to avoid stifling innovation and new forms of competition. The definition included coverage of basic services, payment on a capitation rather than fee-for-service basis, standards for promptness in the delivery of care, an open enrollment period to make HMOs accessible to a large population, and preemption of state laws that had the effect of interfering with group practice (Falk 1970, 687). In particular, the Department of Health, Education, and Welfare (HEW) strategists devised the term *health maintenance organization* to avoid limiting the covered organizational forms to the current prepaid group practice plan models, mostly developed by employers, consumer groups and unions as non-profit plans. The Nixon HMO definition (see table 18) included medical foundation plans organized by local medical societies, where customers paid on a capitation basis and doctors were reimbursed on fee-for-service basis as well as for-profit HMOs (see Havighurst 1970, 727–28).

Inefficiencies in the Health Care Market

In the period when the Nixon administration launched its health strategy, the health research community wrote extensively on the clear analytical inefficiencies in the market for health care delivery. At the time, Americans clearly committed considerable resources to health care. As *Time* magazine reports:

> If gross medical product alone guaranteed physical well-being, Americans would be the healthiest people in the world. The U.S. has more than 7,000 hospitals, many of them with the most advanced and elaborate equipment available anywhere. The nation's 330,000 doctors, one for every 650 people, are the products of the most rigorous training. In sheer dollar terms, health has become the second largest industry in the U.S., last year turning over $67.2 billion, or 6.9% of the G.N.P. ("Health Care" 1971, 86).

The enormous costs of health care and the questionable returns on health expenditures on their face suggested the presence of market inefficiencies. By the early 1970s, Americans were paying more for medical care, both in absolute terms as well as in the proportion of the gross national product devoted to health, then ever before, while "statistics . . . reveal[ed] that America's health is growing steadily worse relative to that of other highly industrialized nations" ("Role" 1971, 889).[3]

Despite having the most advanced technology for health delivery, in 1971 the United States ranked eighteenth among industrialized countries in life expectancy for males and eleventh for females, six-

TABLE 18.   Nixon Proposal HMO Definition (1972)

• Provides, either directly or through arrangements with others, health services to [enrollees] on a per capita prepayment basis;

• Provides, either directly or through arrangements with others, . . . (through institutions, entities, and persons meeting the applicable requirements of section 1861), all of the services and benefits [listed in the title];

• Provides physicians services (A) directly through physicians who are either employees or partners of such organization, or (B) under arrangements with one or more groups of physicians (organized on a group practice or individual practice basis) under which each such group is reimbursed for its services primarily on the basis of an aggregate fixed sum or on a per capita basis, regardless of whether the individual physician members of any such group are paid on a fee-for-service or other basis;

• Demonstrates to the satisfaction of the Secretary proof of financial responsibility and proof of capability to provide comprehensive health care services, including institutional services, efficiently, effectively, and economically;

• Except as provided [elsewhere], has at least half of its enrolled members consisting of individuals under age 65;

• Assures that the health services required by its members are received promptly and appropriately and that the services that are received measure up to quality standards which it establishes in accordance with regulations; and

• Has an open enrollment period at least every year under which it accepts up to the limits of its capacity and without restrictions, except as may be authorized in regulations, individuals who are eligible to enroll . . . in order in which they apply for enrollment (unless to do so would result in failure to meet the requirements of paragraph (5)).

Note: Summary of H.R. 1 as amended sec. 226(A), proposed sec. 1876(b).

3. "Role" 1971, published in the *Harvard Law Review,* is an extraordinary study of the HMO policy problem, and this chapter relies heavily on that work.

teenth for death rates for middle-aged males, and thirteenth in infant mortality ("Role" 1971, 892). The distribution of physicians also was uneven, and an estimated 40 million Americans lacked access to a doctor ("Health Care" 1971, 86). The published health policy literature noted that these comparative statistics, while suggestive, were not readily interpretable, since the United States had the most comprehensive reporting system, and there are variations among countries in environmental circumstances and behavioral patterns, among other factors that affect public health ("Role" 1971, 892). But even in this country, life expectancy had barely increased since 1954 despite the massive increases in spending and infusions of medical technology ("Role" 1971, 893; see also Falk 1970, 673).

To the health policy community of the late 1960s, the basic reason for inefficiencies in the delivery of health care lay in the near absence of a competitive market to allocate health system resources efficiently (Arrow 1963). Health care providers could manipulate demand for health care services, since the consumers of health care—the patients—generally lack the specialized training to know what health services they need. Consumers have no way to compare health services or prices because they do not make the decision about which services to purchase (Kissick and Martin 1972, 152). But consumers also had little incentive to compare services because third-party insurance paid the bills. In the early 1970s, insurance carriers almost exclusively paid physicians retrospectively or a fee-for-service basis for any services provided, based on the usual and customary fees of all physicians in the area ("Role" 1971, 907).

Furthermore, the major carriers, Blue Cross for hospital coverage and Blue Shield for physician services, were organized by hospitals and physician societies, respectively, and consequently had a professional rather than a consumerist orientation: the price of health services remained simply a professional concern. Cost-efficiency has never been a hallmark of the organized health profession, because physicians see providing the best care possible as an ethical obligation ("Health Care" 1971, 87) and because hospitals frequently are run as nonprofit and charitable institutions.

This professional orientation in third-party payment for health services had several distorting effects in the delivery of health services. First, and obviously, it tended to drive up prices for any given service. Because fee-for-service insurance carriers reimburse on the basis of "reasonable costs," "reasonable charges," "cost-plus," or "customary and prevailing rates," physicians do not have a financial incentive to economize (Berki and Heston 1972, xii). This form of payment instead creates a financial incentive for physicians to over-provide services, to favor costly resource-intensive services, and to bid up prices. In addition, fee-for-service financing also creates dis-incentives for referral, since each referral means lost business, which implies incentives for doctors to practice outside of their areas of spe-cialty.

Coverage for hospitalization created similar incentives in the administration of hospitals as well. Both Blue Cross and the hospital coverage under part A of the Medicare program reimburse hospitals based on their costs. Hospitals that economized on costs would sim-ply reduce their income, and since the past record of costs affected current reimbursements, economizing would harm the hospital's income for years to come. "Thus hospitals were encouraged to solve financing problems, not by minimizing costs but by maximizing reimbursements. What was individually a solution for hospitals was, in aggregate, a problem for society" (Starr 1983, 385). In the absence of cost-minimizing pressures, hospitals built facilities and purchased the latest and most expensive high-tech equipment to attract the best physicians. As a consequence, hospitals had redundant and under-used facilities ("Role" 1971, 896).

Second, the pattern in the provisions for third-party coverage introduced distortions into patients' and physicians' choice of ser-vices. Private insurance often would cover expensive inpatient hospi-talization rather than low-cost ambulatory care, or patients might have only hospitalization coverage; in such cases, both patient and physician have incentives to have basic tests and minor surgery done on a costly inpatient basis (Berki 1972, 126; Feldstein 1971, 95; see also Andersen and May 1972, 71; Berki and Heston 1972, xii; Falk 1970, 672–73; "Role" 1971, 892).

Third, health care delivery was poorly organized, and there was lit-tle coordination of the specialized services available for individual patients ("Role" 1971, 891). The practice of medicine had by the early 1970s become highly specialized; the number of physicians in specialties increased from 11 percent to 71 percent between 1923 and

1967 (R. Stevens 1971, 11).[4] Fewer and fewer patients had access to a primary care physician who could be responsible for the patient's overall care and could coordinate referrals. With a majority of doctors in solo practice, specialized services tended to treat the separate body parts and symptoms rather than the health of the whole patient. Further, without coordination and a single health record, doctors might apply redundant tests and procedures and might even administer counterindicated drugs and treatments ("Role" 1971, 900). The organized health profession never took on coordination of services as a policy concern. In Berki and Heston's words, "The vertical integration of separate yet integrally related production processes is absent. . . . It is as if in the construction industry there were no general contractors or architects to coordinate the work of the masons, plumbers, carpenters, and electricians." Instead, "with multiple and uncoordinated entry points to an increasingly mass production system of fragmented care, the patient is lost in a maze" (1972, xiii, x).

The supply of physicians also was unevenly distributed, with inadequate access to physicians primarily in rural and inner-city areas. Health policy researchers traced the distribution of physicians once again to the inefficiencies of professional control of delivery in place of a market-allocating system, since reimbursement on the basis of prevailing fees in the area created incentives for doctors to locate in relatively wealthy urban areas ("Role" 1971, 895; Starr 1983, 387). The main federal program to promote health care in rural areas was the Hill-Burton hospital construction program, but the effect often was state-of-the-art facilities with inadequate staffing (Geiger and Cohen 1971, 33).

In sum, in the fee-for-service health care system with third-party payment, according to the health policy literature of the late 1960s, prices did not serve the usual market function of allocating scarce

---

4. This trend toward specialization began after the turn of the century with the reorganization of medical education that was recommended in the Flexner Report of 1910. Mechanic (1972, 2) argues that specialization was a response to the increased sophistication of health care training and delivery. The trend toward specialization was driven further by federal funding of research through the National Institutes of Health, with new funding that strengthened clinical specialty departments in hospitals. These considerations led D. L. Madison (1971, 519) to declare that specialization simply reflected the absence of a well-ordered market for health care: "The growing specialization of medical practice has arisen entirely from within medicine. It is not a response to changing medical needs of our society."

resources in a rational or efficient manner. The health policy research community began to define the organizational design and market structure for the delivery of health care—and not simply its financing or the quantity of research and technology development—as a policy-making concern. As a model for a better design, by the late 1960s the health research and policy community began to turn its attention to a form of health care delivery called prepaid group practice as a possible organizational solution to the identifiable inefficiencies in solo practice and fee-for-service delivery.

Prepaid Group Practice as an Efficient Organization for Health Care Delivery

As an organizational form, prepaid group practice in theory creates incentives to overcome many of the inefficiencies of the solo practice, fee-for-service form of health care delivery. As I next show, the health policy research community determined that prepaid group practice plans, through better organization and improved financing incentives, had incentives to deliver health care less expensively without sacrificing a high quality of care.

A prepaid group practice plan takes responsibility for the organization, financing, and delivery of services for a defined population in exchange for a fixed annual per capita fee ("Role" 1971, 901). The basic prepaid group practice model combines prepayment financing, where a subscriber pays a fixed fee to cover all health services irrespective of their frequency of use, with delivery of services in the form of a multispecialty group practice (see generally Coburn 1973, 28; Greenlick 1972, 103). The group practice, through its administration, owns its facilities, contracts with physician groups, and hires staff, administrators, and management. This form of health care financing contrasts with financing through risk-sharing insurance, since prepaid group practice bears the financial risk and takes responsibility for delivering a pattern of care to a defined population of subscribers (Phelan, Erickson, and Fleming 1970, 797; "Role" 1971, 902).

The standard model of prepaid group practice has the health care organization pay its physicians by the number of subscribers, referred to as capitation payment, rather than for each discrete service rendered ("Role" 1971, 907). This form of compensation removes the incentives to perform unneeded services and encourages application of the most economical form of care (Greenlick 1972, 104; Newman 1972, 123; Phelan, Erickson, and Fleming 1970, 800). Prepayment builds in an incentive for doctors to keep patients healthy, since services become more costly when a patient becomes sick (Havighurst 1970, 718). As a result, prepaid group practices emphasize low-cost but highly effective preventative medicine ("Role" 1971, 924–25). And because members do not pay a fee for each visit to the doctor or pay only a very small fee, there is no economic barrier for subscribers to seek treatment early, when conditions are cheaper and easier to treat ("Role" 1971, 903).

Having comprehensive coverage removes some of the distortions in health care delivery caused by particular patterns of coverage in indemnity plans. Prepaid group practices provide comprehensive benefits to members for the fixed prepaid fee, including tests and services in both office and hospital ("Role" 1971, 905). In most group plans, this coverage is more comprehensive than similarly priced indemnity plans such as Blue Cross–Blue Shield ("Role" 1971, 906). Neither physicians nor patients have incentives to seek services in hospitals, since the costs are higher for the plan and because out-of-pocket expenses are the same for patients ("Role" 1971, 924). Comprehensive coverage encourages early consultation and treatment and allows physicians discretion to apply medically necessary procedures (Phelan, Erickson, and Fleming 1970, 801). Finally, closed-panel group practice with specialists on staff also encourages referrals because the plan does not lose money in making the referral (Phelan, Erickson, and Fleming 1970, 798).

The health policy research community at the time argued that delivery of care through group practice yielded some efficiencies through economies of scale and through improved organization as well. Because prepaid group practices provide comprehensive care, they can emphasize primary care, can make efficient referrals to specialists, and can have facilities on a large enough scale to provide ambulatory care for all but the most severe cases (D. L. Madison 1971, 522; Phelan, Erickson, and Fleming 1970, 798; "Role" 1971, 904). In contrast, in fee-for-service medicine, physicians occupying a single office would have to hospitalize a patient for procedures slightly more complex than may be accommodated in the office ("Role" 1971, 927). The larger group practices that own hospital facilities also do not have incentives to hospitalize patients when care could be given on an ambulatory basis. Fee-for-service hospitals require a certain level of occupancy to remain solvent, whereas group-practice hospitals see hospitalization as a cost ("Role" 1971, 924).

Some health policy researchers note that in theory, prepayment can create the opposite incentives to overeconomize on health care services. One researcher notes, "The clearest example would be in the temptation to let a patient die of a cardiac arrest rather than place him in the intensive care unit at a cost of $300 per day" (Havighurst 1970, 723). In response, health policy researchers point out that a reduction in services does not necessarily indicate poorer quality of care, especially considering that overprovision of care through unnecessary surgery or overmedication can also harm health ("Role" 1971, 926).

In addition, prepaid group practice plans, through their organization, have countervailing pressures against overeconomizing on health services. Proponents of this sort of organization emphasize that the group practice has incentives to keep patients well, so norms of consultation and peer review develop among the physicians on the closed panel ("Role" 1971, 926). By a similar logic, these plans tend to take special care in physician selection because bad physicians who do not keep patients well will become a liability to the plan as a whole (Greenlick 1972, 104; Phelan, Erickson, and Fleming 1970, 798; "Role" 1971, 928). In a group-practice setting, patients have a single medical record that is shared among the physicians on the closed panel. This makes the patient's record available to all caregivers and provides another form of peer review in which physicians know that other physicians will observe treatments given (Greenlick 1972, 105; "Role" 1971, 929). Finally, malpractice suits, consumer pressure (especially in a consumer-controlled plan), and competition with other plans and delivery systems tend to ensure quality of care.

One can observe an almost identical litany, as outlined in table 19, of these causal incentives arguments repeated in the health policy literature available at the time (e.g., Havighurst 1970). This socially

TABLE 19. HMO Policy: Causal Framework

- Reverses the incentives inherent in fee-for-service medicine (especially where health insurance removes the doctor's direct fiduciary obligation to his patient) for physicians and hospitals to provide unnecessary services in order to increase their income;

- Introduces incentives, particularly absent where third-party insurance is available, for physicians to consider cost effectiveness and to avoid overusing expensive facilities and resources for such purposes as (a) obtaining an incommensurate medical benefit for the patient, (b) adhering uncritically to "routine" practice, (c) minimizing perceived malpractice risks, (d) rendering a certain service in such a way (for example, on an inpatient basis) as to bring it within the terms of the patient's insurance coverage, or (e) catering to the nonpaying patient's perceived preference that "everything possible" be done whatever the expense;

- Creates a decision maker with both the knowledge and the incentive to discriminate on the basis of price and value in the purchase of needed goods and services—particularly drugs, hospital services, and specialists' care—thus strengthening competition and economic performance in markets adjacent to the market for primary care;

- Strengthens incentive for realizing available efficiencies in the use of manpower and other resources, incentives that are weak where providers are not subject to substantial price competition due to the structure and customs of the marketplace of where cost-reimbursement is more or less assured by government or private health insurance;

- Creates an organizational structure in which available efficiencies and improvements in performance can be more readily realized in such areas as (a) maintenance of complete, up-to-date, and nonduplicative medical records; (b) manpower and equipment utilization; (c) utilization of specialists' services; (d) continuing education for personnel at all levels; and (e) administration generally, particularly in billing and in freeing physicians of business details;

- Creates an incentive for providers to keep patients well by such preventive measures as are economic, to detect disease at an early stage, to treat causes rather than symptoms, and generally to effect an early cure;

- Improves incentives affecting referrals and outside consultations, whereby fee-for-service physicians may only lose income from a patient but prepaid providers may gain protection against the financial costs of a subscriber's worsened condition;

- Offers the opportunity for organizing care more conveniently for consumers by providing an accessible and continuously available "entry point" into the health care system and responsible guidance for the patient through the system so that he may obtain promptly and centrally such services as he requires;

• Provides, by encouraging larger organizations of physicians in the place of solo practitioners, a better vehicle for maintaining the quality of care rendered outside the hospital; and

• Provides stronger incentives for maintaining effective peer review and other quality controls in hospitals than exist in the present system of hospital practice.

Source: Reproduced from Havighurst 1970, 720–22; footnotes omitted.

efficient logic of the prepaid group practice form, renamed HMOs, was widely known by the time the Nixon administration began to search for its health strategy.

The Nixon health strategy relied on this decentralized, competition-based approach to create efficiencies in the market for health care. Nixon lodged his faith in the belief that in competition with traditional medicine, HMOs would have the effect of driving all health care prices down. As one observer noted, "President Nixon's spokesmen interpret available studies as justifying the expectation that the HMO strategy will economically and otherwise re-orient the health industry so that its natural forces are compatible with the public's interest" (Flash 1971, 512–13).

Prospectively Gaining Groups Are Diverse

Support for this form of health care delivery came from a wide range of sources, including liberal members of Congress, market-oriented conservatives in the administration, and organized labor, the business community, and insurance companies. The HMO concept gained the active support of nearly all interested health policy groups, with the exception of organized medicine.

The policy leadership in the administration vigorously endorsed this model of government incentives regulation, and Nixon at least initially made HMOs the cornerstone of his new national health strategy ("Changing the System" 1972, 10). Nixon's enthusiasm for HMOs was reflected in his early speeches promoting the initial legislation, which included a goal to have 1,700 HMOs enrolling 40 million peo-

ple by 1976 and to have them available to 90 percent of the population by 1980 (Starr 1983, 396).

In addition, both organized labor and the business community
favored HMO development. Both business firms (e.g., Kaiser) and
labor (e.g., the United Auto Workers in Detroit) had initiated prepayment plans. Business in particular was growing concerned with
the increased health costs in traditional medicine because of the
increased costs of health care benefits for employees (Wolkstein
1970, 714). Insurance carriers also were beginning to become interested in and to invest in this method of financing (Flash 1971, 515).
The business press and the business-sponsored Committee for Economic Development also advocated HMOs (Starr 1983, 396).

Opposition

The AMA opposed giving prepaid group practice plans new competitive advantages over the group's predominantly fee-for-service constituency ("Role" 1971, 953). "In late 1970, the AMA warned President Nixon that emphasis on developing prepaid group practice
would drive doctors out of active practice, inflate costs, and lower
physician productivity" ("Role" 1971, 955). The AMA's counterproposal, Medicredit, only intended to strengthen the dominance of fee-
for-service delivery. In its counterproposal, the AMA proposed no
mechanism to rationalize the market for health care delivery and
included language forbidding any federal control of the practice of
medicine. Havighurst notes, "The AMA's preference for maintaining
the many existing barriers against HMO formation is manifest" (Havighurst 1970, 736).

Experience with Prepaid Group Practice

As in all complex policy areas, the effects of new health care legislation were uncertain prior to implementation. According to Wolkstein, "There is little basis for knowing in advance the effectiveness of
various steps we might take to change the economic and social factors involved in medical care" (1970, 702). The Nixon plan for
restructuring the health care market, however, was purposefully

modeled on existing prepaid group practice plans. Havighurst writes, "The administration's proposals . . . incorporate models of health care delivery organizations that are at least subspecies of HMO, indicating the breadth of the consensus that has embraced this mode of rendering health services" (Havighurst 1970, 716; see also Greenlick 1972, 101; "Changing the System" 1972, 7; Wolkstein 1970, 713). The basic argument of the administration's proposal was that HMOs stood as a viable form of health care delivery and could safely be promoted as an alternative to fee-for-service medicine. Thus, research data on plan enrollments, costs, utilization, and outcomes of current HMOs helped to clarify the likely workings of the Nixon plan if it were implemented.

Given the clear logic embodied in the prepaid group practice organizational form for health care delivery and the demonstrable success of existing programs such as Kaiser-Permanente, HIP, the Group Health Cooperative of Puget Sound, and many others (both in their success as businesses and through statistical studies), the health policy research community reached a near unanimity in endorsing this form as a model for good public policy.[5] Table 20 gives representative quotations.

In addition, the proposals before Congress contained little risk for government policymakers. The Nixon proposal would not entirely supplant the existing fee-for-service forms of practice with organized group practices but instead sought only to promote HMO development. Still, members of Congress have an interest in promoting HMOs if it is known that HMOs will deliver health care efficiently without harming the quality of care in practice. Groups try to speak to this concern in their testimony before the committee.

HMO policy, because of its greater efficiency than fee-for-service delivery, appealed to a wide cross-section of interest groups. In addi-

---

5. The major prepaid group practices in operation at the time were nonprofit plans such as Kaiser Permanente; the Group Health Cooperative of Puget Sound; the Group Health Association of Washington, D.C.; the Community Health Association of Detroit; HIP; various plans at university hospitals such as Harvard and Johns Hopkins; physician-run plans such as the Ross-Loos Medical Group of Los Angeles; medical foundation plans sponsored by county medical societies; and for-profit plans such as Omnicare. For details and evaluations, see Phelan, Erickson, and Fleming 1970; "Role" 1971.

TABLE 20. HMO Policy: Research Community Assessment (as of 1972)

- The development of group practice systems . . . may be the basic solution to what we have called the absence of integration in production, the smoothing of the maze (Berki and Heston 1972, xiv).

- [Prepaid group practice plans] do have strong potential for eliminating many of the abuses and inefficiencies of the current organization of care, for providing greater continuity between preventative and other aspects of care, for moderating patterns of excessive use of hospitals and for facilitating a high level of treatment making optimal use of ancillary assistance and good technical facilities (Mechanic 1972, 5–6).

- [There is] widespread agreement—the medical societies excepted—on the need to steer away from preponderant reliance on fee-for-service medicine toward a system in which consumers, if they wish, may obtain care by prepaying (or having the government pay) the provider. The enthusiasm for this approach has been prompted in large part by the apparent success over a period of time of the prepaid group practice plans which, though existing in only some parts of the nation, now serve around eight million people and have generated some impressive statistics on the per capita cost of providing care of a generally high quality (Havighurst 1970, 720).

- In the early seventies . . . the sense of crisis in health care was accompanied by considerable optimism about the possibilities for successful reform. The record of Kaiser Health Foundation suggested it was possible to provide high quality prepaid health care at 20 to 40 percent lower cost than fee-for-service medicine (Starr 1983, 383).

- Although the way in which physicians are paid probably is the matter over which they will fight hardest, it is likely that prepayment of health services will come to supplant fee-for-service medicine (Mott 1971, 506).

- There was the Kaiser experiment on the West Coast, HIP in New York, something on the order of six or seven million people covered by prepaid group practice arrangements. And it worked! The patients were reasonably satisfied. The quality of services appeared good, at least there were fewer unnecessary operations when audited, lower infant mortality comparatively, and higher quality of inpatient hospital care when studied and evaluated objectively. The cost was far less on average, too, per family, because hospital use was so much less than the average for the United States, which saves a good many dollars (Silver 1971, 1731).

- Skeptics argue that the experience of prepaid group practices is not applicable to the country at large, in part because their membership tends to be characterized by groups representing lower medical risks than some other segments of society. Nonetheless, few proponents claim more than that the HMO concept is a tested alternative to fee-for-service practice that holds promise of helping ease strains on the delivery system ("Changing the System" 1972, 8).

tion, there was a clear consensus in the health policy research literature that HMOs fit well with the basic goals of health care reform: they
held the promise of reducing the cost of health care while maintaining its quality. In the early 1970s, however, the AMA held a rhetorical
advantage in that it could claim its unique capacity to pronounce on
what counts as quality care and appropriate standards of care. This
rhetorical advantage gave the AMA the capacity to interpret the scale
of the benefits from the program in debates before Congress, particularly on the dimension of quality of care. In doing so, they claimed
that the likely benefits from increased participation in the health care
market were small relative to the costs as an empirical matter. In
addition, the AMA testimony attempted to dispute the applicability
of the results of previous studies that compared costs between group
practice and traditional financing, arguing the methodological point
that patients self-select into HMOs and consequently could be
expected to be healthier and cheaper to treat on average, irrespective
of the financing plan. Unfortunately, as the AMA soon discovered, its
era of unquestioned authority in health care politics was on the wane,
and these methodological critiques ultimately did not prevail.

Analysis of 1972 Hearings Testimony

This section analyzes the testimony from the April 12, 1972, hearings
on the Nixon administration bill, H.R. 5615, before the House Subcommittee on Public Health and the Environment.[6] The analysis in
this section has a more limited goal than the analysis found in the
previous two chapters. Rather than an exhaustive accounting of all
groups' claims in testimony, here I offer a simple contrast in the types
of arguments made by the AMA and by all other groups, thereby illustrating the AMA's rhetorical strategy. The AMA's basic public position
was that prepaid group practice was an unproven experiment (Bauman 1976, 136; "Changing the System" 1972, 8; "Coming on Fast"

---

6. All citations in this section are to U.S. House of Representatives, Interstate and
Foreign Commerce Committee, Subcommittee on Public Health and the Environ-
ment, *Hearings on H.R. 5615 and H.R. 11728, Bills to Amend the Public Health Service
Act to Promote Assistance and Encouragement for the Establishment and Expansion of
Health Maintenance Organizations, and for Other Purposes,* April and May 1972.

1973, 54), despite the preponderance of the evidence in support of the program and despite health policy researchers' consensus to the contrary. Established professional organizations can have an authority in politics to reinterpret the available evidence using alternative methodologies to support a line of attack. To demonstrate this phenomenon, I show the extent to which all other groups carefully support their arguments with accurate evaluation data and careful interpretations and compare these efforts to the counterarguments made by the AMA. This contrast illustrates debate under a form of ambiguity that arises when advocates can locate and use competing expectations, and in particular expectations that come from alternative methodological approaches.

Prospectively Gaining Groups

The supporters of the HMO proposal reiterated the logic of the program model, marshaled facts and data in support of the logic, and extensively cited the published evaluation literature to construct instrumental arguments on behalf of the program.

Consistent with the available literature, lobbyists speaking in favor of HMOs clearly state that there is sufficient evidence to support the concept of HMOs as national policy. The lobbyist for the American Federation of Labor and Congress of Industrial Organizations (AFL-CIO) argues that "our experience has demonstrated to us that HMOs can provide better quality medical care at lower cost than the fragmented fee-for-service system" (AFL-CIO 648). Lobbyists speaking on behalf of the HMO concept outline the basic logic of the policy model, noting the origins of efficiencies that will arise. Dr. Edward Saward, the lobbyist for the Group Health Association of America (GHAA), the trade association for group practices and an obvious constituency for HMO promotion, forcefully argues that HMOs by this time had a long track record of proven success.[7]

---

7. Representatives from GHAA argued against several provisions in the administration bill. First, the community-rating requirement put HMOs at a competitive disadvantage with insurance plans that used experience ratings. Second, required services should not be so comprehensive as to price HMOs out of the insurance market. Third, a requirement for community involvement could make the beginnings of

WILLIAM ROY [D-CO]: Some have said that the HMO is not a proven concept. I think you have testified that at least the non-profit HMO is a proven concept. Is that correct, Dr. Saward?

SAWARD: There is no question, in my opinion, that . . . prepaid group practice on a nonprofit basis . . . is a proven concept and proven many years ago. . . . I also believe that the decentralized form of HMO in the medical foundations, again of which there is no single one kind, but there are many kinds of that medical foundation movement, are successful HMOs as well. (GHAA 201)

Likewise, the GHAA representative from the Group Health Cooperative of Puget Sound testifies,

This year our program . . . celebrates its 25th anniversary. It has survived the baptism in a medical community in the late 1940's and early 1950's which tried in every way possible to kill the organization. It has competed with the very best plans that are available in the area. It has hardened itself and it has grown and prospered. It is not a test tube baby. It has survived and prospered because it offers care and efficiency in a competitive environment. (GHAA 208; see also testimony from HIP 201, and GHAA 225).

The full set of arguments in the GHAA's testimony exactly follows the analytical social efficiency logic for HMOs found in the health policy literature (e.g., Havighurst 1970, 1971). All of the GHAA's arguments closely parallel claims empirically well established in the health policy literature. For example, the GHAA argues that HMOs have incentives to minimize costs because they bear the full cost of care under capitation payments. "Full-time hospital based medical groups functioning on a budgetary basis have every motivation to use ancillary personnel wherever possible. Manpower savings are, therefore, substantial" (GHAA 183). Consistent with the health policy literature on prepaid group practices, the GHAA argues that HMOs have incentives not to overprovide care. "If insurance coverage is

---

non-community-sponsored plans too turbulent. Finally, a thirty-day unrestricted enrollment period, beyond the basic dual-choice provision, created an adverse selection unless traditional insurance was also held to the requirement (see, e.g., GHAA 184–85).

comprehensive and a capitation or other budgetary method is used to pay for services, the less expansive, most effective services can be and usually will be used" (GHAA 183). At the same time, HMOs have incentives not to underprovide care since they must pay claims for more expensive treatment sought elsewhere and are vulnerable to malpractice suits, and any harm to the group's public image can lead to lost membership. "Poor quality of care in our experience is the most expensive item we can provide. On the other hand, good quality of care is the least expensive" (GHAA 206).

Saward even quells a moment of levity in the hearing by invoking the scientific authority of the research on which his testimony is based:

PETER KYROS [D-ME]: There has been talk, I understand, about using physicians' assistants to expand physician productivity.

SAWARD: I would like to respond in regard . . . to the nurse-mid-wife. The experience we have had in Portland in the past 18 months with registered midwives is that of 600 people consecutively asked at the appointment center, new obstetrical cases wishing to be seen for the first time, 340 have chosen the nurse midwife, out of 600, which has been somewhat deflating to the obstetrician.

WILLIAM ROY [D-CO]: I cannot help but comment we wiped out gynecological surgery and obstetrics in one fell swoop.

SAWARD: This is reported in this month's *Journal of the American Public Health Association*. (GHAA 311)

Unlike the AMA, the groups that support the HMO concept—such as nurses, group health practitioners, labor unions, and insurance companies—lack the rhetorical capacity to interpret or place a scale on the relative costs and benefits of health care reform. Consequently, supporters carefully state their arguments in a scientifically accurate manner, noting issues of research design and limits of the available scientific knowledge. These groups make literal use of the evaluation literature because they do not have a plausible rhetorical capacity to reinterpret findings to support their position. Their instrumental arguments parallel and accurately restate the findings in the policy literature regarding cost and quality comparisons, along with HMOs' demonstrated ability to serve diverse populations.

Cost Comparisons with Fee-for-Service Financed Care

Cost was a particularly important outcome dimension at the hearing, given that steeply rising costs constituted the basic precipitating factor of the 1970s health care crisis and led to the urgency behind the corresponding crush of legislation. The research available at the time documented the cost-efficiencies of HMOs. For example, one study found that for similar packages of services, the Group Health Cooperative of Puget Sound charged approximately two-thirds as much as insurance carriers in the nation as a whole ("Role" 1971, 922). The Kaiser-Permanente Program in Oakland, California, which enrolled more than 2.5 million members, increased rates 19.1 percent between 1960 and 1965, compared to 43.5 percent in the nation as a whole ("Coming on Fast" 1973, 54). Greenlick cites a study showing that Kaiser-Portland had a physician/population ratio of about 1/1,300 compared to the national average of about 1/750–800 people (1972, 112). In sum, "the data are fairly consistent in indicating that prepaid group practice plans have been able to supply care for substantially less dollar outlay than has the predominant fee-for-service system" ("Role" 1971, 921; see also Greenlick 1972, 110).

Testimony by the bill's supporters closely reflects these themes regarding costs and the effective use of health care personnel. The GHAA lobbyist states, "While increases in the cost per day in Kaiser Foundation hospitals have paralleled increases in community hospitals generally, the lowered utilization of the health plan members has meant that the costs of hospitalization for a member per year has increased only about half as fast as the public at large" (GHAA 183). The AFL-CIO lobbyist testifies, "Prepaid group practice plans require on the average 1.7 hospital beds per 1,000 subscribers. The national standard under Hill-Burton is about four beds per 1,000" (AFL-CIO 648). Regarding the effective use of staffing, the AFL-CIO lobbyist asserts, "The Kaiser Portland plan operates on the basis of one full-time physician for every 1,500 persons, compared with a national ratio of one patient-seeing physician for every 700 persons. If this ratio of physicians could be applied to the country as a whole with a proper distribution of physicians, there would be too many, not too few, patient-seeing doctors" (AFL-CIO 648).

Of course, the administration bill did not intend simply to foster cost-effective HMOs but more importantly to engender reform in the market for health care through competition with these cost-effective delivery organizations. The available research evidence suggested that the market for health care indeed responds to competition whenever it occurred. "The very first foundation plan was established in response to rumors that Kaiser would enter the San Joaquin Valley. . . . The state of California has been blanketed by foundation plans in all areas where Kaiser has not yet expanded" ("Role" 1971, 920 n.121). On this point, a union representative marshals empirical evidence to show some empirical support for the causal logic behind the assertion that HMOs can favorably affect health care market incentives.

JAMES SYMINGTON [D-MO]: What do you think will prove to serve as the major stimulus to efficient performance, or what I might call the lack of feather hospital bedding, as it were?

RICHARD SHOEMAKER [AFL-CIO]: I don't think there is any question that the development of prepaid group practice stimulates competition in any community with regard to the delivery of health care both in terms of quality and in terms of price. I think if Dr. Harrington, for example, from the San Joaquin Medical Foundation has testified before this committee, he frankly admits that the reason that the San Joaquin Medical Foundation got off the ground is because they are afraid of Kaiser coming in there and thought they had better do something about controlling quality and costs or otherwise they would find themselves in competition.

It is a direct kind of competition. Historically you find that the medical foundations follow prepaid group practice. When Kaiser went to Hawaii, a medical foundation followed creating a competition which I think is healthy to both. I am quite sure that in the communities that prepaid group practice exists, I think the cost of medical care outside the prepaid group practice also tends to be held in line. (AFL-CIO 657–58)

Quality of Care

It is often noted in health services research that health outcomes are difficult to measure, consumer evaluation is unreliable, physician evaluation is subjective, and comparative mortality and morbidity statistics are crude. In general, however, by the available outcome

measures, the research community found that "prepaid group practice plans supply good medical care" ("Role" 1971, 927–28). One
study showed that HIP has a slight but statistically significant lower
prenatal mortality rate than average (Neuhauser and Turcotte 1972,
60). Greenlick cites studies showing reduced rates of surgery among
prepaid group practice physicians and increases in the use of preventative services (1972, 105). "It can only be said that the population
using medical care services in [prepaid group practice plans] with a
hospital base between two and three beds per 1,000 does not appear
to be any less healthy, or appear to have any higher mortality rates,
than do populations receiving hospital care in a system using 4.5 hospital beds per 1,000" (Greenlick 1972, 112).

Lobbyists' testimony at the hearing reflects these findings. The following exchange is illustrative.

PAUL ROGERS [D-FL]: Do your studies show that the people in
    your plan are in better health than those outside of your plan?
JOHN SMILLIE [GHAA-Kaiser]: We are just beginning to collect
    that information. We have some information on infant mortality
    in that program. We have a favorable infant mortality when com-
    pared with that of the community.
ROGERS: About how does it compare; do you recall?
SMILLIE: Our infant mortality ranges from 10 to 13 per thousand
    live births. It is usually about 15 to 20 deaths to 1,000 live births
    in the community. So we have a favorable track record in that
    area. (GHAA 242)

The careful use of data in an argument is well illustrated in this
exchange. Here the member solicits a factual response from the lobbyist, and the lobbyist very carefully avoids overstating what the data
show.

Ability to Serve Diverse Populations

The available research evidence also suggested that the government
would be able to supply care to the elderly and poor through HMOs.
"Prepaid group practice has been able to acquire and retain Medicare
enrollees despite the fact that the elderly have only a limited cost savings incentive to join such plans" ("Role" 1971, 990). The Social

Security Administration reported in 1968 that Medicare costs per beneficiary in the Group Health Cooperative were $209.96 less than the national average ("Role" 1971, 990). In addition, in the late 1960s HEW sponsored demonstration research programs at HIP and Kaiser of Oregon, among others, to test the whether group practice plans could incorporate the poor into the service population (see Coburn 1973, 32–33; Greenlick 1972, 109; Phelan, Erickson, and Fleming 1970, 810). Shragg et al. describe the 1968 Southern California Kaiser study and give the statistical results, finding that "the hypothesis that this particular low-income group, after an initial adjustment to the Kaiser-Permanente medical care system, would utilize services in a manner similar to that of regularly enrolled Health Plan members is substantially supported" (1973, 59).

In this vein, the lobbyist from HIP testifies, "We are rather proud of the fact that in HIP in New York, through arrangements with the department of social services for medicaid, and with social security for medicare, we have a population that breaks down roughly on economics, on age, on sex and race, that very closely parallel the whole city's population—11 percent over 65 in contrast with the city's 10 percent" (HIP 203).[8]

Opposition: The AMA

The published evaluation research notwithstanding, the AMA argues that this information is not sufficient to warrant legislation at the time.[9] The lead AMA lobbyist, Dr. John Kernodle, states, "What disturbs us is the prospect of a headlong rush into a large scale HMO program *without hard evidence* that it would fulfill the anticipated hopes" (AMA 334). He went on to state:

---

8. The HIP lobbyist was arguing against the inclusion of a requirement that 40 percent of plan members come from underserved areas. Pro-HMO lobbyists also argued that this provision would make start-up difficult for most plans and that experience shows that prepaid group practice plans become more representative over time.

9. Short of killing HMO legislation, the AMA wants to ensure that medical foundations, organized by local medical societies on a fee-for-service basis, will be included in the HMO definition.

Conceivably the HMO could solve some of our problems. But that is *not yet proven.* HMOs could represent a giant step backwards to a type of contract medicine the public rejected half a century ago. . . .

All I am saying is that we should first gain experience with test models and see if they fly before we order a whole fleet. (AMA 337; emphasis added)

Kernodle and the AMA's other lobbyist, Dr. Russel Roth, testify that insufficient information exists to know how HMOs would work in practice and that this information will become available only after the completion of some HMO demonstration programs funded by HEW. Roth argues,

The Federal Government has already made some 110 grants for planning and for feasibility studies for HMOs. But the results of these studies and plans are as yet unknown in terms of the quality and extent of the services which can be provided, their accessibility to beneficiaries, the cost of providing them, and their acceptability to consumers and providers alike. Our flat assertion is that it is unduly hasty and most unwise to propagate by legislation a remedy which has not as yet passed any necessary tests. (AMA 339)[10]

Kernodle concludes his testimony by saying, "Considerable funds have already been allocated for HMOs [in the HEW demonstrations]. What is urgently needed now is a sound, objective mechanism with which to evaluate the *initial efforts.* Rather than new legislation, the need is for thorough, exhaustive evaluation of the projects underway" (AMA 337; emphasis added).

The AMA lobbyists imply that there had been no experience with prepaid group practices prior to the Nixon proposal or prior to the HEW experiments. Why did the AMA believe it could make this kind of testimony credibly?

---

10. Roth's statement adds further uncertainty, pointing out that the issues that remain unresolved include questions about the size of the area that can be covered, problems of access, recruitment of physicians, whether HMOs can cover poor and high-risk populations and compensation for personnel (AMA 340).

Professional Control of Health Care Delivery and Policy

The AMA, representing the established medical profession, in the early 1970s could evoke professional authority to interpret health policy research information in politics to support the group's opposition. Prior to the health crisis of the early 1970s, there was no precedent for federal government involvement in the organization and delivery of health care. Instead, the regulation and control of health delivery was the responsibility of the medical profession itself (see Arrow 1963; Starr 1983). In the general model of professions, professionals have nearly complete control over conditions of work, and the rest of society cedes the profession autonomy from regular market forces and from direct government regulation, since nonprofessionals cannot directly observe the effectiveness of professional practices (Alford 1975, 194). The enduring characteristic of professions is to gain as much control over the market as feasible, not only to raise incomes by limiting competition but also to maximize professional autonomy and stature. A profession claims to hold itself to higher standards than the market otherwise would require and that only its members can judge each other; this judgment is outside of the capacity of nonprofessionals.[11]

Over time, this sort of self-regulation creates a shroud of legitimacy in the political sphere. Absolute control over the definition of the substantive policy area gives organized professions considerable power relative to the state. According to Morone, "The American Medical Association and its constituent state societies used both public and private power to extend the primacy of medical judgment into a professional hegemony over the American health care system" (1995, 182). In Alford's (1975, 195) words, "Physicians have extracted an arbitrary subset from the array of skills and knowledge relevant to the maintenance of health in a population, have successfully defined these as their property to be sold for a price, and have managed to create legal mechanisms which enforce that monopoly and the social beliefs which have mystified the population about the appropriateness and desirability of that monopoly." Organized med-

---

11. In the aggregate, this self-regulation creates a market failure. "The shift from clients to colleagues in the orientation of work, which professionalism demands, represents a clear departure from the normal rule of the market" (Starr 1983, 23).

icine's hegemony over its own organization, according to sociologists of medicine, extends beyond mere expertise almost to a matter of faith. This is reflected in the language found in the health policy literature, excerpts from which appear in table 21.

The language contained in this table suggests the strength of organized medicine's control over its sphere in the early 1970s, since this kind of absolute language would be an exaggeration if applied to other occupations, even to other professions such as law or accounting. Once this hegemony is ceded to the profession, the state has difficulty intervening in the profession's business via regulation. This sort of historical hegemony over professional organization and regulation, evidenced by the enacting of professional ethics into positive law, gave organized medicine a unique interpretive authority in health policy matters at the time. "Legislators and public administrators have thus far taken the expert advice of private health profes-

TABLE 21. Traditional Authority of Medical Profession

- Medicine traditionally has been as much a spiritual as a scientific endeavor. It is not accidental that health and religion are inextricably intertwined in many primitive societies, and even modern medicine has always been a mixture of science, religion and magic (Mechanic 1972, 2).

- Historical considerations . . . have suggested that medical care is a discrete, narrow, and somehow mystical phenomenon (Geiger and Cohen 1971, 34).

- Medicine is becoming a major institution of social control, nudging aside, if not incorporating, the more traditional institutions of religion and law. It is becoming the new repository of truth, the place where absolute and often final judgments are made by supposedly morally neutral and objective experts. And these judgments are made, not in the name of virtue or legitimacy, but in the name of health. Moreover, this is not occurring through the political power physicians hold or can influence, but is largely an insidious and often undramatic phenomenon accomplished by "medicalizing" much of daily living, by making medicine and the labels "healthy" and "ill" *relevant* to an ever increasing part of human existence (Zola 1972, 487).

- Within the health field, and to a considerable degree outside it as well, it has been considered inappropriate for government to interfere with the functioning of private health organizations. To an important degree private agencies have been viewed as performing a public function and often a charitable and religious one as well (Mott 1971, 503).

sionals at face value as serving the public interest" (D. L. Madison 1971, 525). As Havighurst puts it, "The mystique surrounding medical care and the 'physician-patient relation' served to validate the profession's assertions of high ethical and quality standards and led many well-meaning persons into becoming . . . 'dupes of the interests'" (1970, 742).

Because of their unique interpretive authority, organized medicine (at least in the late 1960s and early 1970s) is less constrained than other groups in testifying before Congress. Instead of citing expert authority contained in peer-reviewed published studies, the AMA lobbyists simply evoke their professional norms and standards—the institutional foundations of traditional professional autonomy—to say that the incentives built into HMO financing should indicate the substandard practice of medicine. The AMA, that is, tried to exploit its capacity to lend interpretations to empirical studies to create the appearance of ambiguities in the state of knowledge regarding HMO effectiveness. In particular, the AMA lobbyists evoke their definition of the standards for the good practice of medicine in an attempt to affect the comparison of costs and benefits that come from promoting HMOs. This is best seen in the testimony of the AMA's Dr. Roth:

JAMES HASTINGS [R-NY]: The study in the [HEW] white paper says, "Studies show that hospitalization is significantly reduced in HMO." This, as I understand it, comes from the American Journal of Public Health in November and the Hospital Monograph Clinic and et cetera.

   Is that an inconsistent statement or is it based on some type of information that is not indicative of the real problem?

ROTH: It has never appealed to me *as being valid in the practice of medicine,* as I have been involved in it and have known an awful lot of people involved in it over 30 years, that there is for most physicians a direct monetary compulsion to decide what they do for a patient on the basis of what the effect on their own pocketbook will be.

   If it does, however, I submit that the one mal-motivation is just as bad as the other. To say I am motivated to operate more or do unnecessary work because I am on fee-for-service is an indictment of me. But to tell him that he is equally avaricious and is motivated to do as little as possible so that there would be that much more money left in the kitty that hasn't been given to the hospitals, is equally bad. (AMA 352; emphasis added)

The literature on health policy often carefully noted that the statistical evidence comparing HMOs to traditional medicine was subject to dispute methodologically on several grounds. In particular, the populations enrolled in prepaid group practice generally are not comparable to populations enrolled in fee-for-service because individuals nonrandomly self-select into one or the other financing scheme (Neuhauser and Turcotte 1972, 54). Roth attempts to exploit this methodological ambiguity by arguing that because of self-selection of the HMO population, the research-based statistical evaluations cannot rule out the competing expectation that HMOs deliver poor-quality medicine to otherwise relatively healthy populations. Roth argues that the HMO concept is unproven as means both to reduce cost and to maintain quality because the population HMOs serve tends to have fewer health risks than the population served by traditional medicine. Making comparisons between the two forms of medicine is like comparing apples and oranges. He states,

> If I were to hold forth a new treatment for diabetes or cancer or kidney disease the burden of proof would clearly be upon me to show my evidence of effectiveness and my assurances of freedom from offsetting dangers. In this far broader proposal for a remedy to national deficiencies it should properly be the role of the proponents to show in fact, rather than in theory, that it will work.
>
> Unhappily, unlike most well-tested remedies in medical practice, there is no true body of experience, testing, or experimentation upon which to base judgment of contract practice in an application to our present problems. Kaiser-Permanente has been reasonably successful in providing a substantial share, but by no means all, of medical services for segments of the population which reflect no major element of adverse risk. (AMA 339)

But one study available at the time, the evaluation of the Federal Employees Health Benefits Program (FEHBP), made a relatively compelling comparison between fee-for-service and prepaid group practice populations. One review of the literature notes,

Since the population base for such comparisons is of critical importance in assessing their validity, special interest attaches to experience under the Federal Employees Health Benefits Program. . . . Data for the 1968–70 period indicate that federal employees enrolled in group practices spend fewer than half the number of days in the hospital (per 1,000 persons) than did those with Blue Cross-Blue Shield coverage. ("Changing the System" 1972, 8)

The health policy research community believed the data from the FEHBP study allowed for valid comparisons between the fee-for-service and the prepaid group practice populations for the cost of treatment and that the results were favorable to HMOs.

At the hearing, the bill's sponsor, William Roy, calls attention to the comparability of populations in the FEHBP study. When Roth attempts to misconstrue the methodological point to argue against the research community's assessment that the populations were indeed comparable, Roy calls Roth to task.

Roy: This troubles me. For example, on the Federal Employees Health Benefits Program. Although I think you are aware of these statistics, I think it is worthwhile getting them in the record and getting your comment on them. [List of results from the study favorable to HMOs] They are very significant statistics. . . .

Roth: I would like to say, Dr. Roy, I am sure you recognize you are, in many instances, contrasting or attempting to compare unlike covered populations. There is a selection factor—

Roy: May I interrupt, sir? We are talking about Federal Employees' Health Benefits Programs. They are extremely comparable groups.

Roth: Then I suspect that the problem is to define what is necessary and what is unnecessary and how much of the shift toward the lower utilization is good medicine. I think that is a relative one. (AMA 353)

Here, very clearly, the AMA is trying to use its professionally based rhetorical advantage in saying what defines the proper practice of medicine to call into question the efficacy of HMOs. When he is called to task on the methodological point, Roth falls back on his professional authority to interpret research findings in politics and to construe the relative costs and benefits of the proposed intervention. The AMA's testimony does not match up with the research found in the evaluation literature on HMOs, as evidenced by Roy's remark, but Roth feels that he has the professional capacity to construe the available information to support the AMA's line of attack.

In addition, Roy's comments serve as another useful illustration of how hearings can serve as a means of demonstrating the committee's expertise to a larger audience. The debate about selection and comparability are not meant to appeal directly to constituents, many of whom would not understand the arcane methodological point.

The Other Groups Interpret the Research with Care

In stark contrast to the AMA's style of testimony, HMO supporters carefully frame their presentation in a very literal interpretation of the health policy literature, using care to cite published studies as accurately as possible. For example, GHAA's lead presenter, Saward, reads word-for-word from a paper he published in the *Hospital Tribune* four years earlier, and he explains his reasoning for doing so:

> To be sure I hadn't clouded my vision of what prepaid group practice expected of itself, after all of the discussion there has been of the health maintenance organization in the last two years, I have gone back to a paper before health maintenance organizations came up as a term in medical parlance to be sure that I would not try to add something into it that we hadn't believed to be there. (GHAA 182)

Rhetorically, quoting from a published article serves to frame the GHAA testimony in a research perspective, lending the testimony the authority of peer review and publication.

The representative of the American Nurses' Association, in arguing for the importance of greater use of nurses found in HMOs, was careful to cite a research-based study to support her arguments.[12]

---

12. If there is any doubt that as of 1972 the American Nurses' Association lacked the same type of authority in politics as the AMA, it is laid to rest by the type of questioning the nurses' representative experiences after her research-intensive testimony: none. Instead, members of the committee make only a few patronizing

"One health maintenance organization—Harvard Community Health Plan, Boston, Mass.—reports that of 4,500 visits made to its center, 65 percent were related to upper respiratory problems, minor trauma, muscle pain and need for psychological support. Their experience indicates that 70 percent of these incidents can be handled by the nurse alone without sacrificing quality care and with full patient acceptance and approval" (ANA 865).

These pro-HMO groups carefully discuss research design issues and the limitations of empirical findings in their testimony—two hallmarks of careful, credible presentations of empirical research findings. HMO supporters state scientifically correct methods in their effort to show that HMOs have been shown to deliver on their social efficiency promises. For example, the GHAA representatives show that the comparisons they make using the FEHBP data are in fact based on comparable populations, again in strong contrast to the AMA testimony.

HASTINGS: We start with a premise that HMOs we hope will provide a better system of health care. Second, hopefully we can produce that system at lower cost. I think those are the two legitimate presumptions we make as we talk of HMOs.

In your experience, do you have anything to indicate that you have been able to improve the quality of delivery of health care?

HAROLD NEWMAN [GHAA]: The only way you can compare the program with the population at large is to try to pick out programs where you have a similar population enrolled, and of course the Federal Employees' Health Benefit program is one of those, where we take our risks and draw from the same population pool that the others do.

There is a volume of statistics that are available that are published on that program, because it has been quite thoroughly studied. (GHAA 302–3)

In addition, it was difficult for the evaluation studies to take into account the amount of services prepaid group practice members

---

remarks: for example, Ancher Nelson (R-MN) states, "I want to join with my colleagues in expressing a thank you. My only daughter is a registered nurse, so I'm a little bit partial to any observations that the nurses make. I also want to comment that that radiant smile of yours would cure almost any person. Thank you very much" (ANA 2:868).

sought outside of the system, known as "leakage," which has the effect of understating usage rates and plan expenditures by some amount (Havighurst 1970, 723; "Role" 1971, 905). Saward carefully notes this methodological limitation and speaks directly to the methodological point.

> I think the social security information is useful on medicare. Medicare . . . keeps tapes on the utilization of all its beneficiaries in this regard. So we have a standard that not only measures the utilization in our program but whenever leakage occurs, as well.
>
> The Kaiser program in Portland, Oreg., has a utilization of hospital days for medicare enrollees that has been quite steady at around 1,800 per thousand per annum, in contrast with 4,000 for that same area in hospital days. That is a marked savings. In trying to measure what leakage there is from the program for medicare, which does not bind people in the program, it is about 8 percent for Kaiser Portland medicare recipients, and 8 percent on top of 1,800 is very little compared to 4,000. That is a marked savings. (GHAA 303)

Another hallmark of the careful presentation of research findings is stating the limits of what can be claimed using available data. HMO supporters carefully pointed out that outcomes in health care are particularly difficult to assess, so there is uncertainty in the comparisons in the effectiveness of fee-for-service and HMO forms of delivery. According to the GHAA's Smillie,

> In regard to the practice of trying to assess quality of care . . . we are at a point in the state of the art where it is rather primitive.
>
> My preceding remarks must not indicate we are not interested in assessment of both the process and outcome type. We are conducting experiments in both these areas and we are not satisfied yet that we are anywhere near an answer in terms of assessment of quality. (GHAA 206; see also 209)

Finally, since newly emerging for-profit HMOs would compete under the proposal with the nonprofit GHAA members for federal grants and for market share, the GHAA had strong incentives to claim that the for-profit HMO would fail. As of 1971, however, there were no proprietary HMOs in operation, so the lobbyists say they simply are uncertain about how proprietary HMOs would work (unlike what the AMA claims in error for all prepaid group practices).

HASTINGS: The question was brought up yesterday . . . the possibility of proprietary HMOs. What is your feeling on this?

SAWARD: The prepaid group practice organizations which have existed in the United States, with one exception, Ross-Loos Clinic in Los Angeles in which the physicians own the program, have been non-profit organizations. My feeling about it is that we are embarking on an experiment when we embark on the for-profit HMO, and I think it is generally recognized that that is an experiment, that we have no experiences with it of substance and, therefore, we don't know its outcome. (GHAA 199)

Overall, the pro-HMO lobbyists attend carefully to methodological questions and do not overstate the findings in available research to support their testimony.

Conclusion

This case demonstrates that the raw availability of favorable program information is not sufficient to limit opposition groups' attacks on program content. On some occasions, methodological ambiguities exist, enabling experts to use different methods to confirm competing expectations. The AMA primarily represents fee-for-service physicians and opposed the promotion of prepaid group practice because this organizational form represented an economically competitive threat. At the time of the hearing, considerable research-based evaluation information (primarily from the Kaiser-Permanente groups) existed that showed the cost-effectiveness of prepaid group practice in the private sector, but the AMA took the lobbying stance that even this information was insufficient to promote HMOs on a large scale through legislation. The AMA had traditional authority to regulate health care and consequently felt itself to be in a position to construe the generality of the available examples and statistical studies for the nation's health care. The AMA attempted to exploit methodological ambiguities regarding the outcome scale for quality, since they had a professional capacity to declare what constitutes good quality of care. In addition, they attempted to exploit the ambiguity of the correct population from which inferences regarding the relative cost and quality of HMOs compared to traditional medicine could be drawn. Conversely, groups that lacked this authority and that supported HMOs backed up their claims in testimony with a literal reading of the policy literature.

In the end, however, the true state of knowledge triumphed over the AMA's attempts to mislead the committee under the guise of professional authority. The AMA's arguments attempting to mislead the committee ultimately had limited effect, and its lobbying efforts eventually failed: in 1973 Congress passed the HMO Act.[13] In many ways, this hearing marked the beginning of the end of an era for organized medicine, which discovered that its monopoly on the interpretation of research findings had come to an end.

---

13. P.L. 93-222, which created Title XII of the Public Health Service Act and established the Federal Health Maintenance Organization Program.

9

Discussion of the Cases

The amended Becker model in chapter 3 shows that interest groups often but not always pressure Congress to enact expert-informed, socially efficient policies and that these groups do so out of self-interest. In this sense, the amended Becker model provides a positive explanation for the use of expert, socially efficient policy ideas in politics. But this is at best only a partial explanation: Congress as an institution of government does not simply do what interest groups instruct. There would be good reason to believe that Congress has this sort of total dependence on interest groups if, for example, there were only one powerful interest group per policy topic, as in a subgovernment. Instead, on all significant policy topics—and even insignificant ones—a great many active groups, each with unique interests, seek to pressure Congress. In relation to interest groups, the problem for Congress is not dependence but complexity, or how to solve problems of multidimensional cycling and persistent conflict among active, informed, and effective interest groups in the issue network.

While complexity and conflict among groups can make life difficult for legislators, complexity also contains the potential solution to cycling through better and more optimal public policies. In particular, Congress has strong incentives to capitalize on socially efficient policy ideas as a way of creating new opportunities to reach social goals, thereby benefiting both interest groups and citizens. Many interest groups care about the real-world outcomes of policies, and among these groups, a socially efficient policy can be expected to create more benefits than harms. If these benefits from greater efficiency are spread wide enough among the active interest groups, efficiency itself can be a solution to cycling problems among interest groups. At the same time, citizens will value the new opportunities and improved means to reach important social goals. As Shapiro puts it, efficiency serves "as a kind of objective, exterior, and substantive measure of the goodness of policy; at least it tells us that whatever deliberation reveals to be good ought to be achieved at the lowest possible cost" (1995, 11).

To benefit citizens and groups, Congress has strong incentives to enact socially efficient policies. Congress can use its agenda-setting authority to solve pressing policy problems that matter to interest groups and to citizens, and this authority gives Congress autonomy from interest groups. But this autonomy is not complete and is potentially something of a house of cards because Congress wants to develop and enact only those innovative policies that are likely to succeed. Congress does not want to be associated with failed or disastrous policies and other unsavory unintended consequences. For example, Congress would like to be known for devising creative solutions for pressing problems involving the environment, education, and health care but does not want to be responsible for environmental disasters, destroying public school systems, or worsening health care, all at higher costs.

The central question in the political economy of expertise, then, is when does Congress have sufficient information and thus the capacity to enact expert, socially efficient policies? More generally, when do policy research ideas and analysis matter in lobbying politics and in the legislative process?

It is relatively easy for Congress to know about the expected outcomes of policies; indeed, the expectations for the policies often are stated in the alternatives themselves. A voucher system should create more effective schools, HMOs should drive down the cost of health care, and so on. But it is relatively difficult for Congress to anticipate how policies will work in practice. To correctly anticipate the likely effects of a policy, one would need to know the informational properties of the policy's causal framework—what I call the state of knowledge—such as the degree of uncertainty or ambiguity. Congress needs to know about the state of knowledge to make correct decisions and to avoid disasters because it cannot see perfectly into the future and know the consequences of its actions.

For their part, interest groups tend to develop the capacity to learn the specialized expertise regarding their policy concerns, and they often know at this expert level of analysis how policies are likely to impact their organizations' core interests. That is, an environmental group will know much better than Congress whether a policy will in fact clean the air, and a trade association will know whether a policy will raise the incomes of member firms. Interest groups have private information regarding the state of knowledge that Congress would like to learn to exercise its authority. In this sense, Congress depends on interest groups to learn about the effects of policies.

Whether Congress can govern effectively through the use of innovative, socially efficient policy depends on whether it can learn useful information about the state of knowledge from interest groups. To communicate the state of knowledge to Congress, lobbyists make research-based, "instrumental" arguments regarding the properties of the causal framework itself and the prospects for success or failure or intended and unintended consequences. These are positive or falsifiable statements regarding the internal logic of the policy and the likelihood that the policy will work in practice as stated in theory. Unfortunately, interest groups might strategically exploit this dependency and make instrumental arguments that are false or misleading for private gains. And of course, interest groups are not angels; they can make instrumental arguments strategically or insincerely.

Fortuitously for Congress, interest groups often—but not always—want to enact public policies that are likely to succeed and to avoid policies that are likely to fail. As the amended Becker model of chapter 3 shows, groups' intrinsic motivation to endorse innovative policies depends on the state of knowledge regarding the causal framework. In particular, groups that might expect to benefit from a socially efficient policy will withhold their support for the policy if there is too much uncertainty or ambiguity. This is true even if they can expect to benefit from the policy, because uncertainty and ambiguity diminish the value of a prospective gain. If a group could expect to benefit from improved efficiency, it also has a strong interest in having the policy work well in practice. In this case, many interest groups have no private interest in misleading Congress into enacting bad public policy. This fortuitous circumstance makes informative debate possible, at least on occasion.

It is nearly always the case, however, that for private reasons, some groups will favor a policy that has a high chance of creating disaster for other groups and inefficiencies for society as a whole or oppose a policy that has a good chance of making other groups and society better off. Again, fortunately for Congress, the incentives and constraints that are inherent in the adversarial nature of public debate help to reveal useful information even when groups seek to be disingenuous. Using the amended Becker model of interest group pressure, chapter 4 shows that the state of knowledge advantages one side or the other in lobbying politics. It is relatively costly to argue against the available research (e.g., to fabricate new favorable research), and such efforts often do not withstand the rigors of adversarial debate. At the same time, it is relatively cheap and more persuasive and compelling to argue on the basis of the available published and received research. If the research shows the policy is likely to be a failure or entails too much risk and uncertainty, opponents can demonstrate this relatively easily with compelling evidence-based arguments. Similarly, if the research shows that the policy is likely to succeed, supporters can demonstrate this relatively easily with compelling research-based evidence. In effect, a group with a position that is not supported by the available research will not have persuasive instrumental arguments available that will withstand the rigors of debate; such a group will be constrained to make noncausal opinion-based normative arguments.

Taken together, interest group motivations as well as groups' capacity to make instrumental arguments to advance their private interests are correlated with the state of knowledge. As chapter 4 shows, groups' interest and ability to make effective instrumental arguments to support their position depend on the informational properties of the causal framework—in particular, the degree of uncertainty and ambiguity. This argument yields three predictions for when Congress can learn about the current state of knowledge from the instrumental arguments of groups.

Certainty: supporters make instrumental arguments to indicate the likely success of the program, and opponents do not counter these arguments with instrumental arguments; Congress learns that the policy is likely to be effective from this informative separating equilibrium.

234 ~ THE POLITICAL ECONOMY OF EXPERTISE

Uncertainty: Opponents make instrumental arguments to indicate that the policy risks failure, and supporters do not counter these arguments with instrumental arguments; Congress learns that the policy is too risky to try from this informative separating equilibrium.

Ambiguity: Both sides of the debate make instrumental arguments (often, pro and con partial truths), so debate simply muddies the waters for Congress, an uninformative pooling equilibrium. Groups with extrinsic preferences over the full set of outcomes will remain ambivalent.

The case studies illustrate how debate under each of these conditions looks in practice. The policies of emissions trading, school choice, and HMO promotion share a very similar causal mechanism—namely, decentralization coupled with a market mechanism to create private incentives for the regulated entities to conform to socially desired goals. These market-oriented policies promise to create new opportunities to meet social goals through greater efficiency than in the absence of a market or than in command-and-control regulation. Even though these policies share these similarities in content, they have very different patterns of debate in congressional committee hearings. In each case, the pattern of debate is explained by the predictions appropriate to the state of knowledge for each policy and each case.

~

Acid rain (1989). With the rise of acid rain as a salient political issue in the 1980s, Congress felt the need to reduce sulfur dioxide emissions, a main precursor to acid rain. Using the command-and-control regulatory framework of the original Clean Air Act, Congress simply could not find a winning coalition among environmentalists, electric utilities, and high-sulfur coal producers to achieve these reductions. In this case, Congress chose to experiment with a sophisticated emissions trading program as a means to reduce sulfur dioxide emissions and to solve the cycling problem among the major interest groups. By the late 1980s, the EPA's prior smaller-scale experiments with emissions trading had produced a considerable amount of evidence regarding their effectiveness as a means to achieve reductions at lesser cost than under command-and-control regulations. As expected, the debate in this case conforms to the certainty predictions, where supporters such as electric utilities, consumer groups, and environmentalists could effectively use instrumental arguments and their opponents could not. Supporters not only argued for the program's effectiveness but also devoted much of their testimony to suggesting ways to refine and improve the program's design. In contrast, the United Mine Workers in effect conceded that the program would work well and focused only on the future plight of high-sulfur coal miners. Drawing on the analogy to statistical thinking, since the state of knowledge showed that there was strong and compelling evidence that the emissions trading program would likely deliver on its promises of cleaning the air at lesser cost, supporters could easily reject the null hypothesis that the policy entailed too many risks for failure.

~

School choice (1991).   The publication of the National Commission on Excellence in Education's *A Nation at Risk* served as a wake-up call for many states and localities to better attend to the quality and effectiveness of public schools. The reforms from this initial effort at the state and local level, however, did not seem to make any headway. At the request of George H. W. Bush's administration, Congress held hearings on the use of a school-choice voucher program as a means to promote effective public schools. At the time, voucher programs simply had not been tried, much less evaluated, and so there existed an informational vacuum on the effectiveness of vouchers as a mechanism for school reform. Again as expected, the debate here conformed to the uncertainty predictions, where opponents such as teachers' unions and school board organizations were advantaged over the supporters, the U.S. Catholic Conference. The opponents argued forcefully and effectively that a school voucher program was too risky to try, an argument that the conference did not contradict. Instead, the group focused its testimony on the normative value of choice in American culture. Sticking with the statistical metaphor, because there was essentially no evidence that the program would work in practice and make systemwide improvements in public education, supporters had difficulty rejecting the null hypothesis that the policy entailed too many risks.

～

School choice (2001). The 1990s witnessed some local-level experiments with school-voucher programs, most notably in Milwaukee, Wisconsin, and education policy researchers carefully analyzed the performance data produced by these experiments, coming up with contradictory expectations regarding the meaning of the data. One set of experts held up demonstrable improvements in student test scores to indicate the program's success, while another set argued that the improvements among the few students who participated in the program indicated that voucher programs endangered the school system as a whole. Here, the debate conformed to the ambiguity predictions, since the expert community held contradictory expectations regarding the likely effectiveness of the school-choice voucher program, and both sides of the debate mobilized research findings to support their position. Furthermore, groups with extrinsic preferences regarding outcomes, such as national business organizations, were simply ambivalent and withheld their support from school choice. Continuing with the statistics metaphor, it is often the case that data are overdetermined or that several theories may be compatible with a given set of findings. In this case, with contradictory expectations, it is possible that the voucher program would improve student test scores and worsen the school system as a whole, but it was simply hard to tell.

～

HMOs (1972). When Congress enacted the Medicare and Medicaid programs in 1965, it placed the high cost of health care and the inefficiencies in the market for health care services on the government's agenda for the first time. The market at the time was dominated by fee-for-service physicians who were reimbursed through third-party insurance, a form of financing that created no incentives

for health care providers to economize on costs. The Nixon administration proposed to rationalize the market for health care delivery by
fostering the growth of highly efficient prepaid group practices,
which came to be called health maintenance organizations (HMOS).
The Nixon proposal was carefully modeled on existing HMOS, which
by the early 1970s had a long track record as an organizational form
for health care delivery and which had been exhaustively studied by
the health policy research community. A growing literature showed
that HMOS performed well compared traditional medicine and could
deliver a high quality of care to a diverse population at lower cost.
The American Medical Association (AMA) was not favorably inclined
toward the administration's idea of fostering the growth of these economic competitors, however, and in the hearings attempted to use
professional authority and expertise to argue that HMOS did not conform to established good medical practices. Furthermore, the AMA
attempted to use a methodological argument that the populations
HMOS serve are self-selected and consequently are healthier and
cheaper to treat than the population served by traditional medicine.
The debate in this case again conforms to the ambiguity predictions,
but this time because the AMA used its specialized expertise in interpreting health care findings to offer a set of competing expectations
at the methodological level and thus countered the HMO supporters
with attempts at instrumental arguments. To complete the statistical
metaphor, experts often disagree about the appropriate methods to
apply to a given set of data, and different methods often can yield different results, none of which rule out competing expectations.

~

Outcomes: The effects of government interventions. Taking the cases
together, it could be argued that Congress's failure to enact an analytically based expert proposal does not in and of itself indicate the
failure of expertise. The flip side of expertise is recognizing policies
that are too risky to try or that engender possible unintended consequences such as policy failure or other surprises. If society prefers to
enact policies that are likely to work and not to enact policies that are
risky or that could have undesired and unintended consequences,

then one can argue that all three cases were decided consistent with the public interest according to the available state of knowledge. Two of the policies have been enacted (emissions trading for acid rain and HMOs) and one has not (the school-choice voucher program).

The emissions trading program in practice has been a remarkable success in reducing sulfur dioxide emissions at lower cost. As of 2001, the program had created an extensive market for allowances, covering nearly 2,300 emissions points at 1,000 separate plants, and sulfur dioxide emissions had been reduced by 6.5 million tons from 1980 levels, a 38 percent reduction (*Clearing the Air* 2002). The Environmental Protection Agency (EPA) projects that these changes will "prevent thousands of premature deaths, and the annual human health benefits in 2010 will exceed $50 billion." In their evaluation of the emissions trading program for acid rain, Schmalensee and his colleagues (1998) found that the Title IV program dramatically reduced sulfur dioxide emissions relative to the command-and-control baseline; that trading in the market for allowances was vigorous; that the price for allowances quickly equilibrated to the marginal cost of control; that the program reduced control costs for the regulated electric utilities by 25 percent to 34 percent; and that the market has driven new innovations in control technology. In the 1990s, scrubber costs dropped by 40 percent, and the devices have become efficient.

In sum, the Title IV program has been quite a success. As the EPA asserts, "The Acid Rain Program has enjoyed an unusually high level of emissions reductions and near-perfect compliance. . . . The success of the Acid Rain Program has spurred the development of numerous cap-and-trade programs based on this model, from the regional to the international level" (*Clearing the Air* 2002, 9). This successful outcome really is no surprise and should be no surprise to participants in the original debate, given the firm empirical foundation for the program prior to enactment.

It can also be argued that the HMO policy has been successful in reducing health care costs. Without question, HMOs are now a part of the everyday landscape in an administered market for health care called managed care, and there also is no question that health care costs would be much higher had the market retained the fee-for-service financing. And while the current number of uninsured is too high, around 14 percent, this number also would be much higher if not for the takeover of managed care. These effects, however, are not necessarily and certainly not fully attributable to the Nixon initiative; by the end of the 1970s, fewer than 10 million people were enrolled in HMOs of any type (Wilkerson, Devers, and Given 1997, 5). Much of the transformation was driven by the purchasing strategies of employers in the 1980s and 1990s, as businesses became increasingly concerned with the cost of providing health benefits. The result has been a near sea change in the delivery of health care: managed care dominates the market, and insurers provide a variety of products such as traditional staff-model HMOs, preferred provider organizations, physician network plans, and provider-sponsored organizations. As a result of these changes, by the mid-1990s health care costs stabilized (Wilkerson, Devers, and Given 1997, 6). Unfortunately, this stability was short-lived; managed care rates currently are returning to the traditional high rates of premium increases, which, coupled with stringent gatekeeping practices, have engendered a managed-care backlash (Dudley and Luft 2001; Mechanic 2001; Robinson 2001). This may portend yet another round of structural reform.

The school-choice voucher program continues its pattern of emerging and then vanishing from Congress's agenda. Most recently, the George W. Bush administration proposed setting aside federal money to fund grants for voucher programs in selected cities. When the mayor of Washington, D.C., announced his receptiveness to accepting the grant money, the city council reacted in disbelief (Strauss 2003; Timberg 2003). Yet the state of knowledge regarding vouchers is no less ambiguous. The Government Accounting Office recently released a report stating that in its review of the research on the Milwaukee and Cleveland programs, there were no definitive research findings indicating that the program raised participants' test scores ("GAO: Voucher Effectiveness Unclear" 2001). Paul Peterson and his partner, Mathematica Research, disagree about the findings of a recent randomized experiment in New York City, where including missing data causes the positive effects on test results to disappear (Winerip 2003). At this writing, the prospects of a national-level school-choice voucher program are at best unclear.

～

Alternative explanations.   The cases in many ways are comparable and so hold constant many important factors that also might explain the pattern of debate across the four topics. In particular, the case studies examine substantively similar policies where the government seeks to establish a market to reach important social goals. In addition, in each hearing the committee considers whether to enact a new policy rather than reauthorize an existing policy, so all of the debates are at the same stage of policy development. By their method, however, the case studies can only illustrate the effects of two the explanatory variables—uncertainty and ambiguity in the causal framework—on the debates. I do not intend to posit a two-variable explanation of politics, and the cases by their method cannot control for the multiple determinants of political debate.

Indeed, there may be other explanations for the pattern of debate in each case that coincide with the state of knowledge, raising the possibility of spurious attribution. For example, there was a sense of inevitability that some acid rain legislation was going to be enacted in the first Bush term, and so perhaps groups in that case felt it best to roll up their shirtsleeves to solve the technical details of the program. Or perhaps school-choice supporters are more comfortable making normative arguments to Democrats, who favor equity and other fairness arguments, and instrumental arguments to Republicans, who tend to worry more about aggregate wealth. Perhaps the AMA felt it could make methodologically incorrect arguments in testimony not because of its professional stature but because at the time it was a politically powerful peak association and very well organized in congressional districts. And finally, for all cases, perhaps lobbyists chose to use or not to use technical expertise to strategically limit or expand participation among nonexperts and attention in the media (see Baumgartner 1989).

In addition, there are counterexplanations based on politics for why the state of knowledge in the acid rain case was believed to be relatively certain and the school voucher and HMO policies were seen as uncertain or ambiguous. In this argument, the state of knowledge is simply an intermediary variable, itself driven by political variables. In the acid rain case, there was a long record of experience at the federal level in regulating emissions. In this case, the major players simply had more available evidence and were more familiar with how the policy operated than in the school-choice and HMO cases, which involved areas where the federal government had had little prior involvement. There also may be a "political" explanation for why experts reached a consensus regarding the benefits of emissions trading, particularly in contrast to the school-choice case. Here, the argument is that economists by their training have an unquestioned belief in the benefits of markets, and economists happened to dominate the evaluations of the EPA emissions trading experiments. Perhaps no similar consensus exists among education and health policy researchers. Education researchers in particular prioritize equity issues, seen in the research interest in efforts to mainstream underachieving students and to integrate public schools. To many of these researchers, market concepts are anathema, since markets inevitably create winners and losers and increase inequalities.

I readily concede that I cannot rule out these and other potential counterexplanations for my results in my qualitative case studies. The cases do reject the strongest claims of the existing literature on positive political economy—particularly the strong claims that the democratic process itself, through its structural features, rejects innovative and efficient policies. In addition, the cases demonstrate the plausibility of my approach, a first and necessary step prior to conducting large-scale systematic research. Finally, future research may well uncover another internally coherent explanation for the role of expertise and policy ideas in politics, perhaps one that does not rely on interest groups in any way. I seek to place a plausible explanation for the use of expertise in legislative politics on the table in hopes of leveraging further research and discussion on this otherwise badly neglected topic.

10

$\sim$

The Political Economy of Expertise

Why Expertise Matters in Lobbying Politics

Some observers—especially those without formal statistical training—may find the state of knowledge for a policy, as I define it, to be an abstract or nebulous concept. But to say that interest groups and legislators care about the consequences of governmental interventions is to say that these political actors care about causality; if they care about how policies work in the real world, they must care about the hypothetical links between a policy alternative and real-world outcomes. These interest group preferences can only be a function of the expert-defined causal framework. And in turn, to say political actors care about these hypothetical causal links between policy and outcome is to say they care about the state of knowledge of how much we know about these links as an empirical matter. Preferences, therefore, are additionally a function of the state of knowledge that describes the causal framework, or what I call the research-based informational properties of the causal framework, such as uncertainty and ambiguity. The policy problem for political actors is not simply to find a new means to desired ends, which alone is difficult enough, but to know the intrinsic quality of the means themselves.

For all involved, lobbyist and legislator alike, the consequences of government action on complex policy problems often are difficult to foresee. This is because people are boundedly rational, and as a consequence, on complex policies one must be very well informed even to know one's interest or preferences across a set of policy proposals. Even if they are not consciously aware of it, since they are boundedly rational, political actors must make inferences about the future effects of policies. Causal inferences inevitably have uncertainty attached to them and often are subject to conceptual and methodological ambiguities. The properties of uncertainty and ambiguity are inherent to some degree in even the best assessments of policy impacts and as concepts are fundamental to any conceivable causal epistemology. If a policy has too much uncertainty, political actors will feel it is too risky to try. And if the causal relationships themselves are ambiguous, the policy could simply increase divisiveness and lead to unintended and undesirable consequences.

While the idea that expertise of this sophisticated nature is central to contemporary politics may surprise some observers, if interest groups and politicians care about policy outcomes, they have no choice but to concern themselves with the state of knowledge about public policies. As Salisbury puts it,

> In today's world of complex, interdependent interests and policies, it is often quite unclear what the "true interests" of a group or an institution may be. The policy that will be maximally advantageous to an association often cannot even be framed without prolonged and searching analysis involving extensive discussion among those who are knowledgeable about both the technical substance of the issues and the feasibilities of the relevant policy situation. (1990, 225)

These aspects of policies—policy ideas and the likely effectiveness of the innovative ideas—often are defined and informed by experts and policy research. Experts propose the sophisticated causal mechanisms that may yield social efficiency, and they conduct empirical research on the most effective way to construct these interventions. Consequently, the preferences and decisions of both Congress and interest groups depend heavily on expertise and the research-based state of knowledge. As a result, research-based analytical ideas and empirical evidence matter in lobbying politics.

The observed constraints on instrumental arguments in the debates, particularly those in the acid rain and the first school-choice cases, lend strong evidence to the claim that the state of knowledge itself is exogenous to the political process. By the division of labor in

American society, the state of knowledge for any policy alternative is socially constructed through peer review and other collegial processes in the expert research community rather than through political processes involving administrative agencies, peak associations, or committee staff. Skocpol (1987, 44–45) notes that "American social scientists have been by international standards unusually 'academic' or university-based, professions, free to innovate theoretically and methodologically in relative isolation from the immediate policy interests of government." The community of policy researchers in the United States essentially has little or no prospect of direct involvement in the political process and so tends to gain rewards from adhering to internal, professional standards rather than to external political standards.

Because the state of knowledge is exogenous, it can but does not always systematically constrain debate. The state of knowledge is disseminated through a variety of channels and thus is common knowledge in the game-theoretic sense. In effect, the state of knowledge is a public good available to anyone. The state of research-based knowledge indeed serves as an explanation for the pattern of debate in all of these hearings as set out in the certainty, uncertainty, and ambiguity predictions. Groups do not and often cannot make any convenient instrumental argument or fabricate analysis to construct arguments to favor their position. Arguing against the state of knowledge is not only costly for a group but often ineffective and potentially could harm its credibility and future access to Congress. This constraint appeared to be binding for the United Mine Workers in the acid rain case and the USCC in the first school-choice case, but the AMA example shows that even the most politically powerful lobbyists ultimately have a hard time manipulating research findings for political gain.

This is not to argue that advocacy analysis and misleading technical-sounding statements play no role in politics. Instead, I am arguing that advocacy analysis is useful to political actors only on those policy topics where members of Congress and interest groups already know what policy they wish to pursue, as on purely distributive, and moral, or highly ideological questions. On these issues, all that matters to legislators and lobbyists is their intuitions and opinions, not the policy analysis itself. In contrast, on complex policy questions, where Congress and groups mutually wish to solve difficult social problems, shoddy analysis will be nearly useless as a means to persuade others and advocacy analysis will be at best a bad investment of time and resources for the group. When legislators wish to learn about how a policy is likely to work on implementation and want to avoid promoting social and economic disasters, they are not likely to be swayed by hack advocacy analysis or poorly received research. And as the case studies show, for the most part, interest groups do not even bother trying. Because lobbyists intend to persuade members of Congress on complex policy questions, they must concern themselves with and make investments in gathering high-quality research.

The theory behind the political economy of expertise is not based on some naive hope that lobbyists and legislators will someday set aside their self-interests for the greater good of society or somehow become overwhelmed by the brute force of academic ideas. Instead, lobbyists care about expert knowledge and policy analysis because they want to promote their self-interests in an effective manner. This is to say that democracy, even in a hard-edged positive worldview, is much more than a set of institutions for aggregating fixed individual preferences that are exogenous to politics or simply a means to distribute public resources. Instead, the core of democracy in contemporary society, even in a strictly positive view, is to provide a forum and institutions for mutual problem-solving efforts among boundedly rational political actors making decisions on complex policy problems. Through the political process, Congress and interest groups often find that they have a mutual need to sort out the good, innovative ideas from the bad ones and discover for themselves whether policy ideas are likely to deliver on their promises.

Social Science in Politics

I have set out the discussion in this book as a counterweight to assertions in the literature on positive political economy that democracy merely parallels market failures with governmental failures (e.g., Shepsle and Weingast 1984). For simplicity, I described my counterargument as one that can explain both the success and the failure of democratic government to use expertise in the public interest. But to say that politics on occasion depends on policy expertise, even for the sake of argument, is by no means to say that this is necessarily a success from the viewpoint of normative democratic theory. There are several components to the debate over whether the use of detached expertise in policymaking is desirable or undesirable in normative democratic theory, and I touch on these issues only briefly here.

The most basic normative issue is whether, by deferring to representatives who use policy expertise, citizens are maximizing their utility in an instrumentally rational sense. It is perhaps uncontroversial that citizens cannot do best for themselves in a direct democracy, since in a direct democracy citizens compel the government to adopt policies that conform to uninformed beliefs. Furthermore, to the extent that the democratic process faithfully and accurately represents the actual, research-based state of knowledge regarding policies, citizen deference in a republican mode of accountability is rational. This is because policy expertise is often the product of peer review and professional judgment about what governmental actions best serve the public interests, professional processes that are not in service of any narrow political goal.

The belief that deference is normatively correct in this context hinges critically, however, on the assertion that political actors indeed faithfully condition their behavior on and accurately represent the research-based state of knowledge. It is a well-established tenet of public administration that one ought to be wary of any political actor who makes claims of faithfully applying expertise to public problems. As Finer remarks, "A system which gives the 'good' man freedom of action, in the expectation of benefiting from all the 'good' he has in him, must sooner or later (since no man is without faults) cause his faults to be loaded on to the public also" (1941, 338). To Finer, accountability could come only through the careful monitoring and oversight of administrative agencies by the legislative branch and ultimately the public, rather than through political actors' claimed adherence to public-interested, professional standards. Unfortunately, this is just to reconnect the circle, since the purpose of delegation in a principal-agent problem is to capture the benefits of allowing better-informed actors to use their discretion.

My argument provides at least a partial way out of this familiar dilemma. While I argue that the political process conditions its use of expertise on the research-based state of knowledge, this argument does not rest on an assumption that interest groups or legislators set aside their private interests in the political process. To the extent that the state of knowledge of a policy is represented in the political process, it is a by-product of the system rather than an intent of any one actor. In my model, there is no central official applying a particular policy bias or ideology in evaluating the adequacy of information for a proposal, but the adequacy of information is shown in the overall pattern of support and opposition among interest groups. In this view, and given Finer's warnings, the proposals of Breyer (1993), Lave (1981), Majone (1989, 6), and others to create new institutions to infuse government with expertise, such as an independent review agency, are neither necessary nor desirable.

Even if one assumes that this argument is correct—that the state of knowledge can be faithfully represented in democratic politics— one can argue that the system I describe contains several inherent biases that may or may not be compatible with anyone's interest or the larger public interest. First, one can argue that scientific expertise contains ideological biases, and the extent to which one favors the use of politics in service of expertise depends to some degree on one's ideological viewpoint. For example, one can argue that efficiency creates a bias in favor of considerations of aggregate wealth over those of equity. Liberals have reason to favor market-oriented policies, provided they work as planned, because these policies create new wealth and new opportunities to meet social aspirations, and they may be easier to use to justify new government interventions into the economy. But at the same time, decentralized markets inevitably create inequality in the distribution of benefits; to the extent that market-oriented policies prevail, the distributional concerns of the ideological Left tend to receive a lesser priority.

Second, I argue that the use of expertise in democratic politics depends heavily on interest group pressure, and it is well-known that the interest group system contains biases in the types of interests that are effectively represented (Schattschneider 1983). This concern about biases in the interest-representation system is qualified in my argument to the extent that policy expertise creates diffuse public goods that transcend the interests of any particular group or set of groups and so in effect represents the interests of the unorganized. Nevertheless, one may have good reasons to object to any imposition

of an expert solution on citizens without their direct input and agreement (Dryzek 1994). To the extent that the interest group system
uses expertise, at best it can only impose expert policies to address
ordinary citizens' assumed needs possibly instead of their actual
wants (Finer 1941, 337).

In the end, several benefits arise from the use of expertise in politics in which everyone perhaps shares a common interest. In particular, politics based on persuasion, expertise, and ideas is inherently
better for society than politics based exclusively on power, ideology,
opinion, and preference aggregation. In itself, the mere aggregation
of uninformed and ideologically determined preferences has no
justification in democratic theory; without debate and the potential
for persuasion, majority rule alone is simply is a system of government where might equals right. In addition, to the extent that the
government uses public-interested expertise to solve difficult problems, this in itself can help to foster and reestablish citizen trust in
political institutions (Breyer 1993, 78).

Conclusion

In common parlance, to say a decision or action is "politically motivated" is meant to imply that the decision was made for expedience
rather than as a response to good arguments or information. This
common view of political decision making in our society in many
ways is ironic, since the idea that political actors may be persuaded
and respond to better or superior ideas is at the core of the intellectual justification of democracy. As Jefferson wrote in the Virginia
Statute for Religious Liberties, from which the First Amendment is a
direct intellectual descendent,

> truth is great and will prevail if left to herself, that she is the proper
> and sufficient antagonist to error and has nothing to fear from the
> conflict, unless by human interposition disarmed of her natural
> weapons, free argument and debate, errors ceasing to be danger-
> ous when it is permitted to freely contradict them. (Jefferson 1823,
> 86)

In the everyday view of politics as well as in the established view of positive political economy, Jefferson is offering an empty justification for democracy. Indeed, if political actors are never persuaded by better ideas, then democracy has no normative justification beyond an appeal to majority rule, which perhaps lends an intuitive sense of fairness that one's position at least had the opportunity to prevail, but nothing more.

In my argument, because political actors seek to solve pressing problems, they are forced to seek out public-interested policy expertise to further their self-interests. This argument suggests that the traditional justification for democracy is founded on much more than naive aspirations for good government. Interest groups can learn about their interests across different policy alternatives both through their own research and, perhaps more importantly, through debate with each other and through their interactions with the state. Congress can take advantage of its agenda-setting power and its autonomy from the demands of any particular interest group to devise superior solutions that solve the many complex problems that arise in the economy and in society. That the legislative process harnesses research to solve social problems is a by-product of and is dictated by the complexity and dynamics of contemporary lobbying.

Congress frequently appears to be unable or unwilling to enact expert-informed, socially efficient legislation, but this is by no means a constitutionally predetermined outcome of democratic politics. Congress's capacity to use expertise to reform public policy depends heavily on the quality of debate among interest groups, and the quality of debate in turn depends critically on the state of knowledge for the policy that has been socially constructed among experts. Even experts often know very little about policies, and they often do not agree among themselves about what is likely to occur in response to a government action. But this is not a necessary state of affairs. The policy research community indeed recognizes and accords greater influence and stature to experts who do careful analyses and who use superior research methods: uncertainty and ambiguity ultimately may be overcome, at least to some degree, with more and better research and analysis. In this view, it is unfortunate that policy evaluation, when done at all, is often at best an afterthought to program design. Evaluation often seems to take a back seat to the much more glamorous exercise of theoretical research.

If this book indeed contains a naive aspiration, it is the hope that a hard-edged positive argument for why policy ideas and evidence matter to the real world of policy-making will lead government, interest groups, society, and the discipline of policy analysis to make a much greater commitment to good-quality empirical evaluation research.

APPENDIX

~

Validity and Reliability Issues

Data from committee hearings have been used in surprisingly few studies in political science—surprising given the vast quantity of such hearings and their ready availability at nearly any university library. The reasons that hearings have been so little studied are unclear, but one possibility is a kind of vicious circle regarding their validity. Because political scientists have so infrequently used hearings as a data source, we know very little about them; because we know so little about hearings, we tend not to use them in our work. In this appendix, I assemble some of what we do know empirically about the hearings process to justify the validity of using them in my study of public debate among lobbyists and the informativeness of these debates for committee members. I also briefly discuss the reliability of my coding of lobbyists' arguments in tables 12 and 16.

Committee Hearings as a Forum for Informative Debate

The basic empirical question in this book is whether committees make use of policy expertise in their work and decision making. All four hearings were as informative as could be expected, given the state of knowledge. There are two possible explanations for this phenomenon: either the committee or the lobbyists wanted the hearings to be informative. As I show next, hearings are a valid data source for my study under either of these assumptions.[1]

---

1. Another possibility, of course, is that the hearings were informative by chance, a mere result of sampling and the natural variation in lobbyists' arguments. The

First, the assumption that hearings were informative because the committee wanted it that way is plausible because committees carefully orchestrate hearings so that the record reflects their work on legislation and so that the hearings shape legislators' understanding of the issue in a manner the committee members find most useful. In particular, the committee controls the scheduling of witnesses, and committee staffers go to great lengths to prepare witnesses to testify. As I discuss in the text, a committee has strong incentives to use the hearing to demonstrate publicly that the legislators have developed the necessary expertise to write good policy, perhaps to expand or maintain committee jurisdiction (Talbert, Jones, and Baumgartner 1995), to extract concessions from the legislature as a whole (Krehbiel 1992), or to help with reelection efforts (Bianco 1994).

Second, the hearing may be informative because lobbyists believe that informative arguments will persuade the committee. Even though committees prepare witnesses to testify, staffers or legislators cannot and do not compel lobbyists to make either instrumental or normative arguments. To some degree, the hearing is informative because lobbyists choose to make it so.

Either way—or both ways—the hearing reflects the committee's relative need for information on an issue. That is, hearings will be either informative or not informative depending on the committee's specific interests regarding and informational needs for the policy topic. Precisely because committees prepare very carefully to ensure that hearings meets goals, the hearings are a valid data source for gauging the nature of committees' interest in policies and the types of statements that interest groups feel will be most persuasive to Congress. Hearings therefore serve as a window on the committee's goals across issues and thus can serve as a means to test hypotheses

---

proposition that the arguments in tables 12 and 16 are independent of the state of knowledge is testable if one assumes that lobbyists' instrumental and normative arguments are independent draws from a distribution of arguments. Although all lobbyists combined make more instrumental than normative arguments in these tables, I make the conservative assumption that lobbyists have a .5 probability of making an instrumental rather than a normative argument. In this case, the hypothesis of dependence is falsifiable by the arguments of the opponents in table 12 and the supporters in table 16. These two sets of lobbyists together made a total of nine distinct arguments. The binomial probability that these lobbyists would make zero instrumental arguments out of nine, under these assumptions, is 0.002, easily rejecting the hypothesis of independence.

stating the conditions for informed debate and members' interests in expertise.

The traditional view of committee goals is that hearings serve only as a forum for advocating a policy the committee has adopted for political convenience. Members use hearings simply as a forum for position taking or advertising (Mayhew 1974; Olezek 1984, 86–87). In this view, committees simply want to assemble a list of witnesses to advocate the chair's predetermined position. If this argument is correct, then the committee will care only about the position that lobbyists take, not the truthfulness or accuracy of the specific arguments by which they support positions given the state of research-based knowledge. This is the view of the established literature: whether lobbyists back up their positions with research or accurate empirical claims is simply irrelevant to the hearing.

If my theory of Congress is correct—that is, if members of Congress seek to draft quality legislation to advance their careers, resolve conflict among interest groups, and improve their reelection chances—then members of Congress will want the hearing record to reflect the best available information on the topic. If the established theory of Congress is true, and committees simply use hearings as forums for position taking independent of the research-based state of knowledge, then lobbyists will never care about the accuracy of their statements. If committee hearings are simply position-taking forums, then lobbyists will say whatever claims are convenient, policy research information will have no systematic effect, and my theory will be falsified by the deviation of lobbyists' arguments from the state of knowledge in the research literature. Consequently, hearings are a valid way of testing claims about the variation in the types of arguments lobbyists make to committees.

But my argument goes further and states that hearings are informative for members of Congress (see Diermeier and Fedderson 2000). It is possible to argue that committee hearings simply reflect what committees already know or that committee members ignore what is said in hearings. Lobbyist debate in hearings in either case would be meaningless to Congress. These, however, are not plausible arguments.

First, members themselves say that hearings are informative. As Kingdon puts it, "Congressmen themselves believe that the hearings do provide them with the bulk of information needed to legislate, and the hearings do affect their decisions" (1989, 213). Second, members of Congress state that their colleagues who sit through hearings have an expertise on the topic; consequently, Kingdon finds, members gain influence over their colleagues through cueing processes: "Congressmen often refer to the opportunity that their colleagues on the committee had to attend the hearings and listen to the experts" (1989, 85–86). Finally, DeGregorio notes from interviews with committee staff members, "According to a sizeable proportion of senior staffers, legislators may decide whether or not to pursue a policy on the strength of the arguments that they receive in testimony" (1992, 978–79).

Given the limits of committee staff resources and time, it is not plausible to assume that committees already have full information about what lobbyists know and will say at hearings—to say the least, this would be an impressive display of analytical prowess. Because committees have jurisdiction over a wide range of issues, and given the sheer complexity of issues and the vast quantity of information possessed by interest groups, committees simply do not have the time and resources necessary to be fully informed on issues or to fully know their positions on issues or how to write highly detailed legislation without consulting with interest groups.

Hearings are a particularly important forum in which members can engage lobbyists because adversarial processes and the public nature of debate ensure that lobbyists make high-quality arguments. Precisely because the hearing is public, lobbyists must present what they feel are the most compelling and persuasive arguments. The adversarial public debate at hearings gives members of the committee a means to check the veracity of lobbyists' private arguments. Perhaps more importantly, new information emerges in debate among lobbyists. One staff member for the House Commerce Committee pointed out to me that hearings are usually the first opportunity for committees to hear how lobbyists respond to each other; committee members often use hearings to see how the various arguments stack up or how lobbyists reply to the arguments of other lobbyists. At hearings, committee members engage lobbyists in this sort of dialectical practice.

Alternatively, the assertion that members simply ignore any new information that emerges in hearings is equally implausible. As can be observed in the case studies, committee members engage in highly detailed discussion about program technical details, design, causal effectiveness, and potential implementation problems. To say that members ignore the information generated in hearings is to argue that after engaging in this arduous exercise, the members retire to smoke-filled rooms and horse-trade specific provisions based on the preconceptions and intuitions held prior to the hearing. Given the obvious and observable interest members have in designing legislation well, this belief is not plausible on its face.

Finally, there is the question of whether there are multiple public debates: are hearings simply one among many debates from which members may learn? Perhaps lobbyists who limit their arguments in hearings are unconstrained in other forums, so hearings are unrepresentative of the legislative process or debate processes in general.

First, consider "debates" that go on behind the scenes, inside Congress, between lobbyists and members. One argument is that the committee members exploit experts in public hearings as political theater and consult nonexperts behind the scenes, where legislation actually is written and where arguments actually matter. In this case, the informative hearings I find would be unrepresentative of debates in the legislative process as a whole.

This argument is also empirically not plausible. Leyden finds that staff are reluctant to schedule witnesses who have not worked with the staffers behind the scenes, since staff members want to know ahead of time how witnesses will respond to questions in hearings and want to trust witnesses to assist in building a record that reflects the committee's interest in the legislation. Leyden also finds that committees generally balance the witness list in a way that reflects what they have been hearing in private (1995, 433–34).

In addition, using the data collected in the Washington Representative Study (Heinz et al. 1995) that I describe in chapter 2, I test the hypothesis that the communication of expertise behind the scenes differs systematically from the communication of expertise in hearings because the data set contains measures of access both through hearings and through behind-the-scenes conversations. Recall that in chapter 2, I use all of these measures of access to construct a scale measure of overall access. Here, I simply reestimate the same model but do so separately for each dependent variable measuring access across the separate channels of access. I list the salient findings in table A1.

In these separate analyses, I find that increasing expertise for centrist or ideologically neutral lobbyists makes them more likely to prepare written testimony as a part of their work, which is to say that they are more likely to write their own or their group's position paper that gets submitted to the committee and is made a part of the hearing record. Similarly, I find that biased expertise improves access through oral testimony—that is, biased experts are more likely to give their positions or those of their groups to the committee orally. It is important to note that hearings systematically capture each type of expertise, either through the written or the oral testimony. In my cases, I examine the oral testimony, which is more likely to be ideologically biased and thus potentially misleading, a conservative aspect of the research design.

More important, I also find that both neutral and biased expertise improves lobbyists' access to behind-the-scenes discussions with members and where the real work of legislation gets done. Furthermore, I find that expertise of both types improves access to these informal discussions slightly more than to hearings, which directly contradicts the cynical expectation that committees are simply stacking hearings with experts to somehow legitimate otherwise uninformed decisions, since expertise improves lobbyists' access through both channels in roughly equal measures. That is, it appears from these findings that members and their staff consult with technically

TABLE A1.　The Effects of Expertise on Access, All Channels of Access

Expertise Improves Access through Hearings
• Neutral expertise improves access through prepared testimony only
• Ideologically biased expertise improves access through oral testimony only

Expertise Improves Access to Behind-the-Scenes Conversations
• Both neutral and biased expertise improve access to behind-the-scenes discussions
• Both types of expertise improve access to informal discussions slightly more than to hearings

Note: All effects significant at $p < 0.05$. Summary of results from statistical models that are identical to the one set out in chapter 2, except here I am modeling the marginal effect of expertise on access separately for each channel of access. See chapter 2 for an outline of the statistical model.

expert lobbyists both while developing legislation behind the scenes and while presenting legislation publicly at hearings. Both qualitative interviews and statistical evidence strongly show that hearings reflect committees' behind-the-scenes work, so (perhaps contrary to popular suspicion) hearings serve as an empirically valid window on the overall legislative process.

Second, members have access to other debate forums outside of Congress, and hearings may differ systematically from these other forums. In particular, lobbyists make public statements to the media and to the insider trade press. I studied the trade press for lobbyist comments in the acid rain case, and all comments at the hearing exactly paralleled those found in the press, as the footnotes to chapter 6 show. Finally, because the committee controls the selection of witnesses, hearings do not measure the full range of interest group support and opposition in the full population of active interest groups (as would be the case if witnesses were randomly selected from the full population of groups active on the issues). In practice, however, hearings capture a large portion of the range of opinion among groups (Arnold 1990, 85).

Coding Reliability

I extensively code witnesses' oral statements to the committee for two sets of hearings: the 1989 acid rain proposal and the 1991 school choice proposal, respectively. To classify the arguments given in testimony into categories, I first use the Congressional Information Service (CIS) published hearings abstracts to identify the major arguments made in testimony, adding other arguments that CIS overlooked. I then use the full text of the hearings to classify groups by which arguments they use. Using this approach enables me to identify the full range of policy dimensions discussed in testimony to and characterize the debate covered in the hearings. I conducted a reliability analysis of the coding by comparing my coding with that of a second coder for these two hearings.[2] In both reliability analyses,

---

2. I am greatly indebted to David Shaffer, a student in my statistics class at Dartmouth College who volunteered his time, for the second round of coding.

the original coding had 77 percent accuracy.[3] In addition, the second coding simply expanded the number of claims listed in the tables for these two hearings, and all of the added claims were consistent with the theoretical predictions. I simply added the arguments picked up by the second coder that I had overlooked in the initial round of coding to the full set of results.

---

3. I divided the number of claims that I had overlooked by the total number of claims coded and subtracted this from one.

References

Aaron, Henry J., Thomas E. Mann, and Timothy Taylor. 1994. "Introduction." In *Values and Public Policy*, ed. Henry J. Aaron, Thomas E. Mann, and Timothy Taylor. Washington, D.C.: Brookings Institution.

"Acid Rain Battle Opens in House as Electric Utility Industry Launches Counteroffensive." 1989. *Public Utilities Fortnightly*, September 28, p. 26.

"Acid Rain Study Pegs Fuel Switching as Least-Cost Method in Likely Reductions." 1989. *Coal Week*, March 13, p. 7.

Ackerman, Bruce A., and William T. Hassler. 1981. *Clean Coal/Dirty Air*. New Haven: Yale University Press.

"AEP Says the Time for Just Studying Acid Rain Has Not Passed." 1989. *Inside Energy/with Federal Lands*, February 27, p. 10.

Ainsworth, Scott. 1993. "Regulating Lobbyists and Interest Group Influence." *Journal of Politics* 55:41–56.

Alford, Robert R. 1975. *Health Care Politics: Interest Group and Ideological Barriers to Reform*. Chicago: University of Chicago Press.

Alvarez, R. Michael. 1998. *Information and Elections*. Ann Arbor: University of Michigan Press.

Ambach, Gordon M. 1993. "Federal Action Essential for Education Reform." In *National Issues in Education: The Past Is Prologue*, ed. John F. Jennings. Bloomington, Ind.: Phi Delta Kappa.

"Analyst Says Bush Acid Rain Bill May Cut Non-Utility Power Out of Energy Market." 1989. *Coal Week*, August 14, p. 3.

Anderson, Ronald, and J. Joel May. 1972. "Factors Associated with the Increasing Cost of Hospital Care." *Annals of the American Academy of Political and Social Science* 399:62–72.

Armor, David J. 1989. "After Busing: Education and Choice." *Public Interest* 95:24–37.

Arndt, Michael. 1989. "Utilities Rake Bush Plan over Coal and Costs." *Chicago Tribune*, June 14, p. 1.

Arnold, R. Douglas. 1981. "The Local Roots of Domestic Policy." In *The New Congress*, ed. T. E. Mann and N. J. Ornstein. Washington, D.C.: American Enterprise Institute.

Arnold, R. Douglas. 1990. *The Logic of Congressional Action*. New Haven: Yale University Press.

Arrow, Kenneth J. 1963. "Uncertainty and the Welfare Economics of Medical Care." *American Economic Review* 53:941–73.

Austen-Smith, David. 1992. "Strategic Models of Talk in Political Decision Making." *International Political Science Review* 13:45–58.

Austen-Smith, David, and John R. Wright. 1992. "Competitive Lobbying for a Legislator's Vote." *Social Choice and Welfare* 9:229–57.

"Back of Nixon Move to Curb Health Costs." 1971. *U.S. News and World Report,* October 25, pp. 38–39.

Banks, Jeffrey S. 1991. *Signaling Games in Political Science.* Chur, Switzerland: Harwood Academic.

Barke, Richard P., and William H. Riker. 1982. "A Political Theory of Regulation with Some Observations on Railway Abandonments." *Public Choice* 39:73–106.

Bator, Francis M. 1958. "The Anatomy of Market Failure." *Quarterly Journal of Economics* 72:351–79.

Bauer, Raymond A., Ithiel de Sola Pool, and Lewis Anthony Dexter. 1972. *American Business and Public Policy: The Politics of Foreign Trade.* Chicago: Aldine Atherton.

Baum, Erica. 1991. "When the Witch Doctors Agree: The Family Support Act and Social Science Research." *Journal of Policy Analysis and Management* 10:603–15.

Bauman, Patricia. 1976. "The Formulation and Evolution of the Health Maintenance Organization Policy, 1970–1973." *Social Science and Medicine* 10:129–42.

Baumgartner, Frank R. 1989. *Conflict and Rhetoric in French Policymaking.* Pittsburgh: University of Pittsburgh Press.

Baumgartner, Frank R., and Bryan D. Jones. 1993. *Agendas and Instability in American Politics.* Chicago: University of Chicago Press.

Becker, Gary S. 1983. "A Theory of Competition among Pressure Groups for Political Influence." *Quarterly Journal of Economics* 97:371–400.

"Behind the Rising Cost of Health Care." 1970. *U.S. News and World Report,* March 16, p. 63.

Berki, Sylvester E. 1972. "National Health Insurance: An Idea Whose Time Has Come?" *Annals of the American Academy of Political and Social Science* 399:125–44.

Berki, Sylvester E., and Alan W. Heston. 1972. "Introduction" [to special issue on health care crisis]. *Annals of the American Academy of Political and Social Science* 399:ix–xiv.

Bianco, William T. 1994. *Trust: Representatives and Constituents.* Ann Arbor: University of Michigan Press.

Biggs, Donald, and Gerald Porter. 1994. "Parental Choice in the USA." In *Parental Choice and Education: Principles, Policy, and Practice,* ed. Mark J. Halstead. London: Kogan.

Bimber, Bruce. 1991. "Information as a Factor in Congressional Politics." *Legislative Studies Quarterly* 16:585–606.

Bimber, Bruce. 1996. *The Politics of Expertise in Congress: The Rise and Fall of the Office of Technology Assessment.* Albany: SUNY Press.

Blaug, Mark. 1980. *The Methodology of Economics; or, How Economists Explain.* New York: Cambridge University Press.

Bohman, James F. 1990. "Communication, Ideology, and Democratic Theory." *American Political Science Review* 84:93–109.

Breyer, Stephen. 1981. *Regulation and Its Reform.* Cambridge: Harvard University Press.

Breyer, Stephen. 1993. *Breaking the Vicious Circle: Toward Effective Risk Regulation.* Cambridge: Harvard University Press.

Brown, Frank. 1991. "Introduction: School Choice and the Politics of Decline." *Education and Urban Society* 23:115–18.

Brown, Frank, and A. Reynaldo Contreras. 1991. "Deregulation and Privatization of Education: A Flawed Concept." *Education and Urban Society* 23:144–58.

Brown, Lawrence D. 1983. *Politics and Health Care Organization: HMOs as Federal Policy.* Washington, D.C.: Brookings Institution.

Browne, William P. 1990. "Organized Interests and Their Issue Niches: A Search for Pluralism in a Policy Domain." *Journal of Politics* 52:477–509.

Bryner, Gary C. 1994. *Blue Skies, Green Politics: The Clean Air Act of 1990 and Its Implementation.* 2d ed. Washington, D.C.: Congressional Quarterly Press.

Bulmer, Martin. 1987. "Governments and Social Science: Patterns of Mutual Influence." In *Social Science Research and Government: Comparative Essays on Britain and the United States,* ed. Martin Bulmer. New York: Cambridge University Press.

"Bush Acid Rain Plan Hits 107 Plants, Emission Swaps in 10-Million Ton SO_2 Cut." 1989. *Coal Week,* June 19, p. 8.

"Bush's Clean Air Proposals Will Allow Tradeable Emission Rights." 1989. *Coal,* September, p. 7.

Cain, Bruce, John Ferejohn, and Morris Fiorina. 1987. *The Personal Vote: Constituency Service and Electoral Independence.* Cambridge: Harvard University Press.

Carpenter, Daniel P., Kevin M. Esterling, and David Lazer. 1998. "The Strength of Weak Ties in Lobbying Networks: Evidence from Health Care Politics." *Journal of Theoretical Politics* 10:417–44.

Carter, David G., and James P. Sandler. 1991. "Access, Choice, Quality, and Integration." *Education and Urban Society* 23:175–84.

"Changing the System of Health Care." 1972. *Morgan Guaranty Survey,* December, pp. 7–14.

Chubb, John E. 1988. "Why the Current Wave of School Reform Will Fail." *Public Interest* 90:28–49.

Chubb, John E., and Terry M. Moe. 1990. *Politics, Markets, and America's Schools.* Washington, D.C.: Brookings Institution.

"Clean Air Act Rewritten, Tightened." 1990. *Congressional Quarterly Almanac,* 101st Cong., 2d sess., 46:229–79.

"Clean Air and Coal." 1989. *Platt's Oilgram News,* September 6, p. 5.

"Clean Air Bill Fails to Move." 1988. *Congressional Quarterly Almanac,* 100th Cong., 2d sess., 44:142–48.

"Clean Air Bill Stalled by Acid Rain Dispute." 1984. *Congressional Quarterly Almanac,* 98th Cong., 2d sess., 40:339–42.

Clearing the Air: The Facts about Capping and Trading Emissions. 2002. Washington, D.C.: Environmental Protection Agency, Office of Air and Radiation.

Cobb, Michael D., and James H. Kuklinski. 1997. "Changing Minds: Political Arguments and Political Persuasion." *American Journal of Political Science,* 41:88–121.

Coburn, A. Stephen. 1973. "Health Maintenance Organizations: Implications for Public Assistance Recipients." *Public Welfare* 31:28–33.

Cohen, David, and Eleanor Farrar. 1977. "Power to the Parents? The Story of Education Vouchers." *Public Interest* 48:72–97.

Cohen, Richard E. 1992. *Washington at Work: Back Rooms and Clean Air.* New York: Macmillan.

Coleman, James. 1981. "Public Schools, Private Schools, and the Public Interest." *Public Interest* 64:19–30.

"Coming on Fast: 'One-Stop' Health Care." 1973. *U.S. News and World Report,* May 21, pp. 52–54.

Congressional Budget Office [CBO]. 1985. *Environmental Regulation and Economic Efficiency.* Washington, D.C.: Congress of the United States, Congressional Budget Office.

Cookson, Peter W., Jr. 1991. "Private Schooling and Equity: Dilemmas of Choice." *Education and Urban Society* 23:185–99.

Cookson, Peter W., Jr. 1992. "Introduction" [to special issue on choice]. *Educational Policy* 6:99–104.

Cookson, Peter W., Jr. 1994. *School Choice: The Struggle for the Soul of American Education.* New Haven: Yale University Press.

Cox, Gary W., and Mathew D. McCubbins. 1993. *Legislative Leviathan: Party Government in the House.* Berkeley: University of California Press.

Cross, Christopher. 1993. "From the Business Roundtable: A Business Perspective on Education." In *National Issues in Education: The Past Is Prologue,* ed. John F. Jennings. Bloomington, Ind.: Phi Delta Kappa.

Dahl, Robert A. 1982. *Dilemmas of Pluralist Democracy: Autonomy versus Control.* New Haven: Yale University Press.

DeGregorio, Christine. 1992. "Leadership Approaches in Congressional Committee Hearings." *Western Political Quarterly* 45:971–83.

Delli Carpini, Michael X., and Scott Keeter. 1996. *What Americans Know about Politics and Why It Matters.* New Haven: Yale University Press.

Denzau, Arthur T., and Michael C. Munger. 1986. "Legislators and Interest Groups: How Unorganized Interests Get Represented." *American Political Science Review* 80:89–106.

Derthick, Martha, and Paul J. Quirk. 1985. *The Politics of Deregulation.* Washington, D.C.: Brookings Institution.

Diermeier, Daniel. 1995. "Commitment, Deference, and Legislative Institutions." *American Political Science Review* 89:344–55.

Diermeier, Daniel, and Timothy J. Fedderson. 2000. "Information and Congressional Hearings." *American Journal of Political Science* 44:51–65.

Dougherty, Kevin J., and Lizabeth Sostre. 1992. "Minerva and the Market: The Sources of the Movement for School Choice." *Educational Policy* 6:160–79.

Dryzek, John S. 1994. *Discursive Democracy: Politics, Policy, and Political Science.* New York: Cambridge University Press.

Dudek, Daniel J., and John Palmisano. 1988. "Emissions Trading: Why Is This Thoroughbred Hobbled?" *Columbia Journal of Environmental Law* 13:217–56.

Dudley, R. Adams, and Harold S. Luft. 2001. "Managed Care in Transition." *New England Journal of Medicine* 344:1087–91.

"Education Vouchers: The Fruit of the *Lemon* Tree." 1972. *Stanford Law Review* 24:687–711.

"EEI: Bush Bill Could Cost $7 Billion a Year; Changes Could Cut It by 30%." 1989. *Electric Utility Week,* September 4, p. 7.

Elster, Jon. 1989. *The Market and the Forum: Three Varieties of Political Theory.* New York: Cambridge University Press.

Falk, I. S. 1970. "National Health Insurance: A Review of Policies and Proposals." *Law and Contemporary Problems* 35:669–96.

Falkson, Joseph L. 1980. *HMOs and the Politics of Health System Reform.* Chicago: American Hospital Association.

Fearon, James D. 1998. "Deliberation as Discussion." In *Deliberative Democracy,* ed. Jon Elster. New York: Cambridge University Press.

Fearon, James D. 1999. "Electoral Accountability and the Control of Politicians: Selecting Good Types versus Sanctioning Poor Performance." In *Democracy, Accountability, and Representation,* ed. Adam Przeworski, Susan C. Stokes, and Bernard Manin. New York: Cambridge University Press.

Feldstein, Martin S. 1971. "A New Approach to National Health Insurance." *Public Interest* 23:93–105.

Fenno, Richard F., Jr. 1966. *The Power of the Purse: Appropriations Politics in Congress.* Boston: Little, Brown.

Fenno, Richard F., Jr. 1978. *Home Style: Members in their Districts.* Boston: Little, Brown.

"FERC Staff: SO2 Allowance Hoarding Unlikely; Remedies Are Available." 1989. *Electric Utility Week,* October 9, p. 13.

Ferejohn, John A., and James H. Kuklinski. 1990. *Information and Democratic Processes.* Urbana: University of Illinois Press.

Finer, Herman. 1941. "Administrative Responsibility in Democratic Government." *Public Administration Review* 1:335–50.

Fiorina, Morris P. 1981. *Retrospective Voting in American National Elections.* New Haven: Yale University Press.

Fiorina, Morris P. 1982. "Legislative Choice of Regulatory Forms: Legal Process or Administrative Process?" *Public Choice* 39:33–66.

Fiorina, Morris P. 1989. *Congress: Keystone of the Washington Establishment.* New Haven: Yale University Press.

Flash, William S. 1971. "National Health Insurance Responses to Health Care Issues." *Public Administration Review* 31:507–17.

Fowler, Linda L. 1993. *Candidates, Congress, and the American Democracy.* Ann Arbor: University of Michigan Press.

Fritschler, A. Lee. 1989. *Smoking and Politics: Policy Making and the Federal Bureaucracy.* 4th ed. Englewood Cliffs, N.J.: Prentice-Hall.

Gais, Thomas L., Mark A. Peterson, and Jack L. Walker. 1984. "Interest Groups, Iron Triangles, and Representative Institutions in American National Government." *British Journal of Political Science* 14:161–85.

Galbraith, John Kenneth. 1967. *The New Industrial State.* Boston: Houghton Mifflin.

Gambetta, Diego. 1998. "Claro! An Essay on Discursive Machismo." In *Deliberative Democracy,* ed. Jon Elster. New York: Cambridge University Press.

Geiger, H. Jack, and Roger D. Cohen. 1971. "Trends in Health Care Delivery Systems." *Inquiry* 8:32–36.

Gilligan, Thomas W., and Keith Krehbiel. 1987. "Collective Decisionmaking and Standing Committees: An Informational Rationale for Restrictive Amendment Procedures." *Journal of Law, Economics, and Organization* 3:287–330.

Goldstein, Inge F., and Martin Goldstein. 2002. *How Much Risk? A Guide to Understanding Environmental Health Hazards.* New York: Oxford University Press.

Goldstein, Judith. 1993. *Ideas, Interests, and American Trade Policy.* Ithaca: Cornell University Press.

Greene, Jay P., Paul E. Peterson, and Jiangtao Du. 1996. "Effectiveness of School Choice in Milwaukee: A Secondary Analysis of Data from the Program's Evaluation." Paper presented at the annual meeting of the American Political Science Association, August 30, San Francisco.

Greenlick, Merwyn R. 1972. "The Impact of Prepaid Group Practice on American Medical Care: A Critical Evaluation." *Annals of the American Academy of Political and Social Science* 399:100–113.

Habermas, Jürgen. 1995. "Reconciliation through the Public Use of Reason: Remarks on John Rawls's Political Liberalism." *Journal of Philosophy* 92:109–31.

Habermas, Jürgen. 1998. *The Inclusion of the Other: Studies in Political Theory.* Ed. Ciaran Cronin and Pablo De Greiff. Cambridge: MIT Press.

Hahn, Robert W., and Gordon L. Hester. 1989a. "Marketable Permits: Lessons for Theory and Practice." *Ecology Law Quarterly* 16:361–406.

Hahn, Robert W., and Gordon L. Hester. 1989b. "Where Did All the Markets Go? An Analysis of EPA's Emissions Trading Program." *Yale Journal on Regulation* 6:109–53.

Hahn, Robert W., and Albert M. McGartland. 1989. "The Political Economy of Instrument Choice: An Examination of the U.S. Role in Implementing the Montreal Protocol." *Northwestern University Law Review* 83:592–611.

Hahn, Robert W., and Roger G. Noll. 1982. "Designing a Market for Tradable Emissions Permits." In *Reform of Environmental Regulation,* ed. Wesley A. Magat. Cambridge: Ballinger.

Hahn, Robert W., and Roger G. Noll. 1983. "Barriers to Implementing Tradable Air Pollution Permits: Problems of Regulatory Interactions." *Yale Journal on Regulation* 1:63–91.

Hahn, Robert W., and Robert N. Stavins. 1995. "Trading in Greenhouse Permits: A Critical Examination of Design and Implementation Issues." In *Shaping National Responses to Climate Change: A Post-Rio Guide,* ed. Henry Lee. Washington, D.C.: Island Press.

Hall, Richard L. 1996. *Participation in Congress.* New Haven: Yale University Press.

Hamilton, Alexander. 1961. "The Federalist, No. 71." In Alexander Hamilton, James Madison, and John Jay, *The Federalist Papers,* ed. Clinton Rossiter. New York: New American Library.

Hamilton, James T. 1997. "Taxes, Torts, and the Toxics Release Inventory: Congressional Voting on Instruments to Control Pollution." *Economic Inquiry* 35:745–62.

Hansen, John Mark. 1991. *Gaining Access: Congress and the Farm Lobby, 1919–1981.* Chicago: University of Chicago Press.

Havighurst, Clark C. 1970. "Health Maintenance Organizations and the Market for Health Services." *Law and Contemporary Problems* 35:716–95.

"Health Care: Supply, Demand, and Politics." 1971. *Time,* June 7, pp. 86–93.

Heclo, Hugh. 1978. "Issue Networks and the Executive Establishment." In *The New American Political System,* ed. Anthony King. Washington, D.C.: American Enterprise Institute.

Heid, C. A., and L. E. Leak. 1991. "School Choice Plans and the Professionalization of Teaching." *Education and Urban Society* 23:219–27.

Heinz, John P., Edward O. Laumann, Robert L. Nelson, and Robert H. Salisbury. 1993. *The Hollow Core: Private Interests in National Policy Making.* Cambridge: Harvard University Press.

Heinz, John P., Edward O. Laumann, Robert L. Nelson, and Robert H. Salisbury. 1995. "Washington, D.C., Representatives: Private Interests in National Policymaking, 1982–1983" [computer file]. ICPSR version. Chicago: American Bar Foundation; Ann Arbor, Mich.: Inter-University Consortium for Political and Social Research.

Hershey, Robert D., Jr. 1989. "New Market for Trading 'Pollution Rights.'" *New York Times,* June 14, p. D1.

Hinich, Melvin J., and Michael C. Munger. 1996. *Ideology and the Theory of Political Choice.* Ann Arbor: University of Michigan Press.

"Hoarding of SO2 Allowances Unlikely Due to Cost-Effectiveness, FERC Says." 1989. *Coal Week,* October 9, p. 8.

Hojnacki, Marie. 1997. "Interest Groups' Decisions to Join Alliances or Work Alone." *American Journal of Political Science* 41:61–87.

Hula, Kevin W. 1999. *Lobbying Together: Interest Group Coalitions in Legislative Politics.* Washington, D.C.: Georgetown University Press.

Hylton, Richard D. 1989. "Who Could Gain in Clean Air Act." *New York Times,* August 4, p. D6.

"Independents to Focus on Fees and 'Offsets' in Acid Rain Bill." 1989. *Independent Power Report,* August 11, p. 15.

"Industrials: Acid Rain Bill Costly, Would Severely Limit U.S. Growth." 1989. *Industrial Energy Bulletin,* August 18, p. 8.

Jackson, John E., and David C. King. 1989. "Public Goods, Private Interests, and Representation." *American Political Science Review* 83:1143–64.

Jefferson, Thomas. 1823 [1726]. "Virginia Statute for Religious Freedom." In *Statutes at Large in Virginia,* ed. W. W. Hening, 12:84–86. Richmond, Va.: n.p.

Johnson, James. 1991. "Habermas on Strategic and Communicative Action." *Political Theory* 19:181–201.

Jones, Bryan. 1994. *Reconceiving Decision-Making in Democratic Politics: Attention, Choice, and Public Policy.* Chicago: University of Chicago Press.

Jones, Bryan. 1999. "Bounded Rationality." *Annual Review of Political Science* 2:297–321.

Jones, Charles O. 1976. "Why Congress Can't Do Policy Analysis (or Words to That Effect)." *Policy Analysis* 2:251–64.

Katznelson, Ira. 1996. "Knowledge about What? Policy Intellectuals and the New Liberalism." In *States, Social Knowledge, and the Origins of Modern Social Policies,* ed. Dietrich Rueschemeyer and Theda Skocpol. Princeton: Princeton University Press.

Kelman, Steven. 1981. "Economists and the Environmental Muddle." *Public Interest* 64:106–23.

Kiewiet, D. Roderick, and Mathew D. McCubbins. 1991. *The Logic of Delegation: Congressional Parties and the Appropriations Process.* Chicago: University of Chicago Press.

Kingdon, John W. 1984. *Agendas, Alternatives, and Public Policies.* New York: HarperCollins.

Kingdon, John W. 1989. *Congressmen's Voting Decisions.* 3d ed. Ann Arbor: University of Michigan Press.

Kissick, William L., and Samuel P. Martin. 1972. "Issues of the Future in Health." *Annals of the American Academy of Political and Social Science* 399:151–59.

Knight, Jack, and James Johnson. 1994. "Aggregation and Deliberation: On the Possibility of Democratic Legitimacy." *Political Theory* 22:277–96.

Kollman, Ken. 1998. *Outside Lobbying: Public Opinion and Interest Group Strategies.* Princeton: Princeton University Press.

Kraft, Michael E. 1994. "Environmental Gridlock: Searching for Consensus in Congress." In *Environmental Policy in the 1990s: Toward a New Agenda,* 2d ed., ed. Norman J. Vig and Michael E. Kraft. Washington, D.C.: Congressional Quarterly Press.

Krassa, Michael. 1990. "The Structure of Interaction and the Transmission of Political Influence and Information." In *Information and Democratic*

Processes, ed. John A. Ferejohn and James H. Kuklinski. Urbana: University of Illinois Press.

Krehbiel, Keith. 1992. *Information and Legislative Organization*. Ann Arbor: University of Michigan Press.

Latham, Earl. 1952. "The Group Basis of Politics: Notes for a Theory." *American Political Science Review* 46:376–97.

Laumann, Edward O., and David Knoke. 1987. *The Organizational State: Social Choice in National Policy Domains*. Madison: University of Wisconsin Press.

Lave, Lester B. 1981. *The Strategy of Social Regulation: Decision Frameworks for Policy*. Washington, D.C.: Brookings Institution.

Lave, Lester B., and Gilbert S. Omenn. 1981. *Clearing the Air: Reforming the Clean Air Act*. Washington, D.C.: Brookings Institution.

Legro, Jeffrey W. 2000. "The Transformation of Policy Ideas." *American Journal of Political Science* 44:419–32.

Leveson, Irving. 1972. "The Economics of Health Services for the Poor." *Annals of the American Academy of Political and Social Science* 399:22–29.

Leyden, Kevin M. 1995. "Interest Group Resources and Testimony at Congressional Hearings." *Legislative Studies Quarterly* 20:431–39.

Lieberman, Myron. 1989. *Privatization and Educational Choice*. New York: St. Martin's.

Lieberman, Myron. 1994. "The School Choice Fiasco." *Public Interest* 114:17–34.

Liroff, Richard A. 1986. *Reforming Air Pollution Regulation: The Toil and Trouble of EPA's Bubble*. Washington, D.C.: Conservation Foundation.

Lohmann, Susanne. 1998. "An Information Rationale for the Power of Special Interests." *American Political Science Review* 92:809–28.

Loomis, Burdett A. 1986. "Coalitions of Interests: Building Bridges in the Balkanized State." In *Interest Group Politics*, 2d ed., ed. Allan J. Cigler and Burdett A. Loomis. Washington, D.C.: Congressional Quarterly Press.

Loomis, Burdett, and Allan J. Cigler. 1986. "Introduction: The Changing Nature of Interest Group Politics." In *Interest Group Politics*, 2d ed., ed. Allan J. Cigler and Burdett A. Loomis. Washington, D.C.: Congressional Quarterly Press.

Lowi, Theodore J. 1964. "American Business, Public Policy, Case Studies, and Political Theory." *World Politics* 16:677–715.

Lowi, Theodore J. 1969. *The End of Liberalism: Ideology, Policy, and the Crisis of Public Authority*. New York: Norton.

Lupia, Arthur, and Mathew D. McCubbins. 1998. *The Democratic Dilemma: Can Citizens Learn What They Need to Know?* New York: Cambridge University Press.

Madison, David L. 1971. "The Structure of American Health Care Services." *Public Administration Review* 31:518–27.

Madison, James. 1961. "The Federalist, No. 51." In Alexander Hamilton, James Madison, and John Jay, *The Federalist Papers*, ed. Clinton Rossiter. New York: New American Library.

Majone, Giandomenico. 1989. *Evidence, Argument, and Persuasion in the Policy Process.* New Haven: Yale University Press.

Manin, Bernard. 1987. "On Legitimacy and Political Deliberation." *Political Theory* 15:338–68.

Manin, Bernard, Adam Przeworski, and Susan C. Stokes. 1999. "Introduction." In *Democracy, Accountability, and Representation,* ed. Adam Przeworski, Susan C. Stokes, and Bernard Manin. New York: Cambridge University Press.

Margolis, Howard. 1996. *Dealing with Risk.* Chicago: University of Chicago Press.

Martin, Michael. 1991. "Trading the Known for the Unknown: Warning Signs in the Debate over Schools of Choice." *Education and Urban Society* 23:119–43.

Martin, Michael, and Diane Burke. 1990. "What's Best in the Schools of Choice Movement?" *Educational Policy* 4:73–91.

Mayhew, David R. 1974. *Congress: The Electoral Connection.* New Haven: Yale University Press.

McConnell, Grant. 1966. *Private Power and American Democracy.* New York: Knopf.

McCubbins, Mathew D., and Thomas Schwartz. 1987 [1984]. Congressional Oversight Overlooked: Police Patrols versus Fire Alarms. In *Congress: Structure and Policy,* ed. Mathew McCubbins and Terry Sullivan. New York: Cambridge University Press.

McCubbins, Mathew D., and Terry Sullivan. 1984. "Constituency Influences on Legislative Policy Choice." *Quality and Quantity* 18:299–319.

McFarland, Andrew S. 1992. "Interest Groups and the Policymaking Process: Sources of Countervailing Power in America." In *The Politics of Interests: Interest Groups Transformed,* ed. Mark P. Petracca. Boulder, Colo.: Westview.

McFarlane, Deborah R., and Kenneth J. Meier. 2001. *The Politics of Fertility Control: Family Planning and Abortion Policies in the American States.* New York: Chatham House.

Mechanic, David. 1972. "Human Problems and the Organization of Health Care." *Annals of the American Academy of Political and Social Science* 399:1–11.

Mechanic, David. 2001. "The Managed Care Backlash: Perceptions and Rhetoric in Health Care Policy and the Potential for Health Care Reform." *Milbank Quarterly* 79:35–54.

Michaels, Sarah. 1992. "Issue Networks and Activism." *Policy Studies Review* 11:241–58.

"Midwest Threatened by Acid Rain Plan, Which Encourages Fuel Switching and Scrubbing." 1989. *Coal Week,* June 26, p. 8.

Milbrath, Lester W. 1963. *The Washington Lobbyists.* Chicago: Rand McNally.

Mintrom, Michael. 1997. "Policy Entrepreneurs and the Diffusion of Innovation." *American Journal of Political Science* 41:738–70.

Mitchell, William C., and Michael C. Munger. 1991. "Economic Models of

Interest Groups: An Introductory Survey." *American Journal of Political Science* 35:512–46.

Morone, James A. 1995. "Elusive Community: Democracy, Deliberation, and the Reconstruction of Health Policy." In *The New Politics of Public Policy,* ed. Marc K. Landy and Martin A. Levin. Baltimore: Johns Hopkins University Press.

Mott, Basil J. F. 1971. "The Crisis in Health Care: Problems of Policy and Administration." *Public Administration Review* 31:501–7.

Mueller, Dennis C. 1989. *Public Choice II.* New York: Cambridge University Press.

Munger, Michael C. 2000. *Analyzing Policy: Choices, Conflicts, and Practices.* New York: Norton.

National Association of Public Administrators [NAPA]. 1994. *The Environment Goes to Market.* Washington, D.C.: National Association of Public Administrators.

National Commission on Excellence in Education. 1983. *A Nation at Risk: The Imperative for Educational Reform.* Washington, D.C.: U.S. Department of Education.

Nestle, Marion. 2002. *Food Politics: How the Food Industry Influences Nutrition and Health.* Berkeley: University of California Press.

Neuhauser, Duncan, and Fernand Turcotte. 1972. "Costs and Quality of Care in Different Types of Hospitals." *Annals of the American Academy of Political and Social Science* 399:62–72.

Newhouse, Joseph P., and Vincent Taylor. 1971. "How Shall We Pay for Hospital Care?" *Public Interest* 23:78–92.

Newman, Howard N. 1972. "Medicare and Medicaid." *Annals of the American Academy of Political and Social Science* 399:114–24.

O'Day, Jennifer. 1995. "Systemic Reform and Goals 2000." In *National Issues in Education: Goals 2000 and School-to-Work,* ed. John F. Jennings. Bloomington, Ind.: Phi Delta Kappa.

Oleszek, Walter J. 1984. *Congressional Procedures and the Policy Process.* Washington, D.C.: Congressional Quarterly Press.

Olson, Mancur. 1965. *The Logic of Collective Action.* Cambridge: Harvard University Press.

Ordeshook, Peter C. 1990. "The Emerging Discipline of Political Economy." In *Perspectives on Positive Political Economy,* ed. James E. Alt and Kenneth A. Shepsle. New York: Cambridge University Press.

Paquette, Pat. 1989. "Senate Sets a Deadline for Acid Rain Bill." *Inside Energy/ with Federal Lands,* March 26, p. 1.

Parker, Glenn R. 1996. *Congress and the Rent-Seeking Society.* Ann Arbor: University of Michigan Press.

Passell, Peter. 1989. "Sale of Air Pollution Permits Is Part of Bush Acid-Rain Plan." *New York Times,* May 17, p. A1.

Peirce, Neal R. 1989. "Bush's Chance to Take the Lead in Education." *National Journal,* September 16, p. 2277.

Peterson, Mark A. 1990. *Legislating Together: The White House and Capitol Hill from Eisenhower to Reagan.* Cambridge: Harvard University Press.

Phelan, Jerry, Robert Erickson, and Scott Fleming. 1970. "Group Practice Prepayment: An Approach to Delivering Organized Health Services." *Law and Contemporary Problems* 35:796–816.

Pitkin, Hanna Fenichel. 1972. *The Concept of Representation.* Berkeley: University of California Press.

Polsby, Nelson W. 1984. *Political Innovation in America: The Politics of Policy Initiation.* New Haven: Yale University Press.

Portney, Paul R. 1990. "Air Pollution Policy." In *Public Policies for Environmental Protection,* ed. Paul R. Portney. Washington, D.C.: Resources for the Future.

Posner, Richard A. 1974. "Theories of Economic Regulation." *Bell Journal of Economics and Management Science* 5:335–58.

"President Nixon's Health Proposals." 1971. *Washington Bulletin,* August 9, pp. 83–88.

"President's Clean Air Bill Seen as Worst Yet for Utility Industry." 1989. *Electric Utility Week,* July 31, p. 15.

Price, David E. 1971. "Professionals and 'Entrepreneurs': Staff Orientations and Policy Making on Three Senate Committees." *Journal of Politics* 33:316–35.

Price, David E. 1978. "Policy Making in Congressional Committees: The Impact of 'Environmental' Factors." *American Political Science Review* 72:548–74.

Przeworski, Adam. 1990. *The State and the Economy under Capitalism.* Chur, Switzerland: Harwood.

Quattrone, George A., and Amos Tversky. 1988. "Contrasting Rational and Psychological Analyses of Political Choice." *American Political Science Review* 82:719–36.

Quirk, Paul J. 1989. "The Cooperative Resolution of Policy Conflict." *American Political Science Review* 83:905–21.

Rabin, Matthew. 1998. "Psychology and Economics." *Journal of Economic Literature* 36:11–46.

Rasmusen, Eric. 1993. "Lobbying when the Decisionmaker Can Acquire Independent Information." *Public Choice* 77:899–913.

Ravitch, Diane. 1995. "Introduction." In *Debating the Future of American Education: Do We Need National Standards and Assessments?* Washington, D.C.: Brookings Institution.

Raywid, Mary Anne. 1984. "Synthesis of Research on Schools of Choice." *Educational Leadership* 41:70–78.

Raywid, Mary Anne. 1992. "Choice Orientations, Discussions, and Prospects." *Educational Policy* 6:105–22.

Ricci, David M. 1993. *The Transformation of American Politics: The New Washington and the Rise of Think Tanks.* New Haven: Yale University Press.

Richards, Diana. 2001. "Coordination and Shared Mental Models." *American Journal of Political Science* 45:259–76.

Riker, William H. 1982 [1988]. *Liberalism against Populism: A Confrontation between the Theory of Democracy and the Theory of Social Choice.* Prospect Heights, Ill.: Waveland.

Riker, William H. 1986. *The Art of Political Manipulation.* New Haven: Yale University Press.

Ritov, Ilana, and Jonathan Baron. 1992. "Status Quo and Omission Biases." *Journal of Risk and Uncertainty* 5:49–61.

Roberts, Marc J. 1982. "Some Problems of Implementing Marketable Pollution Rights Schemes: The Case of the Clean Air Act." In *Reform of Environmental Regulation,* ed. Wesley A. Magat. Cambridge: Ballinger.

Robertson, David Brian. 1991. "Political Conflict and Lesson Drawing." *Journal of Public Policy* 11:55–78.

Robinson, James C. 2001. "The End of Managed Care." *Journal of the American Medical Association* 285:2622–28.

"The Role of Prepaid Group Practice in Relieving the Medical Care Crisis." 1971. *Harvard Law Review* 84:887–1001.

Rose, Richard. 1993. *Lesson-Drawing in Public Policy.* Chatham, N.J.: Chatham House.

Rothenberg, Lawrence S. 1992. *Linking Citizens to Government: Interest Group Politics at Common Cause.* New York: Cambridge University Press.

Rothenberg, Lawrence S. 1994. *Regulation, Organizations, and Politics: Motor Freight Policy at the Interstate Commerce Commission.* Ann Arbor: University of Michigan Press.

Rueschemeyer, Dietrich, and Peter B. Evans. 1985. "The State and Economic Transformation: Toward an Analysis of the Conditions Underlying Effective Intervention." In *Bringing the State Back In,* ed. Peter B. Evans, Dietrich Rueschemeyer, and Theda Skocpol. New York: Cambridge University Press.

Salisbury, Robert H. 1984. "Interest Representation: The Dominance of Institutions." *American Political Science Review* 78:64–76.

Salisbury, Robert H. 1990. "The Paradox of Interest Groups in Washington— More Groups, Less Clout." In *The New American Political System,* 2d ed., ed. Anthony King. Washington, D.C.: American Enterprise Institute.

Salisbury, Robert H. 1991. "Putting Interests Back into Interest Groups." In *Interest Group Politics,* 3d ed., ed. Allan J. Cigler and Burdett A. Loomis. Washington, D.C.: Congressional Quarterly Press.

Samuelson, Paul. 1954. "The Pure Theory of Public Expenditures." *Review of Economics and Statistics* 36:350–56.

Schattschneider, E. E. 1983. *The Semisovereign People: A Realist's View of Democracy in America.* Fort Worth, Tex.: Holt, Rinehart, and Winston.

Schick, Allen. 1976. "The Supply and Demand for Analysis on Capitol Hill." *Policy Analysis* 2:215–34.

Schlozman, Kay Lehman, and John T. Tierney. 1986. *Organized Interests and American Democracy.* New York: Harper and Row.

Schmalensee, Richard, Paul L. Joskow, A. Denny Ellerman, Juan Pablo Montero, and Elizabeth M. Bailey. 1998. "An Interim Evaluation of Sulfur Dioxide Emissions Trading." *Journal of Economic Perspectives* 12:53–68.

School Choice: A Special Report. 1992. Princeton, N.J.: Carnegie Foundation.

Schultz, Kristin L. 1993. "States Experiment with School Choice." *Comparative State Politics* 14:12–23.

Schultze, Charles L. 1977. *The Public Use of Private Interest.* Washington, D.C.: Brookings Institution.

Schwartz, Stephen E. 1989. "Acid Deposition: Unraveling a Regional Phenomenon." *Science* 243:753–63.

Schwartz, William B. 1972. "Policy Analysis and the Health Care System." *Science* 177:967–69.

Shabecoff, Philip. 1989a. "An Emergence of Political Will on Acid Rain." *New York Times,* February 19, sec. 4, p. 5.

Shabecoff, Philip. 1989b. "President's Plan for Cleaning Air Goes to Congress." *New York Times,* July 22, sec. 1, p. 9.

Shapiro, Martin. 1995. "Of Interests and Values: The New Politics and the New Political Science." Baltimore: Johns Hopkins University Press.

Shepsle, Kenneth A., and Barry R. Weingast. 1984. "Political Solutions to Market Problems." *American Political Science Review* 78:417–34.

Shepsle, Kenneth A., and Barry R. Weingast. 1995. "Positive Theories of Congressional Institutions." In *Positive Theories of Congressional Institutions,* ed. Shepsle and Weingast. Ann Arbor: University of Michigan Press.

"Shortage of Emission Credits Projected." 1989. *Coal Outlook,* August 7, p. 2.

Shragg, Harry, Myrna E. Fagenbaum, Joel W. Kovner, Helen M. Caro, and Edward D. Bunting. 1973. "Low-Income Families in a Large Scale Prepaid Group Practice." *Inquiry* 10:52–60.

Silver, George A. 1971. "National Health Insurance, National Health Policy, and the National Health." *American Journal of Nursing* 71:1730–34.

Skocpol, Theda. 1985. "Bringing the State Back In: Strategies of Analysis in Current Research." In *Bringing the State Back In,* ed. Peter B. Evans, Dietrich Rueschemeyer, and Theda Skocpol. New York: Cambridge University Press.

Skocpol, Theda. 1987. "Governmental Structures, Social Science, and the Development of Economic and Social Policies." In *Social Science Research and Government: Comparative Essays on Britain and the United States,* ed. Martin Bulmer. New York: Cambridge University Press.

Smith, David G. 1992. *Paying for Medicare: The Politics of Reform.* New York: Aldine De Gruyter.

Smith, Richard A. 1984. "Advocacy, Interpretation, and Influence in the U.S. Congress." *American Political Science Review* 78:44–63.

Smith, Richard A. 1993. "Agreement, Defection, and Interest-Group Influence in the U.S. Congress." In *Agenda Formation,* ed. William H. Riker. Ann Arbor: University of Michigan Press.

Stanfield, Rochelle L. 1991. "Reading, 'Riting and Roadblocks." *National Journal,* May 11, p. 1141.

Starr, Paul. 1983. *The Social Transformation of American Medicine.* New York: Basic Books.

Steinbach, Carol. 1990. "New Corporate Activism on Schools." *National Journal,* April 7, pp. 850–52.

Steinbach, Carol, and Neal R. Peirce. 1989. "Multiple Choice." *National Journal,* July 1.

Stevens, Beth. 1988. "Blurring the Boundaries: How the Federal Government Has Influenced Welfare Benefits in the Private Sector." In *The Politics of Social Policy in the United States,* ed. Margaret Weir, Ann Shola Orloff, and Theda Skocpol. Princeton: Princeton University Press.

Stevens, Rosemary. 1971. "Trends in Medical Specialization in the United States." *Inquiry* 8:9–19.

Stigler, George J. 1975 [1971]. "The Theory of Economic Regulation." In *The Citizen and the State: Essays on Regulation.* Chicago: University of Chicago Press.

Stokey, Edith, and Richard Zeckhauser. 1978. *A Primer for Policy Analysis.* New York: Norton.

Stone, Deborah. 1989. "Causal Stories and the Formation of Policy Agendas." *Political Science Quarterly* 104:281–300.

"Stormy Clean Air Debate Stirs Praise, Outrage." 1989. *Coal Outlook,* June 19, p. 1.

Strauss, Valerie. 2003. "President to Push Vouchers for D.C.; Bush Moving ahead Despite Opposition." *New York Times,* February 8, p. B1.

Sunstein, Cass R. 1988. "Beyond the Republican Revival." *Yale Law Journal,* 97:1539–90.

Sutton, John R. 1996. "Social Knowledge and the Generation of Child Welfare Policy in the United States and Canada." In *States, Social Knowledge, and the Origins of Modern Social Policies,* ed. Dietrich Rueschemeyer and Theda Skocpol. Princeton: Princeton University Press.

Talbert, Jeffrey C., Bryan D. Jones, and Frank R. Baumgartner. 1995. "Nonlegislative Hearings and Policy Change in Congress." *American Journal of Political Science* 39:383–405.

Tietenberg, T. H. 1985. *Emissions Trading: An Exercise in Reforming Pollution Policy.* Washington, D.C.: Resources for the Future.

Timberg, Craig. 2003. "Williams Sheds Light on Vouchers Stance; Mayor Cites Need for New System." *Washington Post,* May 3, p. B1.

Toppo, Greg. 2001. "GAO: Voucher Effectiveness Unclear." Associated Press, October 1.

Truman, David B. 1951. *The Governmental Process: Political Interests and Public Opinion.* New York: Knopf.

Trumka, Richard L. 1989. "Pass That Compromise on Acid Rain." *Washington Post,* January 23, p. A19.

Tversky, Amos, and Daniel Kahneman. 1981. "The Framings of Decisions and the Psychology of Choice." *Science* 211:453–58.

Tversky, Amos, and Daniel Kahneman. 1988. "Rational Choice and the Framing of Decisions." In *Decision Making: Descriptive, Normative, and Prescriptive Interactions,* ed. David E. Bell, Howard Raiffa, and Amos Tversky. New York: Cambridge University Press.

"Utilities Give Draft Acid Rain Bill Very Low Marks in Every Department." 1989. *Electric Utility Week,* July 17, p. 16.

"Utilities Hit 'Polluter Pays' Concept; Industry Reaction to President's Clean Air Provisions." 1989. *Coal Outlook,* August 21, p. 3.

VanDoren, Peter. 1989. "Should Congress Listen to Economists?" *Journal of Politics* 51:319–36.

Wald, Matthew L. 1989. "Largest Coal User Criticizes Bush's Acid Rain Proposal." *New York Times,* August 18, p. D1.

Walker, Jack L., Jr. 1969. "The Diffusion of Innovations among the American States." *American Political Science Review* 63:880–99.

Walker, Jack L., Jr. 1977. "Setting the Agenda in the U.S. Senate: A Theory of Problem Selection." *British Journal of Political Science* 7:423–45.

Walker, Jack L., Jr. 1983. "The Origins and Maintenance of Interest Groups in America." *American Political Science Review* 77:390–406.

Walker, Jack L., Jr. 1991. *Mobilizing Interest Groups in America: Patrons, Professions, and Social Movements.* Ann Arbor: University of Michigan Press.

Wawro, Gregory. 2000. *Legislative Entrepreneurship in the U.S. House of Representatives.* Ann Arbor: University of Michigan Press.

Webber, David J. 1984. "Political Conditions Motivating Legislators' Use of Policy Information." *Policy Studies Journal* 4:110–18.

Weingast, Barry R., and William J. Marshall. 1988. "The Industrial Organization of Congress; or, Why Legislatures, Like Firms, Are Not Organized as Markets." *Journal of Political Economy* 96:132–63.

Weingast, Barry R., Kenneth A. Shepsle, and Christopher Johnson. 1981. "The Political Economy of Benefits and Costs: A Neoclassical Approach to Distributive Politics." *Journal of Political Economy* 89:642–64.

Weir, Margaret, Ann Shola Orloff, and Theda Skocpol. 1988. "Understanding American Social Politics." In *The Politics of Social Policy in the United States,* ed. Margaret Weir, Ann Shola Orloff, and Theda Skocpol. Princeton: Princeton University Press.

Weiss, Carol H. 1989. "Congressional Committees as Users of Analysis." *Journal of Policy Analysis and Management* 8:411–31.

"Western Fuels Coop: Acid Rain Bill Could Foreclose Future Use of Coal." 1989. *Electric Utility Week,* September 11, p. 4.

Whiteman, David. 1985. "The Fate of Policy Analysis in Congressional Decision Making: Three Types of Use in Committees." *Western Political Quarterly* 38:294–311.

Whiteman, David. 1995. *Communication in Congress: Members, Staff, and the Search for Information.* Lawrence: University of Kansas Press.

Wildavsky, Aaron. 1979. *Speaking Truth to Power: The Art and Craft of Policy Analysis.* Boston: Little, Brown.

Wilkerson, John D., Kelly J. Devers, and Ruth S. Given. 1997. "The Emerging Competitive Care Marketplace." In *Competitive Managed Care: The Emerging Health Care System,* ed. John D. Wilkerson, Kelly J. Devers, and Ruth S. Given. San Francisco: Jossey-Bass.

Winerip, Michael. 2003. "What Some Much-Noted Data Really Showed about Vouchers." *New York Times,* May 7, p. B12.

Witte, John F. 1992. "Public Subsidies for Private Schools: What We Know and How to Proceed." *Educational Policy* 6:206–27.

Witte, John F., Troy D. Sterr, and Christopher A. Thorn. 1995. "Fifth Year Report: Milwaukee Parental Choice Program (Executive Summary)." Photocopy. Department of Political Science and the Robert M. La Follette Institute of Public Affairs, University of Wisconsin–Madison.

Witte, John F., Christopher A. Thorn, and Kim A. Pritchard. 1995. "Public and Private Education in Wisconsin: Implications for the Choice Debate." Photocopy. Robert M. La Follette Institute of Public Affairs, University of Wisconsin–Madison.

Wittman, Donald. 1995. *The Myth of Democratic Failure: Why Political Institutions Are Efficient.* Chicago: University of Chicago Press.

Wolkstein, Irwin. 1970. "Medicare 1971: Changing Attitudes and Changing Legislation." *Law and Contemporary Problems* 35:697–715.

Wright, John R. 1996. *Interest Groups and Congress: Lobbying, Contributions, and Influence.* Boston: Allyn and Bacon.

Zaller, John R. 1992. *The Nature and Origin of Mass Opinion.* New York: Cambridge University Press.

Zola, Irving Kenneth. 1972. "Medicine as an Institution of Social Control." *Sociological Review* 20:487–504.

Zuckman, Jill. 1992. "New Bill Kills Federal Money for Private School 'Choice.'" *Congressional Quarterly Weekly Report,* February 29, pp. 471–72.

Author Index

Subject Index

A. E. Staley Manufacturing (AES), 140, 155
Acid deposition, 114n. 1. *See also* Acid rain
Acid rain: effects, 116; politics, 14, 107, 116
Advocacy analysis, 3, 81, 85, 89, 244
Agenda cycling, 46–47, 60, 119
Allowance, 123; emissions reduction credits (ERCs), 131, 133, 136
Ambach, Gordon, 179
Ambiguity: definition, 8, 65–66, 86; effects, 12, 13, 16, 54–56, 66–67
Ambiguity predictions, 112, 234
America 2000, 112, 163–64
American Association of School Board Administrators, 171, 191
American Educational Research Association (AERA), 174
American Electric Power (AEP), 118, 140, 144, 147, 156–57
American Federation of Labor and Congress of Industrial Organizations (AFL-CIO), 212, 215
American Federation of Teachers (AFT), 171, 176, 177, 179–81, 184, 191
American Gas Association/Interstate Natural Gas Association of America (AGA/INGAA), 140, 143–47
American Medical Association (AMA), 16, 194, 208, 211–12, 214, 218–20, 222–25, 228–29, 237, 240, 244
American Nurses' Association (ANA), 225–26

American Public Power Association (APPA), 140, 158
Argument types, 79
Ayres, Richard, 144, 146

Babbling equilibrium, 95, 113
Bailey, Keith, 192
Barker, John, 144, 146
Bates, Jim, 145–46
Becker model, 58–61, 68–69; amended, 61–67, 69–71, 230, 232
Benefit function, 58
Black Alliance for Educational Options, 190
Blue Cross/Blue Shield, 201, 204
Bounded rationality, 48, 82
Bush, George H. W., 5, 14, 119, 163
Bush, George W., 16, 189, 239
Business Coalition for Excellence in Education, 192
Business Roundtable, 162, 171
Byrd, Robert, 117–18

California Teachers Association, 172
Carnegie Foundation for the Advancement of Teaching, 173, 175
Causal epistemology, 8, 243
Causal framework: boundedly rational preferences, 48, 86; definition, 6–8, 48–49; informational properties, 7, 86
Certainty predictions, 111, 139, 233
Chicago school of regulation, 27, 103
Citizen political knowledge, 2, 29